STO

ACPL ITEM
DISCARDED

SO-BKX-539

*The first industrial research laboratory in the United States was housed in a barn in Schenectady; from this beginning grew General Electric's phenomenal research and development program.

*In 1858 a stubborn Yankee opened a fancy dry goods store on New York's Sixth Avenue with the simple—and revolutionary—merchandising policy of no credit and the lowest possible prices. Today that store is a billion-dollar retail empire, with sixty-three branches across the country. It's called Macy's.

*Less than twenty years ago the highly successful and well-established Coca-Cola Company still had a one-product line; management took a deep breath and decided to diversify, with astonishing results in the marketplace and in profits.

Somewhere in the history of all successful companies are moments when the future hangs in the balance. The difference between fortune and failure lies in the hands of the men who, in Peter F. Drucker's words, have "the willingness to risk and the ability to seize opportunity."

Pioneers of American Business pro-files some of these men and their crucial decisions that marked turning points in the development of America's top companies. Trailblazers in marketing, science, and industry, they were not tycoons but individuals of imagination and initiative. Here are the stories of Marcellus Berry, an employee of American Express, who devised the traveler's cheque as a replacement for the troublesome letter of credit; George Clowes, a young chemist at Lilly and Company who recognized and developed the potential of insulin; Henning W. Prentis, Jr., of Armstrong Cork, a far-sighted manufacturer whose creative marketing revolutionized an industry.

Illustrated throughout with period photographs, historically important and nostalgically delightful, *Pioneers of American Business* stands as dramatic witness to the force of ideas whose time is come, and as tribute to the determination and vision of the men of American commerce.

Pioneers
of American
Business

compiled by
Sterling G. Slappey
Senior Editor, *Nation's Business*

GROSSET & DUNLAP
A National General Company

Publishers   New York

Contents

1799098

Foreword

ARCH N. BOOTH
CHIEF EXECUTIVE OFFICER
CHAMBER OF COMMERCE OF THE UNITED STATES

Good ideas are a dime a dozen; men put them into effect, millions of dollars apiece.

We often think that the moment in which a great idea or invention is conceived is the happy end of the story. It is not. It is just the beginning. More than the idea is required.

Edison said inventing is "one percent inspiration and ninety-nine percent perspiration." It takes a lot of work to experiment with an idea, prove it out, refine it, put it into effect. The inventor has to have faith in his invention. He has to have persistence. He has to be willing to work.

And even that is not enough. History is full of great ideas that died in infancy.

• Hero of Alexandria described both turbine and pressure forms of the steam engine in the first century A.D. The Greeks built models of them for toys. Yet nearly two thousand years would pass before steam was harnessed to perform useful work. Why?

• Roger Bacon may have invented both the telescope and the microscope in the thirteenth century. Nevertheless, the microscope had to be re-invented at the dawn of the seventeenth century. Why?

• Leonardo da Vinci sketched plans for various types of aircraft, including the helicopter. So did many others, before the Wright brothers. Something stopped them all. What?

In some cases the barriers were cultural. The ancient Greeks did not see the point in labor-saving devices. They had slaves. Besides, a Greek gentleman was expected to use only his mind, not his hands. Tinkering was for the lower classes.

Sometimes the barriers were religious. Religious traditionalism and mysticism halted the progress of Arab science in the eleventh century. Roger Bacon, too, was a victim of religious hostility.

Often the barriers were technological. Leonardo could have constructed a successful airframe—kites have been flown for thousands of years. But he lacked a lightweight power source for it, as did all would-be aviators before the development of the internal combustion engine.

The point is that while good men with good ideas are essential to progress, that combination alone is still not enough. The context in which both occur is equally important. A good idea may well be useless in a society which does not value—or cannot exploit—good ideas.

An innovator needs the stimulus of peers who appreciate his ideas. He needs freedom to think and to experiment. He needs resources to support his work. He needs a technological and commercial base to build upon. He will probably need capital for production. And ultimately, he will need consumers who are receptive to new methods, new products.

Our country's commercial and industrial history, properly told, is an exciting story. The men who made that history were no less pioneers than those on the wagon trains, trekking west. They were pioneering a new kind of society, one with both the incentive and the technical capacity to create a better way of life for the average citizen, where earlier artisans had reserved their gifts for the wealthy and the aristocratic.

The stories within these pages cover a long span of time, from our early days to comparatively recent years, but further chapters of that history are still to be written. The stories for the next edition are taking place right now, out there. It's not too late to become a part of one.

Preface

PETER F. DRUCKER

There is much discussion these days on "decision theory." But there is little mention, in all these books, of courage and judgment and of the willingness to risk. There are countless books on "management" that discuss organization structure, personnel policies and teamwork. But rarely is there mention of the man, the individual entrepreneur, out of whose commitment and act of courage the big organization grew. And as a result American business history, which should be one of the most exciting stories around, tends to be a dull subject, left to specialists, replete with figures, trends and financial data, but sans people, sans excitement, sans drama.

This book attempts to redress the balance. It is not, fortunately, a "systematic" history. Instead, it is a collection of exciting and crucial moments, an introduction to men who literally made history. It is a reminder that even the largest company started small, with one individual, and that even the biggest "corporate giant" grew out of an act of faith. It is also a testimony to the diversity and variety of American business leadership and should go a long way toward rectifying the popular but mistaken belief that a few "tycoons" —the J. P. Morgans and John Rockefellers—created and dominated the American industrial scene. All kinds of peo-

ple built American business, and very few of them were
"tycoons." What they had in common was the willingness to
risk and the ability to seize opportunity.

The sketches brought together in this volume are, so to
speak, "still photographs" snipped out of a moving film. They
capture single moments of an unfolding drama. And of course,
they all have "happy endings"; the failures leave behind no
monuments. But this book is a fast-paced introduction to the
human drama that underlies every entrepreneurial achievement.

Introduction

STERLING G. SLAPPEY
SENIOR EDITOR, *Nation's Business*

History rewards politicians, presidents, prime ministers, princes and warriors with long biographies in the best encyclopedias. Contemporaries reward them with fame, fortunes, stately homes with sweeping lawns and even with adoration.

But for the men of commerce there often has been little reward beyond the money they earned, despite the fact that their exploits were as beneficial for mankind as the exploits of the diplomats and generals.

Hannibal crossed the Alps and conquered nearly all of Rome, and he is secure in history. But who sold Hannibal the elephants that took him over the mountains?

That Carthaginian businessman of 218 B.C. is lost to history, yet his role was as necessary as Hannibal's.

It is rightful that Dwight Eisenhower, George Marshall, George Patton and Chester Nimitz have their places in military history, but what about the men at General Motors, Ford, Lockheed, Douglas, Bell and the shipyards who supplied *their* elephants—the trucks, ships, planes that made victory possible?

During the summer of 1969 an editorial meeting of *Nation's Business* in Washington discussed the deplorable fact that the history of American business and the lives of outstanding American businessmen are so little known, not only

xi

by the general public but by other American businessmen and even professors in our business schools.

The editors agreed that any of us could walk into the best graduate business school in the country and fail to get correct answers to such simple and basic questions as:

Who was Mr. Swift? Mr. Reynolds? Gospodin Smirnoff? Mr. Factor? Mr. Hertz? Mr. Singer? Why is the world's biggest bank in San Francisco of all places? What sent New York Life Insurance Co. ahead at the very time other insurance firms were dropping out like flies? Of the tens of thousands of jitneys, taxis and one-truck transportation systems, why did Greyhound prosper?

Another discouraging point was made during that editorial meeting. A reporter could walk into many a business, ask almost any employee for the name of the company founder and get the blankest of stares. If he pursued the point further and asked some of the company executives what it was that made their particular company prosper while other similar companies failed, he would get only an embarrassed "I don't have a clue."

Because of these deficiencies I proposed that *Nation's Business*, with its nearly one million circulation, dig around in the history of American business to discover some of the little-known heroes and pinpoint the decisions that turned ordinary companies into prosperous firms.

Editor Jack Wooldridge and Managing Editor Wilbur Martin immediately agreed. They said to take all the time necessary and spend whatever was needed to get twenty-five or thirty company stories down on paper.

The articles would be short, concise histories describing why and how the companies went on to greatness. The series would be stories of success, not failures, and would be titled, "Great Men and Great Moments of American Business."

We agreed that the companies need not necessarily be the largest in their fields. But the companies would each have to be well known, highly respected, have an interesting history to tell and be successful.

The three of us selected twenty-seven firms fitting that

description. We telephoned each and invited participation. Companies quickly accepted and soon the articles were coming in.

They made magnificent reading.

Each article was accompanied by two or three pictures, usually of a historic nature. Many of those pictures had never been published before. They had lain in company archives for fifty to one hundred years, forgotten or disregarded.

The first twenty-seven articles appeared in the January, 1970, issue and were a tremendous success. Community, school and university libraries all over the country wrote in for reprint rights or additional copies of the issue. Many of the featured companies ordered thousands of reprints to distribute to their stockholders, customers and suppliers.

Soon telephone calls were put through from other companies asking if *Nation's Business* intended running more articles of the same nature, and if so, how those companies could go about getting themselves included.

Once you're riding a good horse, gallop on.

Yes, we said, *Nation's Business* would keep the series going—since it was a success and in such demand. We were onto a good thing, so a second collection of articles was lined up and published in the January, 1971, issue.

Response was even greater than in 1970, especially in the number of firms asking that they be considered for inclusion.

In February, 1972, the third collection of articles appeared and in January, 1973, the fourth collection was printed.

You should never ride a good horse to death. Don't overdo a good thing. Quit while you're winning.

But, at the same time, don't let go of a good thing either.

Today, in the *Nation's Business* files in Washington is a large folder entitled, "Great Men and Great Moments—197?????" Inside are letters from companies saying, "If *Nation's Business* revives the series, think first of us."

Maybe we will someday, considering there are at least another one hundred and fifty companies that could qualify for later inclusion.

Amusing incidents took place during the putting together of the series.

One year a well-known, respected company was invited to participate. The company accepted but a month later the vice president telephoned to say the firm was withdrawing from the series. The company would the next day, he said, bring suit for more than $100 million against one of the very founders who would have to be mentioned in the article.

As in the best of families, there had been a falling out on the corporate level.

"We don't think our suit would be helped if we were out in print with glowing words about Mr. So-and-So at the same time the case is being heard," he said.

This being undeniably true, a different company was substituted.

Another company accepted the invitation to do an article, but immediately thereafter the vice president for public affairs retired. He neglected to tell his successor about the project. When the information did not appear a call went to the company and the new man got on the line.

"You can still make the issue if you have your information in our hands by this time tomorrow," he was told by *Nation's Business*. That night he assembled his facts and flew to Washington from the Midwest with them the next day. The article made the issue.

Books are more permanent than newspapers or magazines —to say nothing of radio and television performances. So Grosset & Dunlap and *Nation's Business* have now collaborated in publishing this book. The idea was to select the best of the articles, have them expanded so that more interesting details would be included and then put them between the hard covers of a book, thereby preserving the stories as no magazine ever could.

In the articles that follow you will find little-known men doing very important things. Here's a sampling.

Marcellus Berry? Well, to him we largely owe the advantages and conveniences of the traveler's cheque. He was an American Express man.

Cyrus Holliday built a city, helped develop a state, established a railroad—The Atchison, Topeka & Santa Fe.

Orville S. Caesar designed a bus that was nearly twice as good as anything else on the road. Greyhound was his company.

George Clowes was a young chemist who recognized in insulin one of the great medications of all time. Eli Lilly and Company was his place of work.

Paul Galvin was an early failure who later became a brilliant man of the marketplace. He put Motorola radios in automobiles.

Rudolph Kunett, a Russian, held the rights to an old vodka formula called Smirnoff, but it took an American businessman, John G. Martin, to know what to do with it.

Many historic events had their impact on business—the San Francisco earthquake on the Bank of America; the resurgence of Dixie after the Civil War on Southern Railway; The Civil War and battle photography on GAF; the California Gold Rush on Wells Fargo; a historic storm over the North Atlantic on Borden, Inc.

Also in this book are stories about the first of the great franchisers—the Coca-Cola Co.—and about one of man's first throwaways—the Gillette razor blade.

Those are the samples, now comes the full treatment on the great men and great moments of American business.

Pioneers
of American
Business

AMERICAN EXPRESS

□ □ □

In Quest of Utopia

Since primitive man first clambered aboard a log and paddled it across a river, travel technology has made massive strides. Men now navigate across space to the moon, and luxurious intercontinental jets have put long-distance travel within reach of the masses. Even so, there are still "little things"—flight delays, lost room reservations and the like— that leave the travel industry striving for its utopia. But whatever travel "systems" shortcomings exist today, they are slight compared to conditions in 1890 when James C. Fargo returned from an overseas trip in a testy mood, his patience run out. Mr. Fargo was the third president of American Express Company, then a famous and respected shipper of goods, specializing in money and valuables.

At that time standard equipment for travelers to Europe was the circular letter of credit, which is still in limited use today. Issued by a number of leading United States banks and negotiable only at specified European correspondent banks, the letter of credit provided protection. But drawing against it was a chore. Letters of credit were honored only by banks and during banking hours. The negotiation process took a lot of time.

Mr. Fargo had had a hard time of it abroad and he went straight to the office of an untitled underling, Marcellus Fleming Berry. "Berry," he said, without even a greeting,

1

Marcellus Berry, who devised the American Express Travelers Cheque as a replacement for the inconvenient letter of credit.

The first American Express Travelers Cheque, dated August 5, 1891, and cashed at the Hotel Hauffe in Leipzig, Germany.

"the moment you get off the beaten track, letters of credit are of no more use than so much wet wrapping paper. If the president of American Express has that kind of trouble, think about the trouble the ordinary traveler has. Something must be done. Do it."

Marcellus Berry then devised the "traveler's cheque"—substantially the same as those in use today—which called for the now familiar signature and countersignature.

In 1891, the first year it was in use, the traveler's cheque (note the spelling, which is still used) enjoyed a sales volume of $9,200. In ten years sales had jumped to $6 million. Now, billions of dollars' worth are sold yearly. The growth of traveler's cheques, which are now issued in Canadian dollars, pounds sterling, Swiss francs, German marks and French francs, as well as in U.S. dollars, led to American Express's entry into the travel business prior to World War I.

President Fargo also told Mr. Berry to devise a money order whose amount could not be raised. Mr. Berry's system called for the issuing agent simply to tear off printed figures along the edge until the figure for the amount of the order was reached. If the order was for $50, then only the $50 figure was not torn off. The system remained in use for many years.

Marcellus Berry was a small, bald fellow who often wore his hat in the office. He talked little, but when he spoke, everyone—including Mr. Fargo—listened. He was the one man sure enough of himself to tell the president to his face when the president was wrong. He rose to become the company's first European division manager.

Fargo's ability to see shortcomings in the system, plus Berry's innovative genius, set the tone for American Express Company down through the decades. They were among the great men of early business. Based on their decisions, American Express Company and its subsidiaries have expanded tremendously in recent years and have moved into fields that not even Fargo and Berry foresaw.

The American Express Card is now carried by millions of travelers around the world. It is currently issued in fourteen different currencies, ranging from American dollars and British pounds to South African rands. This travel and entertainment card exemplifies the company's main concern—to make things easier for people who travel. American Express Company and its subsidiaries—through their respective divisions—offer travel, traveler's cheques and card services locally to the traveling public all over the world.

In 1959 The American Express Company, Inc., a wholly-owned subsidiary, decided to strengthen and expand its overseas financial activity to provide a full range of banking services to individuals, banks and corporations abroad. Since it had access for lending purposes to the world's major currencies, the overseas subsidiary was in a position to respond to the financing requirements of international firms throughout the world. By February, 1968, international banking constituted the principal business of The American Express Company, Inc., and its subsidiaries. Reflecting this development, the name was changed to American Express International Banking Corporation (AEIBC). Today AEIBC is a billion-dollar institution that specializes in the financing of international trade and investment in Europe and the Orient. The Military Banking Division of AEIBC, operating offices, suboffices, mobile units and conversion points at U.S. military installations in Europe and the Far East, provides retail banking services for American servicemen, their dependents and authorized civilians.

American Express Company acquired the assets and properties of the Fund American Companies in 1968. These property-liability subsidiaries, now known as Fireman's Fund American Insurance Companies, offer a complete range of property-liability protection. Fireman's Fund American Life Insurance Companies provide both ordinary and group life protection as well as a full range of disability policies throughout the country.

American Express Investment Management Company (AEIMCO), a wholly-owned subsidiary, manages and distributes five domestic mutual funds, acts as adviser to a fund sold abroad and provides other investment management services. Another subsidiary, W. H. Morton and Company, Inc., specializes in the underwriting and distribution of corporate bonds and preferred stocks, while the W. H. Morton Company Division of American Express Company underwrites and distributes state and municipal securities.

The Space Bank® international computer reservation service of American Express Reservations, Inc., provides immediate hotel, motel and car-rental reservations all over the world. With one toll-free phone call, a travel agent or individual traveler can reserve a room or rent a car almost anywhere in the world.

American Express has come a very long way from being a simple shipper of goods. But American Express Company and its subsidiaries—now doing business in 125 countries—must be going in the right direction, because they have been imitated by so many others, and imitation, it is said, is the sincerest form of flattery.

ARMSTRONG CORK

□ □ □

A Theme of Success:
"Let the Buyer Have Faith"

Great decisions that alter business organizations—like great battles that change history—are rarely spur-of-the-moment phenomena. They usually involve a host of closely related individual decisions, each requiring insight, courage and planning, but all implementing a single objective.

Such was the case with the "great decisions" made for Armstrong Cork Company by Henning W. Prentis, Jr., in the early 1920s. The series of decisions he made brought a number of innovative practices into the resilient flooring business. They were all based, essentially, on two philosophical concepts— "Let the buyer have faith" and the "equality of competitive opportunity" in the distribution of goods.

Looking back today we would say that Prentis was a modern marketing man well ahead of his time.

He joined Armstrong in 1907 and spent his entire business career with the company, serving as president from 1935 to 1950 and as chairman of the board from then until his death in 1959. Along the way he found time to make valuable contributions to business in general, to serve in dozens of public service positions and to become nationally known as a spokesman for private free enterprise.

Prentis felt strongly that the manufacturer's job didn't end with making a product, but extended to helping the wholesaler and retailer sell it, as well as helping the consumer use

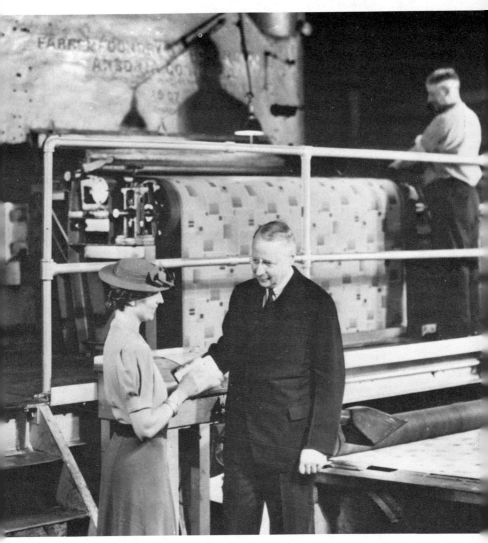

Henning W. Prentis being interviewed by a reporter in the 1920s.

it. One of his first moves was to encourage the editors of *The Dry Goods Economist*—a trade magazine for retail department stores—to run a series of articles designed to help wholesalers and retailers sell more floor coverings.

Going a step further, Prentis reasoned that even if the wholesaler and retailer were well trained, consumers still wouldn't buy unless the retail salesman understood how to present the product to the customer. Characteristically, Prentis wrote a series of articles called "Told in the Store." These described successful selling techniques, including a section on home decoration.

He also became a pioneer in consumer advertising. He asked the board of directors at Armstong for the then unheard-of sum of $50,000 to invest in a consumer magazine campaign over a three-year period. He got the money, and on September 1, 1917, the first national consumer advertising for Armstrong linoleum appeared in the *Saturday Evening Post*. To help homemakers get the most from Armstrong advertising, Prentis set up a bureau of interior design to answer requests as to which linoleum designs were most suitable for individual customer's needs.

While Prentis was carrying forward his advertising ideas, the company was moving ahead in other areas. One thing that made possible his advertising theme—"Armstrong's Linoleum for every room in the house"—was the company's effort to bring style to a previously utilitarian product. Another was the company's adherence to high standards of quality. Still another was the company's traditional long-range point of view—the insistence that every act must be based on principle, and on a "willingness to make temporary sacrifices for the sake of substantial future gain." Prentis had merged these elements in his advertising efforts, and now he got the chance to express them in another area—distribution.

In the 1920s the general practice in the flooring business was for retailers to purchase linoleum wherever they could get the best price. The price in each transaction depended on who could bargain best, and *caveat emptor* was the rule of the game. It was like an oriental bazaar. The consumer was at the mercy of the marketplace in such a situation, and found it almost impossible to be sure he was getting good value in his purchase.

Prentis believed strongly in fairness, responsibility and honesty. Instead of "Let the buyer beware," he thought the rule should be: "Let the buyer have faith." He not only was confident that homemakers would welcome color and good design, but also felt that a more orderly system of distribution would enable consumers to benefit from a wide choice of patterns.

If a bulky product like linoleum were to be made in a variety of styles, colorings and gauges, he reasoned, the most efficient means of distributing it would be through wholesalers who would maintain stocks in strategic locations throughout the country. But he was convinced this system could operate effectively only in an atmosphere of mutual trust and respect between the wholesaler and his source of supply—something decidedly lacking in those days.

In the chain of distribution, he said, compensation received should be determined by the function performed. Consequently, even the smallest wholesaler—if he truly fulfilled his service function—should be assured a price proportionately lower than that given the largest retailer, to compensate the wholesaler for the services he rendered. In short, he believed in extending "equality of competitive opportunity" to all Armstrong customers.

To replace the secret "deals" between buyer and seller that were then customary in the flooring business, Prentis set up openly published price lists. He was widely criticized for this open-book approach. But retailers began accepting the new idea as soon as they realized that for the first time they could know what competing dealers were paying for their merchandise. Now they could spend less time buying and more time selling. Now they could devote their attention to serving the needs of customers rather than haggling with suppliers.

To carry forward the new marketing approach, Prentis

felt that something was needed beyond the typical selling agent of the time. He decided to develop a sales staff that would reflect the company's own character—a radical departure from the personal selling practiced by the typical salesman of the time. He went to colleges and universities and sought out outstanding men who were about to graduate (coincidentally launching one of the early corporate college recruiting programs). Then he trained these men in Armstrong methods for careers—rather than jobs—with the company. There was doubt and even ridicule about this practice in the trade, but Prentis and his "college boys" persisted. The program of recruiting on campus has been greatly expanded and widely copied. One of the first men Prentis hired and trained, Clifford J. Backstrand, was ultimately to succeed him as president of the Armstrong Cork Company.

The recruits were trained in almost every phase of the flooring business as well as in the importance of meeting consumer needs. This proved so successful that soon Armstrong was being called on to offer training programs for wholesalers and retailers. Then the company established an installation school to develop skilled flooring craftsmen to assure consumers greater satisfaction.

With the spread of wholesale distributors, enabling retailers to offer their customers a broad range of flooring patterns, the floor became an important element in home decorating.

By the end of the twenties Armstrong had opened the door to a new era of growth; the flooring business had reached a level of maturity and responsibility never before achieved; and Henning W. Prentis Jr., had made his mark.

BANK OF AMERICA

□ □ □

The Largest Bank Was Once
a Plank on the Waterfront

A thirty-second earthquake had shattered all the careful safeguards of man. Telephones and electric lights were useless. Water and gas mains burst. The streets of San Francisco were a maze of ridges, gaps and debris from fallen walls. The time was 5:12 A.M., Wednesday, April 18, 1906.

Most of the city's well-built structures survived the shock. Many people returned to bed, thinking the danger over.

But as thousands of workers headed for the financial district at 8 A.M., flames raced through the poor area of the city south of Market Street, where buildings squatted on "filled" tidal flats and flimsy frame houses dated back to the days of the Forty-niners. These shacks fell, and the wreckage nourished fires from overturned stoves, downed electric wires and severed gas pipes.

Firemen found no water in the mains. Hoses were rigged to draw water from the bay, but the flames were already past control.

Refugees began dragging trunks up the horribly steep hills, supposedly to safety. Troops from the Presidio urged the exhausted families to move on, just ahead of the shifting line of fires. The mayor ordered that looters be shot on sight.

The people in the business section finally began to worry that the flames would reach their area. At noon Amadeo

11

Amadeo Peter Giannini, founder of the Bank of America.

Giannini's first banking enterprise, the Bank of Italy, occupied these temporary quarters on San Francisco's Montgomery Street for fifteen months after the 1906 earthquake.

Peter Giannini, the young man who had started the Bank of Italy two years earlier, reached his little bank on Montgomery Street. He had walked most of the seventeen miles from his home in San Mateo. No trains were running and travelers were headed hysterically in the opposite direction.

The bank had been opened by two employees. Giannini watched the blaze on Market Street and decided to get out. There was no vault to protect the funds; the Bank of Italy stored money overnight in a larger bank's vault. Giannini got two teams and wagons from a produce company and stowed the bank's $80,000 in cash under crates of oranges.

They waited until dark to start the journey to Giannini's home, thinking that travel would be safer then. The roads were so packed with refugees that the two wagons didn't reach San Mateo until 7 A.M. Thursday. The money was hidden in the ashes trap of the Gianninis' fireplace.

The banker returned to the charred city to find the Bank of Italy office in embers. One third of San Francisco was demolished. The fires were finally halted Friday at wide Van Ness Avenue, where a last stand with dynamite and wet rugs saved the rest of the city.

More than 500 were dead. There were 250,000 homeless camped at the edges of the city. Property loss was about $400 million.

Giannini remained confident about the future, though he had only $80,000 to cover deposits and meet requests for loans to rebuild North Beach, the Italian area of fruit vendors and merchants the bank served. As the big bankers waited for their vaults to cool, and then put a month-long bank holiday into effect, he set up a temporary bank—a plank counter and a bag of money—on the waterfront.

He did more. He searched out ship captains, gave them funds and told them to get lumber. This foresight aided reconstruction considerably.

At his "wharf" branch Giannini encouraged the earthquake victims: "We are going to rebuild San Francisco . . . greater than ever." The comforting voice booming from this tall, well-known man brought confidence to those who had given up in despair.

When a listener said he was ready to do his part, Giannini praised him: "That's the spirit! We'll fix up a loan immediately." Security was often merely a man's character. If a borrower asked for $3,000, the banker offered half that amount. Holding up a sheaf of papers, he would say: "Look at all the requests. If we give everybody all he wants there won't be enough to go 'round."

Surprisingly, deposits came in. Italians who had always distrusted banks knew their hoards would be safer with Giannini than in the refugee camps. Six weeks after the earthquake the Bank of Italy's deposits exceeded withdrawals.

So the bank grew, under Giannini's leadership, and became Bank of America, the largest bank in the world. And it was due to the response from the people of North Beach after the fire that Giannini decided to be a banker for life.

While one man does not make an institution, he can, as A. P. Giannini did, cast a very long shadow, imbue an institution with a quality that affects it far into the future, and set enduring standards for dealing with his fellow men. Though he died in 1949 his influence is still felt, and the quality that chiefly characterized A. P. Giannini is the quality the bank's management seeks to emulate today—humanity.

It was the humanization of banking that Giannini often said he considered his proudest achievement. He believed that business could be transacted more quickly and satisfactorily if done humanely and simply, and he recognized the fact that banking, like any other business, is fundamentally the mutual fulfillment of material human needs. He knew that the bank of the future would have to be a more human institution, more in touch with the rank and file of the population, and more quickly responsive to its changing needs.

In order to bring banking closer to the people he conceived and pioneered a statewide system of banking offices. The first Bank of America branch office was opened in San Francisco in 1907, and the first out-of-town office in San Jose in 1909. Today there are more than 1,000 offices throughout the state. In keeping with the Giannini philosophy of serving the community, these are known as community banking offices rather than branch banks.

Giannini's foresight and shrewd business sense also enabled him to start Bank of America on the way to international leadership. A branch bank was opened in London in 1931. At the end of World War II others were opened in Manila, Bangkok, Guam, Düsseldorf, Tokyo, Yokohama, Kobe and Osaka. At the close of 1972 there were 124 branches and other facilities plus 84 subsidiaries and other equity investments outside the United States, giving the bank representation in 78 countries and territories. BankAmerica Corporation, Bank of America's parent company, has a number of subsidiaries that provide additional services outside but related to the field of banking.

Despite this growth and expansion, the management of Bank of America has never lost sight of A. P. Giannini's guiding principle of service to the community. Nearly all of the banks' employees, both in California and overseas, are from the communities in which their offices are located. The bank is a part of the community, and it supports the community's activities.

Since the founding of Bank of America the role of banks and bankers has changed. The public expects community leadership from banks; the demand is not only that bankers perform well in their own area but also that they assume a major role in efforts toward the solution of the larger problems of society. First-rate service to customers is no longer enough; bankers are expected to serve their communities too.

Just as A. P. Giannini took the lead in the rebuilding of San Francisco after the devastating earthquake and in the revolutionary approach to banking that offered wage-earners and small businesses the services traditionally reserved for wealthy individuals and large companies, so the bank he founded assumes leadership and responsibility in the development of the communities where it operates and in alleviating their pressing social problems.

Since the complexities of modern urban life and the scope of Bank of America's operations make it impossible today for one man to guide both the financial and social concerns of the corporation, a Social Policy Committee within the bank and a Public Policy Committee of the BankAmerica Corporation board of directors have been established to guide activities in social areas.

Formation of the two committees followed an earlier decision to channel resources and expertise into four areas of pressing public concern: social unrest, equal opportunity, decent housing for everyone, and preservation of the environment. Issues under special consideration have included the problems of women in obtaining consumer credit and the impact of restrictive environmental standards on bank lending policies; their priority projects have included broadening opportunities for advancement for women and minority employees, expansion of the home loan program for low-income families, development of an experimental program to improve bank communication with borrowers under the Small Business Administration's minority enterprise program, and improving the student loan program.

All these activities are consistent with the Giannini tradition. He insisted that the bank constantly adapt its services to the needs of its changing clientele. He believed that the majority of loans would become smaller in size but would be used for a wider variety of purposes, and he knew that small loans meant there would be more loans and thus more people would be served.

"Any banker can make a sound loan for a million dollars," he once said, "but you don't get real constructive banking until you put up five hundred dollars for some fellow who has nothing but imagination and ambition."

Bank of America looks forward to the celebration of the seventieth anniversary of its founding next year, carrying on a tradition started in 1904 and summed up forty years later by its founder in these words:

"It is my earnest wish that the bank be preserved for these purposes: to serve all classes of people, to promote all worthy enterprise, to be watchful always of the interests of the bank's shareholders, to provide permanence and opportunity for those who are devoting their lives to building it, and to maintain its greatest possible usefulness to the nation."

BORDEN

□ □ □

How Babies' Cries Helped
Launch an Industry

The ship carrying Gail Borden home from England rolled and lurched, its sails dipping into the chilly Atlantic waves. Several immigrant babies were crying in the dank hold. After a few days four of them died as a result of drinking contaminated milk from diseased cows kept on board ship.

Gail Borden, who had witnessed the babies' misery, was deeply troubled. He couldn't get their cries out of his mind. He began to dream about a milk that would be safe for shipboard use, and "as common on shipboard as sugar." He meant to find a way to treat milk that would keep it fresh and pure over a period of time, and still retain its body-building qualities.

Back in New York, where he was then living, he began to seek a method of removing the water from milk, and concluded that using a vacuum pan was the only good way. As his determination increased, he boarded his family and moved upstate to New Lebanon, a Shaker community, where he thought he could learn something from the way the Shakers were using a vacuum process to preserve fruit.

In 1853, after two years of experimenting, he had a new product which he called "condensed milk." It was pure, fresh milk from which most of the water had been removed under vacuum at a low temperature. It contained sugar as a preservative.

*Gail Borden, 1801–1873,
had a varied career. As
a Texas newspaperman,
he wrote the headline,
"Remember the Alamo."*

*After two years of experimentation, Borden successfully
condensed milk by removing the water and adding sugar.
He set up operations in Connecticut in 1857; this is his first
condensery.*

Borden sought a patent for his process, but was told that it lacked novelty. There were dozens of patents on file for "evaporated milk," including one for "evaporation in any known mode." A second application was turned down when the Patent Commissioner ruled that "evaporation *in vacuo*" was not essential to the process. Borden was credited with merely using more care in preparation. A third appeal was refused because Borden had failed to prove that "milk taken fresh from the cow and evaporated in the open air" would not serve the same purpose as his process. A fourth effort, backed by affidavits from General Sam Houston and Robert McFarlane, editor of *Scientific American,* was successful. The date was August 19, 1856.

Now it was time to market the new product. In October, 1856, Borden set up a factory in a converted carriage shop in Wolcottville (now Torrington), Connecticut. He chose the site because the rent was cheap and there was an abundant supply of pure, wholesome milk from the surrounding countryside. He took in two friends as partners, Thomas Green and James Bridge, who provided financial backing, but ran the new enterprise himself, designing and supervising the construction of equipment, overseeing production and personally managing sales. He set up a New York City sales office at 173 Canal Street.

Borden selected his first customer with care—a community leader whose opinion of the product would help solidify this strange company's position in Wolcottville. Charles McNeal, owner of the town's general store and drugstore and operator of the telegraph and post offices, thought well of the product, but few New York City customers did. Accustomed to the watered output of cows kept in distillery stables and fed on fermented mash, a product doctored with chalk for whiteness and molasses for "creaminess," they found Borden's pure condensed milk strange, and therefore suspect. Few bought.

Partners Green and Bridge lost heart. Mr. Borden went to Texas, and the first condensed milk factory closed.

In the spring of 1857 he returned North for another attempt. On May 11, 1857, at Burrville, Connecticut, this time in an abandoned mill, Gail Borden, Jr., and Company, manufacturers of condensed milk, opened for business. It is still in business today, as Borden, Inc., having undergone a succession of corporate names: from the New York Condensed Milk Company (1858), the Borden Condensed Milk Company (1899), The Borden Company (1919), to its present title in 1968.

Gail Borden was fifty-six years old, and on what he called the "downhill side of life," when he started his successful business. It was the last in a series of ventures and adventures that began while he was still in his teens.

He was born on November 9, 1801, in Norwich, New York. Following a family tradition, he became a surveyor. He helped to lay out Covington, Kentucky, and became the official surveyor for Jefferson County, Indiana, when he was only twenty. In time, however, he developed a persistent hacking cough from the constant outdoor work.

Although he had only about two years of formal education, he got a job as a schoolteacher in Amite County, Mississippi, where the warm climate would be good for his health. His students were especially lucky. To strengthen his lungs he ran full speed to school each day, stopping occasionally to scoop up a child, deposit him on his shoulder and take off again at the same pace. Often, he arrived at the schoolhouse door with a delighted youngster on each shoulder.

Then he began to invent. He originated a sort of "prairie schooner," or wagon with sails, which was supposed to travel equally well on land or water. Unfortunately, on its first voyage the unusual vessel tipped over, dumping a cargo of influential occupants into the Gulf of Mexico. Later he invented a "Lazy Susan" table, with two revolving concentric rings for the top, but his wife rejected the device because it couldn't be used with a tablecloth.

In 1835 he became publisher of the *Telegraph and Texas Register*, the first permanent newspaper in Texas. One of his headlines—"Remember the Alamo!"—rallied recruits to the

Lone Star standard, and when the Texans finally won their republic he helped draft its constitution. Later he became collector of customs for the port of Galveston.

But at heart Borden was an inventor. He became obsessed with the desire to find a way to preserve food. First he developed a dehydrated meat biscuit as a replacement for pemmican, the staple of troops, prospectors and scouts. It traveled with the miners to California in the Gold Rush of 1849, but it was never accepted as part of army rations and a large market never developed.

The meat biscuit, however, was considered by many a technical achievement, and unique enough to be awarded a gold medal at the Great Exposition in London in 1851. Borden traveled to London to accept the medal from Queen Victoria, and it was on the voyage back to America that he was inspired to develop a process to preserve milk.

His new condensed milk business was a financial struggle. He had spent too much money on his unprofitable meat biscuit. But soon a chance encounter occurred that gave his business the push it needed. On a train he met Jeremiah Milbank, a conservative New York banker. Milbank liked Borden and, intrigued by his stories of troubles and successes, agreed to back him. As Borden's partner, Milbank invented $100,000 in the condensed milk business. When he died some years later his investment was worth $8 million.

Borden worked constantly, putting in eighteen-hour days at his plant, always talking—to anyone who would listen— about the need for cleanliness in milk production. He insisted that farmers who wanted to sell him milk meet strict conditions of cleanliness for their animals, barns, feed and equipment. In teaching them how to produce milk for his company, he also taught them the possibilities of quantity milk production, as well as saving them long hours of churning and cheese-making.

When he died in 1873 his company was firmly established as the leading milk-condensing company in the United States, and the modern dairy industry had begun. From his first successful factory in Burrville, which offered one product, employed three people and had total sales of $48,000 the first year, grew a corporation that ranks among the nation's fifty leading manufacturing companies. Borden, Inc., had worldwide sales of $2.2 billion in 1972. Of its almost 47,000 employees, some 12,000 are overseas. It has more than 67,000 shareholders, nearly 100 profit centers, more than 300 manufacturing locations and more than 7,500 products.

In August, 1856, a week before his patent was granted, Borden wrote to a friend: "I shall, if I live, within one year either be a citizen of the world, known in every civilized country, or, I shall be a retired, humble individual in the back woods of Texas."

He lived to be a citizen of the world. His condensed milk was being sold in Australia before the Civil War. Philippine natives in Grover Cleveland's time thought the label on Borden condensed milk, a bald eagle rampant, was the American flag. Borden condensed milk went with Peary to the North Pole, and with climbers to the top of Anapurna, the world's second highest mountain.

A few years before his death Gail Borden selected a gravesite in New York City's Woodlawn Cemetery. On it he had placed a large stone shaped like a can of condensed milk. He could see it from the train, high on a knoll, as he passed the cemetery each morning on his way to work. When he died, the stone was removed, and in its place was put a simple marker inscribed with words he had written to a friend, which the friend had chosen for an epitaph: "I tried and failed. I tried again and again, and succeeded."

BURLINGTON INDUSTRIES

□ □ □

Threading Your Way to the Top

In 1923, J. Spencer Love, with the encouragement and backing of the townspeople of Burlington, North Carolina, built a plant there for production of textile fabrics. It was a time when cotton textile prices were low, so Love turned to a new and untried fiber—rayon. In 1924 the new mill began weaving a blend of rayon and cotton and produced its first new product, a bedspread.

The foundation for the future growth and development of Burlington Industries was formed. It was the unique blend of the man, the moment and the decision that combined to breathe life into a new enterprise.

During those early days Burlington Mills grew steadily, if not spectacularly. Within a relatively short span of time it gained a wealth of knowledge in working with the new man-made fiber, so that by 1925 a second plant was making rayon dress goods. Two years later a third plant was opened in order to accommodate the thriving demand for these goods.

Even though these early Burlington Mills plants were not comparable in structure and design to the present-day models, they did have one particularly practical feature. While exterior supporting walls were constructed of bricks and mortar, internal walls were made of wood so they could be easily moved or knocked out for expansion. The walls continued to tumble down with an amazing degree of regularity.

By 1937 Burlington was the world's largest weaver of rayon fabric with twenty-two rayon weaving plants in operation and sales volume of $27 million. That same year, as Burlington Mills, it was listed on the New York Stock Exchange.

From synthetic "greige" (unfinished) goods, Burlington moved to the manufacture of finished fabrics. Further expansion and diversification carried the company into fancy cotton fabrics, hosiery, worsteds, plain cotton goods and blends of all fibers. Thus by 1945, when the newer man-made fibers began to account for an ever-increasing volume

Early employees of Burlington Mills, around 1924.

of business for textile producers, Burlington had more than twenty years of experience in man-made fibers and yarns.

Along with production experience, innovation and know-how, the company continued to develop its management capabilities. Particular stress was placed on merchandising concepts, new and improved methods of distribution, and service to customers. These moves marked a change from the old commission house form of selling textiles. Traditionally, textile mills did not do their own selling; almost all sales were handled by independent commission houses. The system was bad for the industry because decisions about what and how much to manufacture were made in situations totally removed from the buyer.

Management realized that the traditional order must change, and that marketing must determine the mills' output, furnishing direction to the needs of the market and to developing fashion trends.

That the thinking and the changes made were valid is evident today, because this is now the accepted pattern of the textile industry.

By 1962 Burlington had become a significant force in the nation's economy. Sales that year reached a new high—$1.3 billion—reflecting increased volume in all product areas and almost all divisions.

After the death of J. Spencer Love, the mantle of leadership was assumed by Charles F. Myers, Jr., president, and Henry Rauch, chairman, both men of strong financial backgrounds. They knew the company possessed the know-how, the equipment, the talent and the resourcefulness capable of producing the textile products demanded by consumers. New emphasis was placed on research, new product development, quality control standards and new machinery and equipment.

The stage was now set for management to make a critical decision that ultimately:

• Established a totally new awareness of Burlington and its products among consumers.

• Provided the company with a new signature mark.

This decision, in 1965, was to move into national network television. Burlington's sponsorship of a major weekly network program became an industry "first."

The growing identification of Burlington and Burlington products at the retail level was further expedited by adoption of the "weave symbol" as the company's official signature.

By the end of 1967 Burlington was not only the nation's largest and most diversified manufacturer of fabrics and textile products for apparel, home and industry, but also was rapidly becoming a household word as a result of its consistent promotional efforts.

The company began its fiftieth year in 1973 with 135 plants in the United States and others in ten countries abroad and in Puerto Rico. Charles F. Myers is now chairman and chief executive, and Horace C. Jones is president and chief operating officer. Employees number 84,000; sales in 1972 were $1.8 billion.

Public recognition of the Burlington name continues to grow through national network advertising and promotion of brand-name consumer products.

Significant changes have been made within the company during the last two years. One of the most important involved changes in product lines as the company moved into markets considered good for growth and earnings potential. One example is the rapid expansion of knit and stretch woven apparel fabric manufacture, which has nearly tripled over the past three years. Another example is the continued growth of home furnishings, which in 1972 constituted one-third of Burlington's total sales volume.

Burlington has moved substantially into the environmental field. Under the guidance of a company safety and health committee, major efforts are under way at each plant location to identify and eliminate potential hazards within the plant. Corporate safety and health personnel have been added to guide division and plant programs.

Occupational health programs include medical screening of employees, hearing protection, control of environmental conditions, and the elimination of materials handling, chemical and physical hazards. Research, engineering and purchasing departments are working with manufacturers of machinery and chemicals to improve employee safety.

In 1971 Burlington invested some $2.2 million in projects to install or improve pollution control facilities.These expenditures totaled $3.5 million in 1972 and are expected to be $4.5 million in 1973.

The company's support of educational, as well as health, social and other public interest programs, has continued, with particular regard to community needs in Burlington's areas of operation. These and other efforts reflect Burlington's concern for and involvement in good industrial citizenship.

CARRIER

□ □ □

Keeping Cool at Ringside

When Willis Haviland Carrier, the father of air conditioning, developed the machine that launched the comfort cooling industry, he was so uncertain anyone would come to see
it that he scheduled a six-round boxing bout to draw an
audience.

The debut was set for May 22, 1922. Dr. Carrier had developed the first air-conditioning system twenty years earlier, but it was designed for industrial use in a printing
plant. There was no suitable cooling device to provide comfort in big buildings.

Previously, cooling machines for factory air conditioning
employed reciprocating ammonia compressors. They were
physically huge, mechanically complex and difficult to control. They could not be directly driven by electric motors
or steam turbines. And they were dangerous in heavily
populated buildings. Ammonia refrigerant is toxic and explosive. Even a small leak of the pungent gas could cause
panic.

Dr. Carrier's new cooling machine used a centrifugal com-
pressor with a safe refrigerant. The system chilled water for
air conditioning, corrected all the other deficiencies and
was more economical to own and operate.

Still, air conditioning was such an infant industry, Dr.
Carrier wasn't sure the 300 invited New York engineers

Dr. Willis Carrier with the centrifugal refrigeration machine he invented in 1922. This model is displayed at the Smithsonian Institution in Washington, D.C.

would travel to the Carrier plant in nearby Newark, New Jersey, to see the new unit's maiden run. To help them decide, he offered a free dinner and the boxing bout.

No one recalls who won the fight, or even the names of the boxers, but some details of that evening are well documented. The dinner tables, set up in the machine shop, were crowded. The new centrifugal refrigeration machine was in operation nearby, behind curtains, when Dr. Carrier rose to tell how it worked.

He had scarcely launched his talk when a loud, long grinding noise erupted behind the canvas curtain. The noise was suspiciously like that of a high-speed rotating device surging. The inventor knew his centrifugal was turning over at 3,500 r.p.m.

Dr. Carrier, maintaining his cool despite his fears, continued talking. Meanwhile, J. Irvine Lyle, a longtime associate and general manager of the company, quietly slipped behind the curtain, expecting to find disaster.

In a moment Lyle reappeared and signaled to Dr. Carrier that all was well. The frightening noise had been caused by a heavy metal shop table being dragged over a rough concrete floor to make room for the boxing match.

The pioneer machine operated perfectly when the dinner guests crowded around it. (After a working career of twenty-eight years, it was placed on permanent display at the Smithsonian Institution in Washington, D.C.)

Immediate industrial sales were made for centrifugal air conditioning systems. Leading candy manufacturers were the first to buy. And it was not long before Dr. Carrier's novel machine had created a huge new market for comfort air conditioning.

In 1924 the J. L. Hudson department store in Detroit bought three units of 195 tons cooling capacity each for its basement sales area. The same year three more centrifugals were sold to cool theaters in Dallas and Houston. The success of these installations set the stage for an appearance at New York's Rivoli Theater in 1925.

Before this showcase job could be completed, however,

Dr. Carrier was faced with an unexpected problem. The New York City building code barred centrifugals because dielene, the perfectly safe refrigerant it used, was not listed as "approved."

The city safety chief would not issue an installation permit, so Dr. Carrier decided to call on him and try an experiment.

"Right in his office," he later recalled, "I poured some dielene into an open container and dropped a lighted match in it. The safety chief got mad, and scared too, I think. He said if we were going to try such stunts, we should go elsewhere. All the while the dielene burned down very slowly —no flare-up, no explosion."

The impromptu demonstration, plus the proved safety record of the machines already in service, finally carried the day. The air-conditioned Rivoli made box-office history and launched the major movie theater market. Comfort cooling was here to stay.

By 1930 293 centrifugal refrigeration machines had been sold to provide 40,000 tons of cooling for skyscrapers, stores, the House and Senate chambers in Washington, the battleship U.S.S. *Wyoming*, Madison Square Garden and even a gold mine in Brazil.

At the New York World's Fair in 1940 Dr. Carrier predicted that within twenty-five years public utilities would sell chilled water piped under city streets to air-condition buildings. Thanks to his centrifugal, this bold forecast came true just twenty-two years later with the development of the first district cooling plant in Hartford, Connecticut.

In 1962 The Hartford Gas Company (now Connecticut Natural Gas Corporation) began delivering chilled water and steam from a district plant to the complex of new skyscrapers and several older buildings that constitutes downtown Hartford following a major urban renewal project. By 1965 this new kind of business required 15,000 tons of centrifugal cooling to serve fourteen customer-buildings connected to the utility plant by pipelines buried under 3,600 feet of Hartford streets. A dozen companies from coast to coast now sell chilled water generated in district plants by centrifugals.

The first seed of the district plant concept was actually sown the same year of the prediction. In 1940 Southern Methodist University in Dallas began operating the world's first true central plant. Other universities followed. Scores of colleges and universities in the United States and Canada now have central cooling and heating plants to serve all types of campus buildings.

Today the centrifugal is the heart of most big building systems around the world. It helped make possible the Houston Astrodome, where major-league baseball and football games, as well as many other events, take place in an ideal atmosphere no matter what the season or time of day.

Centrifugals go to sea in oceanliners and help provide healthful comfort below the sea in nuclear submarines. Miniature versions smaller than a basketball, their rotors spinning at 85,000 r.p.m., even serve in the sky to cool jet airliners.

At this writing, more than 38,000 centrifugals, providing more than 15 million tons of cooling capacity, have been sold. And air conditioning for human comfort is by far the biggest part of the $6 billion climate control industry.

Equipment now ranges from small-room units with less than a half-ton of cooling capacity to giant centrifugals with a capacity of 10,000 tons each. In between these extremes literally thousands of different types of packaged units and system components are available for every conceivable space occupied by people.

Meanwhile, the machine that gave comfort cooling such a boost has continually played a vital role in industrial processes. This is true of products as diverse as chewing gum, beer and penicillin. Centrifugals have been particularly useful in the manufacture of synthetic substances.

The manufacture of rayon, well advanced prior to the centrifugal, nevertheless was greatly benefited by the high-capacity chiller as early as the twenties. In the thirties it was nylon's turn.

In the forties butadiene, essential in making artificial rubber, owed its mass production to compact, efficient centrifugal refrigeration. During World War II, when America was cut off from sources of natural latex, air-conditioned stores, including Tiffany's in New York, gave up their Carrier centrifugals so butadiene production could be more rapidly expanded. Shoppers and clerks sweltered for the duration while soldiers rode on rubber-tired trucks and jeeps.

Low-temperature centrifugal air conditioning, down to —40° F., quick-freezes the baked goods of Sara Lee in Chicago and herring and halibut in one of the world's largest fish freezing plants in Bergen, Norway.

Special industrial centrifugal refrigeration machines, in basic design kissing-cousins to the one Carrier conceived for climate control, turn natural gas into a liquid at —260° F. Liquefaction reduces the volume of natural gas 600 times, so the fuel may be shipped overseas in cryogenic tankers.

The air-conditioning industry has come a long, long way since Willis Haviland Carrier introduced his revolutionary centrifugal water chiller a half-century ago, with a boxing bout to lure his audience. Nowadays air conditioning is the added attraction at boxing bouts.

COCA-COLA

□ □ □

Letting the Genie Out of the Bottle

In 1955 The Coca-Cola Company faced perhaps the most difficult decision in its corporate history. Although it had only one product in two packages—the familiar 6½-ounce bottle and the fountain glass—it was a highly successful business enterprise. Volume continued its steady increase from 400 drinks sold in its first year to 50 million drinks worldwide every day in 1955. Profit growth had kept pace.

Amid this success, a somewhat strange concept—change —entered the picture. To change at this stage, many felt, would be to tamper with success. But the reasons for diversification overshadowed those doubts.

This decision was no spur-of-the moment move. As the entire top echelon of management weighed the long-range results of diversification, they studied the statistics of failure. They knew that of the 6,000 new consumer items introduced each year, only about 500 lived beyond their first twelve months. But at the same time, they knew that the world was moving and changing. The world was Coca-Cola's customer and they knew that the company must move with it.

The first change was in its own way so radical a switch that it amounted almost to the introduction of a new drink. Changing the size of a bottle of Coke meant tampering with a bottle that had been called with justification "the most perfectly designed commercial package in history." To put Coca-

The evolution of the world's most familiar bottle. The characteristic bulbous shape of the modern Coke bottle design (patented in 1915) was inspired by the contours of the cola nut.

1799098

The "family-size" Coke bottle, introduced in 1956.

Cola into another dimension, some felt, was almost heresy. A genie had been kept in the same bottle, so to speak, for nearly three-quarters of a century and no one knew what would happen if he were let out.

Based upon a great deal of market research and a series of highly successful tests, the company felt somewhat akin to prospectors who had uncovered gold after months and even years of sloshing through the Klondike. Now the consumer can buy (besides the original 6½-ounce bottle) 10-ounce, 12-ounce, 16-ounce and 26-ounce, 28-ounce, 32-ounce and 48-ounce one-way bottles; a 32-ounce returnable-resealable bottle; 12-ounce and 16-ounce cans, and a 5-gallon pre-mix container for food counter dispensers. A plastic bottle for Coca-Cola is being developed.

Making Coca-Cola available to consumers in a variety of packages, then, was the first cautious step toward diversification for The Coca-Cola Company.

When it came to the second step, marketing new soft drinks, the company also moved carefully. It turned to an item it already had in the house and knew something about. This one, the Fanta line of flavored drinks, had begun in Germany when World War II made the concentrates from which Coca-Cola syrup is produced completely unavailable there. After the war, Coke came back and Fanta was filed but not forgotten. It was brought back in 1955 when the company decided to launch new soft drinks. Today, the Fanta line reaches most of the markets in this country. Fanta Orange is one of the world's most popular and widely distributed brands of orange carbonated soft drinks.

In rapid succession came Sprite, a lemon-lime drink, and TAB, a low-calorie beverage—rapid in the sense that they were introduced into the marketplace quickly. Actually, from the standpoint of money invested and time spent, no market research program leading to new product introduction moves more slowly or with greater in-depth consideration than does that at The Coca-Cola Company.

After the introduction of Sprite and TAB came the third step, venturing outside the company. In 1960 Coca-Cola ac-

quired the Minute Maid Corporation, the firm that held the
top position in the citrus processing industry. Minute Maid
itself had been doing some diversifying and had previously
acquired an instant coffee company. As a result, Coca-Cola
was automatically in the coffee business. A logical next step
was to keep looking down that road and in 1964 Coca-Cola
joined with Duncan Foods Company, which made and distributed a top line of coffee and tea products on a regional
basis.

A second low-calorie drink, Fresca, made its appearance
in 1966. Before introduction, the product and its marketing program had been four years in the making. First came
the testing of citrus-based calorie-free drinks in company laboratories, followed by wide-ranging tests with company personnel around the country. This led to the final choice of a
formula and more tests on thousands of potential customers
at fairs, shopping centers and finally "in home use tests."
Full-scale test markets at widely separated points of the
country came next. Meanwhile, the marketing specialists
were experimenting with various approaches to the launching of the new product. The winner was: "Fresca tastes like
a Blizzard."

As the record proves, Fresca was one of the most spectacular successes in the history of soft drinks, achieving 95
percent national distribution in one year. The Food and
Drug Administration's 1969 ban on cyclamate, the artificial
sweetener used in both Fresca and TAB, produced minimal
effect on total company business. Reformulated versions
without cyclamate were prepared and on the market in a
relatively short time.

In 1968 the company undertook the development of
nutritional beverages which could benefit not only the
people in developing countries, but also people everywhere
who don't receive enough nourishment for sound bodies and
healthy minds. A long-range objective is to develop a variety
of good-tasting nutritional beverages that are compatible
with different consumer food preferences around the world,
and toward this end every effort is being made to utilize

locally available protein sources. The company's first protein-based beverage, placed in a South American test market in 1968, used local soybeans as a protein source. Future ones will use other protein sources in the research and development program which continues in this highly important nutritional beverage field.

In 1970 the company introduced in Surinam a protein-based beverage under the trademark "Samson," which utilizes casein as its protein source. Tai, which derives its protein from milk whey, was introduced in 1971 in Brazil.

In 1969 a major branded line of mixers under the trademark "Santiba" was introduced in test markets. Available in four flavors, Santiba was the first line of products introduced by the company in one-way packaging with easy-open caps.

In product tests conducted in homes prior to test marketing, Santiba gave an impressive performance. Over 65 percent of consumers tested preferred the mixer to their present brand, and 75 percent like the new line's extra "hint" of added citrus flavor which consumers usually add to spice their mixed drinks. The allure of a tropical isle where the living is relaxed and leisurely is used in introducing the product.

As much preparation, testing, feedback and retesting goes on with marketing programs as goes on in the laboratory. To put millions of dollars behind a product that does not give reasonable evidence of consumer acceptance would be wasteful. At the same time, to have a product that consumers tell you they like and then not give it everything you've got would be an even greater waste.

The Coca-Cola Company has an extremely important extra motive for taking greater care. Whenever a new product is to be introduced through the franchise bottler system, it has a responsibility not only to itself but also to the independent business concerns that are bottlers of the products it develops. (There are 750 bottlers of Coca-Cola in the United States. Outside the United States there are some 850 bottlers.) So a new introduction is like an am-

phibious landing—there is no turning back. Either a successful beachhead is established, or the result is a shambles.

A vital part of the company's business is to keep satisfying,
and holding, customers with new and worthwhile products.
However, the results of research and development must be
carefully balanced against the abilities of marketing specialists to position the new product with the consumer . . . and
all this has to be done at a profit.

Today the world calls for Coca-Cola over 155 million times
a day in more than 80 languages, and that includes only
Coca-Cola and not the seventeen other soft drinks manufactured by The Coca-Cola Company nor the other beverage
products of the company's Foods Division and Tenco Division. The Coca-Cola Company's soft-drink business reaches
into more than 130 countries around the world.

In addition to its business of carbonated beverages, The
Coca-Cola Company is the world's largest processor and
marketer of citrus concentrates and drinks, a cultivator and
harvester of thousands of acres of citrus groves, the world's
largest producer of private-label instant coffees and teas and
one of the foremost U.S. coffee importers and roasters.

The company acquired through merger in 1970 Aqua-
Chem, Inc., based in Milwaukee, which manufactures packaged steam and hot-water generators, equipment for de-
salting seawater and pollution-control equipment for the
purification of water.

This diversity of products, 250 in all, has pushed corporate
sales to a record $1.87 billion in 1972, with a net profit of
$190 million—a lengthy sprint for a venture that netted $50
in the first year of its lifetime.

DU PONT

□ □ □

Encourage the Seeker
and Find Nylon

With a history dating back to 1802, the Du Pont company has experienced many critical periods in its evolution from a small producer of black powder to its present role as the world's largest manufacturer of chemicals and allied products. One such date, 1902, the company's anniversary year, has been celebrated as the time when a century-old family ownership yielded to a publicly-held corporation and the producer of the country's premier explosives began to diversify its operations.

But the great moment of decision, the time of maturity, for Du Pont came a quarter-century later, when a Du Pont research manager's vision crystallized into a bold proposal, and that proposal was approved by the company's innovative president.

Dr. Charles M. A. Stine, not yet forty-four although a twenty-year veteran of Du Pont research, had been chemical director (the title "research director" had not yet achieved its present aura of respect) since 1924. Small, intense, already of acknowledged stature among U.S. industrial scientists, Dr. Stine believed that the time had come for chemical manufacturers to stop depending on research departments in academic institutions as sources of discovery.

In his three-year stint as chemical director he had been sounding out his colleagues on what the company needed to

Dr. Charles M. A. Stine, who argued that a company such as Du Pont should not have to depend on universities, won approval for a program of "fundamental research."

revitalize itself. The conclusion he drew from this process of self-examination: Du Pont needed a program of *fundamental* studies, principally in organic chemistry, chemical engineering and catalytic processes.

He defined fundamental research as "a quest for facts about the properties and behavior of matter, without regard to a specific application of the facts discovered."

To most interpreters, "without regard to a specific application" is the heart of the matter. Dr. Stine, however, carefully pointed out in all discussions of his dream program that "fundamental research properly carried on is bound to add to the sum total of knowledge, some . . . results of which may be immediately useful and all of which will eventually be so." He added that "fundamental research . . . is not . . . a labor of love; it is . . . a sound business policy, a policy that should assure the payment of future dividends."

Dr. Stine first tried to put his theory to work in his own department budget, by including a special allotment of $30,-000 for "basic research." He quickly realized, however, that the program he envisioned needed much bolder financing. He framed a letter to the company's executive committee in December, 1926, and carried the message personally to the president.

Lammot du Pont, forty-seven, company president for one year, was himself a chemist who was well informed of the new directions and challenges of the chemical industry. His family had produced many innovations in the development of the explosives industry, and applied research had long been a company tradition. After listening to Dr. Stine's proposal that the Du Pont company undertake a program of research studies previously practiced only by universities and a few foundations, Lammot du Pont agreed. Moreover, he agreed without reservation to Dr. Stine's condition that the work be carried out regardless of the immediate practical value it might have for Du Pont. He continued his strong support throughout the Depression years which followed.

His historic decision set a course which profoundly affected future research throughout the chemical industry.

Companies especially alert to the seemingly unlimited possibilities of polymer chemistry, to which Du Pont's program gave new life and strong practical application, were to become fierce competitors later through their quick pickup of Du Pont's pioneering approach.

Dr. Stine's catalytic role, however, did not end with the reception of the first $250,000 budget (with a pledge of a minimum of $750,000 over five years) for exploratory work. What makes great moments "momentous" is often the judicious and energetic follow-up of the original decision.

Among his first tasks was to recruit exceptional scientists from the universities to give his program a good start. Principal among them was the man who was to head the organic chemistry group—Dr. Wallace H. Carothers. Already receiving wide attention for his interest in long-chain molecules, Dr. Carothers elected to explore the synthesis of these superpolymers with his staff in the Du Pont laboratories.

Though Carothers was given complete freedom to proceed on his own, he found his subject matter already relevant to Du Pont's going business. Several of Du Pont's basic product lines—smokeless powder, rayon, cellophane, "Duco" paints and lacquers—were based on cellulose, a natural polymer containing several thousand molecular units linked in a chain. But Carothers and his associates set out to create synthetic chains containing atoms of nitrogen and oxygen along with carbon. Building upon "difunctional" organic acids and bases, Carothers' group created a number of new superpolymers falling into two major classes: the polyesters (containing oxygen in the chain) and the polyamides (containing nitrogen).

As early as the third year of the program the research team noted that some of the superpolymers could be drawn into tough fiberlike materials. Dr. Stine, well aware of the fruitlessness of projects in applied research that had sought practical analogues of rayon and acetate, urged the fundamental group to think of fibers as one "useful" end result of the exploration.

Concentrating first on the polyesters, Carothers found that

some could be drawn out into fibers, but their low melting points and susceptibility to a wide range of solvents made them impractical. So he turned to the polyamides. Finally, in 1935, five years after the first curious interest in fiber properties and eight years after the establishment of the fundamental research program, Carothers setttled on a highly promising polymer, derived from hexamethylene diamine and adipic acid. The polyamide was given the name nylon.

Four years of frenetic activity in the classical procedure of translating laboratory discoveries into commercial realities followed. Some 230 organic, physical and analytical chemists, mechanical, chemical and electrical engineers, physicists, statisticians and other skilled technical personnel scrambled over and around each other to create the industrial process and the industrial plant. Nylon was offered to the world in 1938.

The first decade of Du Pont fundamental research also produced neoprene, the first successful general-purpose synthetic rubber. In fact, neoprene preceded the more widely celebrated nylon into the marketplace. The search for a man-made elastomer had gone on for decades, with seemingly endless disappointment. But Carothers' group, applying their fundamental knowledge in superpolymers to the chemistry of acetylene, were able to produce a "rubber" which still offers a unique combination of desirable characteristics.

Dr. Stine and his bright young men were able, too, to report other "substantial contributions," both to the scientific literature and to the company's progress. Most important of all to Du Pont's future was the penetration of high-polymer thinking into the company's operating departments, thereby assuring a continuity of practical effort. Thus were created whole new families of fibers, films, plastics, paints, elastomers and related products.

The moment of decision in 1927 transformed a company somewhat provincial in its interests and operations into an international corporation which today has over 100,000 employees and 1,600 product lines serving every industry.

EATON

□ □ □

The Ideas Whose Time Had Come

In 1911, when the fledgling automotive industry was putting the nation on wheels, a young man in New Jersey noted with some dismay that the only difference between a passenger car and a truck was the body style.

Joseph Oriel Eaton foresaw a nation where not only people, but food, manufactured products, raw materials and every manner of goods would be transported over the roads. He was sure that trucks had to be sturdier, bigger and more versatile than passenger cars.

With a group of associates he attacked the problem by developing truck axles in a small machine shop in Bloomfield, New Jersey. Customers were few and doubtful at first. About the only way to sell a truck axle was to build an entire truck around it. This is what he did, and it worked; seven axles were sold in the first year.

Eaton, the son of an Ohio farmer, had helped pay his way through Williams College by painting protraits. After graduation in 1895 he held a variety of selling jobs. For a time he was an $8-a-week clerk at the American Express Company. It wasn't until he was in his mid-thirties that his creativity and administrative skill found fertile ground in, of all places, the making of truck axles.

Eaton's small company soon outgrew its quarters and moved to Cleveland to be nearer truck manufacturers. Other

J. O. Eaton, founder of Eaton Corporation.

The original Eaton Corporation factory in Bloomfield, New Jersey, where, in 1911, J. O. Eaton and his associates began manufacturing truck axles.

elements and components for cars and trucks were developed and the Eaton Manufacturing Company was well on the way to becoming a leading supplier in the vital fields of moving men and materials.

Early in his career Eaton developed a philosophy that still guides the company that bears his name: "The highest quality products at the most economical prices in the most competitive markets."

The company grew through development and acquisition. Over the years many famous names of American industry joined its ranks and added their quality products to the company's growing competence.

On January 1, 1966, Eaton merged with Yale & Towne, the famed lock and hardware company. There were similarities in the men involved in conceiving both enterprises. Both Eaton and Linus Yale, Jr., were portrait painters in their youth and both embarked on business careers with ideas "whose time had come"—Eaton with the truck axle, Yale with the pin-tumbler cylinder lock, which to this day remains the basic element of security the world over.

Yale, son of a well-known lockmaker and inventor, was a devoted angler, and it was probably during a fishing session that he first sketched his ideas for the pin-tumbler lock. This locking principle, which was known to the ancient Egyptians, was perfected by Yale into the secure and inexpensive mass-produced lock of today, virtually unchanged in design after a hundred years.

A modestly successful dreamer, Yale looked to Henry Towne, a young engineer and administrator, for the successful management of the company. When Yale died of a heart attack at forty-seven, Towne carried the Yale name and products throughout the world. The company became Yale & Towne in 1883 and Henry Towne served as its president for an amazing fifty years.

Recognizing the international market for axles, valves, transmissions, locks and lift trucks, Eaton embarked on a program of international manufacturing in the late fifties. Today the company has manufacturing operations in twenty-two Free World nations.

About 28 percent of the company's sales are generated outside of the United States. These operations are managed for the most part by citizens of the host nation along with a number of "third nation" managers, most of whom are not Americans. The products are made for the market served by each facility and are not imported into the United States.

Eaton feels very strongly that the cooperation of men and women of many nations in attacking the problems of productivity and marketing will go much farther in assuring world peace and understanding than a century of diplomatic conferences.

Although it began as a supplier to the automotive and truck manufacturing industries, Eaton has expanded into many fields. Today industrial power transmission, construction and forestry equipment and a wide range of materials-handling systems and security systems for homes and business bear the mark of quality that Joseph Eaton insisted upon. It is a tribute to his foresight that no car or truck made in the United States comes off the assembly line without some Eaton-manufactured parts in it. This is true also of a large percentage of cars and trucks produced outside this country. The average family car today has more than a hundred parts and components manufactured by Eaton.

In 1971 the company was faced with a major decision—a name change. Known for five years as Eaton Yale & Towne, and by various other names prior to that, it had not succeeded in making its name, the scope of its activities and its role as a corporate citizen fully known to its many publics. And there were many more directions it was planning to take. In order to unite all its activities and products under a single, readily recognized name, the company became known as Eaton Corporation. Efforts are being designed to make that name one of the best known in the world.

Today Eaton has taken on a new challenge, one Joseph Eaton would have championed. A detailed and comprehensive program has been designed to correct one of the most serious problems that has ever faced the business sector of our economy—the lack of understanding and the overall distrust of business among the general public. Entitled "Comm/Pro," this program was started in mid-1972 when several national surveys established this lack of confidence. The surveys indicated that in 1966 55 percent of the general public had confidence in business and felt that business was fulfilling its role in the economy and the society. The same poll conducted in 1971 revealed that only 27 percent of the public had confidence that business was functioning as it should. The prime source of this disapproval of business by an overwhelming majority of Americans is profits. Unfortunately the public's information has been sorely inaccurate on this score—studies reveal that the average American believes that corporations make profits seven times greater than what they actually do make.

In Comm/Pro more than a hundred of Eaton's top managers all across the country, including every officer in the company, have been trained to speak to communities about business. These executives speak at meetings of Rotary Clubs, P.T.A.'s, church groups, and just about anywhere else they can get an audience. They discuss profits and the necessary part they play in rejuvenating and furthering the growth of our economy. They answer questions relating to imports and exports, multinational companies, youth in business and environmental issues. They explain the role of business in correcting social ills and meeting the needs of society.

It is not the type of program that will sell more axles or transmissions or Yale locks tomorrow . . . or next month . . . or even next year. But it is an effort that must be undertaken not only by Eaton, but by businessmen everywhere to guarantee the survival of our free enterprise system of economic government. Through this effort Eaton hopes to tell the true story of business, to get the facts before the people. For business has been and will continue to be the prime growth factor in our economy. Eaton wants American business to regain the credibility that it truly deserves. Joe Eaton, a onetime $8-a-week clerk who had a good idea, would be proud of this effort.

EXXON

□ □ □

Striking It Big—the Unorthodox Way

In the summer of 1921 Exxon USA's first geologist, Wallace E. Pratt, felt insecure. The four-year-old oil company, expecting him to find the oil it critically needed, had backed him in a multimillion-dollar venture near Ranger, Texas. Although a technological success, the gamble proved to be an economic failure, and the pressure on Pratt from his employers mounted. As he recalls, "The future was black and my stock was at a low ebb." Pratt and Exxon USA both very badly needed a discovery.

An opportunity had developed earlier that year when a wildcatter completed a flowing well on a block of leases near Mexia in east central Texas. A north-south trending anticline (a type of geological structure capable of trapping oil) which was shown on a U.S. Geological Survey map had been tested. In the following months more good wells were drilled. Interest in the area heightened, with most observers believing the bulk of the field lay to the east of the discovery well.

As chief geologist, Pratt had been aware of the Mexia anticline but at first was unimpressed, writing in April, "We do not consider this well . . . particularly significant." However, he decided to watch the development more closely and assigned Dwight Edson, a geologist just graduated from Dartmouth, to study the area.

The Famous Golden Lane, Mexia, Texas.

The young man began gathering some disturbing, apparently conflicting, geological data. Confused, he notified Pratt, who journeyed from Houston and joined him at his home in Mexia.

As Pratt recalls, "We were in his tiny kitchen late Saturday night. Mrs. Edson had gone to bed. We were tired and frustrated, but still puzzling over our astounding data when suddenly the light broke and there was the complete explanation, simple and plain as day."

The answer was this: First, the oil accumulation was not controlled by the anticline, but was trapped in the east-dipping Woodbine sand against the east side of the fault. Second, the fault plant was not vertical, as others had assumed, but was inclined at a flat angle, dipping to the west. This meant that the fault had to intersect the oil sand far to the west of where its surface indications were to be found.

The point at which the fault plane cut through the sand some 3,000 feet below the surface would determine the western limit of the field.

Pratt then realized that the most prolific oil sand would be close to the fault at the western edge of the field's dimensions, and not to the east, as others believed.

It was midnight, but Pratt telephoned Houston and woke his boss, Will Farish, to request the authority he needed to proceed. Since Pratt's ideas contradicted popular opinion, it seemed he was taking an awful gamble. But Farish was convinced. Exxon USA scraped together $400,000 for him and Pratt began leasing heavily west of the fault.

The drill proved Pratt's judgment to be flawless. The best part of the field lay under Exxon USA's leases.

From Mexia, Pratt moved northeastward up the same fault zone to lease what became about one-third of the prodigious Powell field. So accurate were his readings that of the first 180 wells drilled by Exxon USA, 175 were producers —a phenomenal record. Exxon USA climbed out of the red as production soared from 7.8 million barrels in 1920 to 17 million in 1923.

In the middle twenties Pratt began to push development of geophysics. He also proposed a new plan calling for the leasing of large blocks of land as opposed to the prevailing checkerboard pattern of that era.

These two ideas came together in the discovery of the Sugarland (Texas) field, the first major oil field found by seismic surveying. Because of Exxon USA's unique lease position, it also became the first field in which the new concept of pressure maintenance to increase oil recovery could be tried.

Pratt's genius as a geologist, trader and organization builder led to discoveries at Raccoon Bend, Anahuac and Baytown, and purchases at Thompsons, Conroe and Tom O'Connor, all in Texas, which increased the company's reserves from 219 million barrels in 1930 to 1,905 million barrels in 1937.

A major Pratt thesis, not widely accepted in that era,

held: "Hydrocarbons are normal constituents of marine sed-
imentary rocks." This idea sustained him in his conviction
that Exxon USA should purchase a wholly unconventional
twenty-year-term oil and gas lease on the one-million-acre
King Ranch in 1933. This vast South Texas property was
situated deep in a region then rated as barren of oil. Pratt's
fellow directors on the board were dubious, but he persisted
until they finally agreed.

Once again, his judgment was correct. Developed with
great care over several decades, the King Ranch now has
over 600 producing oil and gas wells and is the site of the
world's largest natural gas processing plant.

But Pratt gave his greatest discovery to the American
people—the geological wonderland and scenic sanctuary of
McKittrick Canyon, heart of Guadalupe Mountains National
Park in the wilderness of West Texas. When the park is open
to the general public in mid-1970s, the Park Service estimates a half-million visitors a year will see the hidden
beauty Pratt first discovered in 1921, just as the young
geologist found it. The park's most spectacular feature
was formed more than 200 million years ago. Framed with a
canyon of utmost majesty, it is a sheer and magnificent exposure of the Captain Barrier Reef, one of the most extensive fossil reefs known. The reef was slowly erected by the
lime-secreting organisms of ancient Permian sea known to
geologists as the Guadalupian. Its warm waters, bursting
with marine life, extended over much of New Mexico and
West Texas. The organic remains of these myriad sea crea-
tures later became, through nature's chemistry, the petroleum found today in the prolific oil and gas fields of the
great geological province known as the Permian Basin.

Naturally this prehistoric paradise is of intense interest to
geologists. For half a century they have come from all over
the world to ponder and interpret the Capitan limestone
formation thrusting as high as 2,000 feet above the floor of
McKittrick Canyon. More than 500 species of fossils have
been found there. It is a geological and paleontological
treasure house. And it is lovely beyond imagining.

"My interest in it was esthetic, not professional," Pratt remembers. "I had been told simply that it was the most beautiful spot in Texas. So I drove a hundred-odd miles in an old Model-T to see for myself." He found the canyon fully as beautiful as he had been led to believe, but the unusual geological significance of it was immediately apparent to him as well. The upshot of that visit in 1921 was that, over the next few years "and largely with borrowed money," Pratt eventually acquired full ownership of McKittrick Canyon and its surrounding acreage.

It has not changed since Pratt acquired it. "Mr. Pratt is an inspiration to the people who are designing and planning this park," says National Park Service Ranger Roger Reisch. "It is a masterpiece of conservation and preservation—which is a tribute to Mr. Pratt's practices here. He kept it pristine and untrammeled."

Pratt's gift of 5,632 acres comprising the heart of the 77,000-acre park (additional acreage was purchased from others for $1.5 million) is officially a "scientific preserve." Pratt says, "For me and my colleagues, McKittrick for many years has been a source of knowledge and understanding of the world about and beneath us." He expresses the hope that the canyon will continue as a timeless source of inspiration.

Pratt, a wise and percipient man who still maintains worldwide contact with the leaders of geological studies, now resides at the foot of the Santa Catalina Mountains just outside Tucson, Arizona. He is pleased that his gift may soon be seen by millions of Americans as a side trip from Carlsbad Caverns National Park, forty-five minutes away, and Lincoln National Forest, which adjoins the new park to the north.

"They can learn a great deal about their world, and about themselves, out there," he says. A practical oilman, a scientist, and a philosopher, he quotes Shakespeare: "And this our life, exempt from public haunt, finds tongues in trees, books in the running brooks, sermons in stone and good in everything."

Alert and active, Pratt is widely esteemed in his profession. Some fellow practitioners consider him one of the world's greatest geologists. This is a mantle he declines to wear, insisting his work was neither great nor innovative. Nevertheless, his pioneering application of practical earth science to oil-finding helped to convert petroleum geology from an esoteric specialty into a scientific discipline of remarkable effectiveness and utility. Simultaneously his accomplishments moved Exxon USA into a major role as the nation's leading producer of crude oil and natural gas with the nation's largest petroleum reserves.

FORD

□ □ □

Riding the Model T to Mass Production

From its incorporation in 1903 Ford Motor Company gave America countless innovations and made innumerable momentous decisions contributing to the ferment and growth of the vast automotive industry in this country.

Some would identify the decision to battle relentlessly against the effort of owners of the Selden patent to dominate the automobile industry as a most striking single step.

Some would give this primacy to the decision, after the Panic of 1907 had prostrated half the motorcar manufacturers of the United States, to undertake a new Model T—distinguished by such improvements as vanadium steel, an improved magneto and carburetor and stronger transmission —and push it by expansion of the sales organization with new branches, dealers and efficient services.

The succession of great new steps led—through the lowering of Model T prices to bring it within reach of the poor mechanic and farmer, the introduction of the V-8 engine in 1932 and the adoption of such liberal policies as Ford's $5 day and its employment of handicapped men and former convicts—to the emergence of Ford Motor Company as one of the greatest money-makers in the United States, amassing profits of over $900 million in 1927, and able to breast the Depression of 1931–1933 triumphantly.

But in the long view of history probably the most original

Henry Ford first used the modern moving assembly line in the summer of 1913. Production was speeded up, and soon a completed Model T was rolling off the line every ten seconds.

and powerful executive action by the heads of Ford Motor Company was a series of steps culminating in the adoption of mass production methods, making Ford not only one of the most productive and richest manufacturing corporations in America, but also the perfector and master of a mode of work that changed the face and value of industry the world over. It enabled Ford to make a tremendous contribution to the success of the United States in World War I, World War II and ensuing struggles.

To grasp the momentous character of these policy decisions it is essential to understand the true character of mass production. It is not merely quantity production, with which it is often confused. It is a modernized mode of manufacture that combines uniformity and continuity of motion in all factory procedures and assembly lines, speed achieved by scientific time studies, and precision of every part and operation. It makes uniformity of design, accuracy of part changes and economy of performance possible.

Mass production also requires such specialization of machinery and machine operation that one task may be assigned to one man, or one separate machine function, with repeated subdivision. Early specialization and standardization enabled the International Association of Machinists in the Detroit area to declare in 1896 that "the all-around machinist" was "dying out," the jack-of-all-trades in the factory was disappearing. Craft unions, once so powerful in Detroit as in other industrial cities, were giving way to the specialist, expert in one small machine activity. Thus a way was paved to automation, which became a prime element in mass production.

Ford Motor Company began to face a really grave manpower shortage when it announced at the end of winter in 1908 that it was working a full force not only on days but at night as well. It had installed ever finer and more elaborate tools. Edsel Ford lost the tip of a finger to a fine Hendy lathe he was using. Henry Ford, a thoughtful man, then read a great deal or, as an associate records, "would sit quietly and think." He knew all about the incessant changes taking place in the metal trades, and in rival motor works; he knew aviation well; he liked experiment and put an experimental department in his factory. He was glad to see a new model give a livelier zeal for efficiency to Ford shop work. In 1911, as *The Detroit News* noted, he slapped a workman on the back, praising his beautifully kept machine and zest for work. In a few days every machine in the Ford department "shone like a diamond." In fact, he shared in the strong wave of enthusiasm for technological advancement and efficiency that swept the automobile industry in 1908–1909.

The Panic of 1907 and the Depression stimulated a movement for simplification and standardization of a limited number of new and highly durable motor parts. Supervision of the badge-wearing Ford employees by strict, experienced plant superintendents P. E. Martin and Charles Sorensen was watchfully stringent. Ford Motor Company was proud that, from a ten-hour-a-day industry (some American factories worked their men longer), the Ford plant went to a nine-hour day between 1905 and 1910, though hours later rose again. On March 19, 1908, the first circulars on the Model T went to Ford dealers. The response was enthusiastic. Ford executives might well have raised a joyous chant: "The car sounds the knell of high prices and big profits."

Various men had played key roles in creating the epochal new machine: Joseph Galamb, C. Harold Wills, C. J. Smith. Some improvements in bearer adjustment, spark and throttle control and planetary transmission were due less to the Ford Motor Company than to the broad advance of the industry. The precise authorship of some main features of the revolutionary new car can never be determined. But the conclusion stated in the most accurate Ford history may be allowed to stand:

> When all allowances are made, we must repeat that general credit for the Model T unquestionably goes to Henry Ford. His was the controlling plan for a light, powerful, trustworthy cheap car; his was the guiding mind; his was clearly the most powerful personality. We might be

tempted to fall back on the usually accurate theory of
social invention, but all the survivors of that era who have
left reminiscences agree as to his leadership and his paramount contributions.

In some mechanical matters, men then—as later—found
in Ford an extraordinary power of divination.

Ford owed much to his fellow workers Wills, Galamb,
August Degener, Smith and others.

He and his associates had created the Model T. The
Model T and its successors created mass production. Of
course, mass production came in by degrees, unevenly and
irregularly. Some early steps were primitively picturesque.
The moving assembly line, for example, appeared in the
Piquette plant as the company was about to move to Highland Park. Ford, Martin and Sorensen were anxious to install
it, as was later described by a veteran:

> At the Piquette plant I remember that they built a line
> . . . out of railroad ties, iron slides and some horses. They
> put the chassis on there (that is, on the iron slides), and
> they pulled it with a rope. . . .
> They made a long line, maybe 20 or 30 feet long, with the
> two rails. They put the front axle and the rear axle on it,
> and they slid it along so they could connect all the parts
> that were necessary—the engine, brake, and other differ-
> ent parts. That was the start of the assembly line.

The summary of Ford operations for the year closing June
16, 1909, recorded a factory space of 12 acres; average number of employees, 2,190; and the number of cars built,
10,660. Ford could well say gleefully to Sorensen: "We're on
the right track here. We're going to get a car now that we
can make in great volume and get the price a way down."
He might have added that the Ford management had
opened a resplendent new chapter in the industrial history
of the Western World.

The final assembly line was first improvised at Highland
Park in 1913. Production of the Model T was then taking on
huge proportions.

In order to keep up with the fantastic demand for his
light cars, Ford and his brilliant staff of engineers designed,

built and bought tools with which they could produce automobile parts by the thousands, perform numbers of machine
operations simultaneously and otherwise make possible the
production of automobiles at high speed and in large quantities. The new tools led inevitably to interchangeable parts,
which again simplified and accelerated production. They
also led to the construction of radically designed new factories where these machine tools could be placed and used
with maximum efficiency; thus there came into being the
so-called crystal palace at Highland Park, into which Ford
moved from the Piquette plant in 1910.

By the time it was completed, the Highland Park plant
almost filled a 60-acre tract with buildings in which parts
were cast, machined and assembled into complete automobiles at an ever more rapid pace (for several years production virtually doubled each year). Gradually this most
advanced of all automobile plants, crammed with 15,000 machine tools, using huge presses that could stamp out steel
frames and bodies in an instant, employing product-flow
techniques and devices ranging from slides and chutes to a
network of craneways, achieved what is now known as mass
production. The essence of this process was the constant
flow of parts and subassemblies into a moving final assembly
line manned by workers who stood still, each performing a
single operation. Movement of components was continuous
and perfectly timed along each tributary as well as the
mainstream, at the end of which the complete car emerged.

So successful were these operations that by 1914 Ford,
with one-sixth of the nation's automotive labor force, was
making almost one-half of the nation's cars. Assembly plants
were multiplying across the land, enabling the company to
ship components instead of finished cars, which cut transportation costs in half. The legendary $5 day was instituted
as a means of sharing profits with the worker; prices were
cut as a means of sharing profits with the consumer. The
unbelievable results were reduced manufacturing costs and
increased profits on sales. Within a decade Model T run-
abouts were to be offered at $260 retail, and the company

was still able to show a net profit exceeding $80 million for the year.

"No other manufacturer had sufficient quantity," declared Alvin Macauley of Packard, "to go into special machinery as Ford did." And, in the words of a New York banker, "The Ford machinery was the best in the world." The mass production thus made possible enabled management to cut prices while making a better product, and simultaneously to double the minimum daily wage to $5 and still make a profit. Model T's came forth in ever-increasing numbers at ever-decreasing prices till they reached the level of a car every ten seconds, a total of two million T's a year and a bottom price of $260 retail. These were some of the realities of mass production.

Yet such miracles performed by Henry Ford more than half a century ago have turned out to be mere lumbering steps toward mass production in an age of automation, electronics and computer technology. Computer-controlled machines now enable the manufacturer to make products of higher quality than ever before possible. A computer, closed-circuit television and a video tape system help Ford manufacture "float" glass today in ribbons miles long. A sophisticated system of computer technology known as "numerical control" has speeded the process of transforming blueprints and clay models into dies which stamp the doors, fenders and many other sheet-metal parts of cars made by Ford Motor Company. Henry Ford may never have envisioned such prodigies of industrial achievement. But the vison he showed in formulating the techniques of mass production back in the primitive years of automobile manufacture led directly into the miraculous epoch that now has come into being.

GAF

□ □ □

Success for Uncle Sam—and for the Photographer

While many corporations can claim to have witnessed this nation's evolution from an agricultural to an industrial society, few have photographic evidence to support their claims. Fewer still can link origins that are more than a century old with participation in the space age.

However, for GAF, the first manufacturer of photographic materials in the United States, the visual record of American history over the past 130 years is synonymous with the development of the company's own photographic process.

In 1842, a young civil engineer named Edward Anthony opened a photo shop in New York that became the precursor of the multimillion-dollar photo products segment of GAF's chemical, building material and industrial products empire. Although he had been out of Columbia University for only two years, he soon performed a signal service, through the medium of photography, in determining the rightful territorial boundaries of this country in a dispute with Great Britain.

Anthony was a promoter of the French daguerreotype technique, which made possible the production of pictures by the action of light on a chemically sensitized surface, and his shop also supplied the necessary materials for it. For those reasons, he was called on to photograph a highland range that marks the boundary between Maine and Canada

The early hand-held cameras were advertised as "light, compact, easy to carry"—though they weighed about thirteen pounds. This early camera helped pave the way for today's more sophisticated models.

Union General R. B. Potter and his staff pose for a Mathew B. Brady photo in the field. Leaning against the tree at right is the famed Civil War photographer, whose habit of stepping into view occasionally has helped determine some of the areas where he was active.

—then a possession of Britain, which denied the existence of the range.

Anthony, hired by the U.S. government in the first practical use of photography by any government, took pictures that substantiated the U.S. claim. Spurred by the popularity that success had won him, Anthony opened a portrait studio in Washington, D.C. Using a Senate committee room, he made portraits of all members of Congress as well as of many other individuals prominent in national affairs.

Established about 1843, his National Daguerrean Gallery eventually made daguerreotype portraits of some one hundred politicians and celebrities, thereby anticipating the later work of Mathew Brady and Frederick Gutekunst. The famous engraving of "Clay's Farewell Speech in the U.S. Senate" used a great many of these portraits as models.

Public exhibition of his work in Washington and New York created a huge demand for portraits and the equipment and materials needed to take them. Quick to recognize the business potential, Anthony in 1853 conducted the world's first photographic contest—a widely publicized event that lent considerable thrust to the marketing of his own photographic products.

Another milestone took place in 1853 when a portrait of Edward Anthony was used as a frontispiece in the April issue of the *Photographic Art Journal*. This was an event of no small importance, as it represented the first time a photograph was used as an illustration in a periodical anywhere in the world.

Less than a decade later, he scored another first when his firm led the way with the introduction of the wet "collodion" process for making negatives on glass, greatly reducing the time of exposure and offering a limitless number of prints from a single negative.

In 1860, Anthony products were used to take the first U.S. aerial photo. Boston Harbor was photographed from a balloon 1,200 feet above the ground. The feat was not to be duplicated for more than a half-century. In World War I, the Allied forces resurrected the technique to photograph enemy troop and gun positions.

The U.S. Civil War added impetus to every aspect of photography. Anthony extended credit to no less a luminary than Mathew Brady, who became the best-known photographer of that war.

He was by no means the only one. With the start of hostilities, Anthony arranged to have his photo shop foreman, Thomas C. Roche, assigned under the special orders of General Meigs to make documentary photographs of the war. Roche made many 10-by-12-inch Anthony glass plate negatives for government use, developing them in his traveling studio—an enclosed horse-drawn wagon—while shots and shells exploded around him. It should be noted, too, that while Roche was engaged in government business, he enjoyed the prerogative of indulging in private enterprise. With the blessing of the Union Army commanders, he took vast numbers of stereo photos for Anthony, who converted them to three-dimensional stereoscopic views that made the war more real for millions of Americans.

It is interesting to note that while Anthony, Brady and Roche were chronicling the Union Army's tides of fortune, there were other photographers working behind the Confederate lines. And since photographic materials were not contraband, it is likely that Anthony was performing a similar public service for the Confederate forces. Cook, of Charleston, South Carolina, and Lytle, of Baton Rouge, Louisiana, were the South's outstanding photographers and since they were partial to Anthony's superior negative plates, it is believed they may have used them during the war.

Brady was a great photographer but not a very good businessman. At war's end, unable to meet his debts for photographic equipment, he presented many of his glass negatives of war scenes and well-known personalities to Anthony in settlement. The negatives were eventually donated by GAF to The Smithsonian Institution.

His lack of business acumen notwithstanding, it was largely due to Brady's creative use of Anthony products that photography became accepted as a serious and profitable business.

After the war, the Anthony firm set about expanding its scope by acquiring companies related to the photographic process. Before the turn of the century, it had introduced a thin, rollable, transparent film that enabled much smaller cameras to be manufactured, which greatly enhanced the popularity of photography.

This forerunner of today's highly sophisticated photographic films, incidentally, led to one of the longest patent suits in court history. Its inventor, the Rev. Hannibal Goodwin, a retired Episcopal minister of Newark, New Jersey, made first application for his invention in the U.S. Patent Office on May 2, 1887, but because of interference claims, it was not until September 13, 1898—more than 11 years later —that the patent was finally issued. The patent office hearings eventually evolved into an infringement suit by the Goodwin firm against Eastman Kodak in 1902—two years after Mr. Goodwin's death. Like the patent itself, the suit had a long and extended history, with final settlement of a $5 million judgment being made by Kodak in March, 1914, more than a quarter-century after the patent application was entered.

Through a series of mergers and acquisitions that included the Goodwin firm, the original Anthony company evolved into Ansco Photo Products, Inc., which in 1929 became part of a holding company owned by German interests. A decade later, the holding company was renamed General Aniline & Film Corporation, which was seized by the U.S. government during World War II. Today, GAF Corporation—now the official name—is an American firm whose stock is widely held.

GAF is continuing to be a factor in breakthroughs in the photography field. GAF film recorded the reactions of Alan Shepard on the nation's first space flight. Astronaut John Glenn, the first American to orbit the earth, used a specially modified GAF camera to photograph Earth's terrain. Those films were used to brief Edward White prior to his momentous "space walk" in 1965.

The company has matched its record in the photographic

field in its other areas of business activity. In 1886, for instance, GAF's building materials division was organized; it developed the first single-layer ready-to-lay roll of asphalt roofing only six years later.

The company's industrial products plant at Glenville, Connecticut, was the miracle of the day when Thomas Edison installed an electrical generator there, making it the first manufacturing plant in the United States to enjoy electric light. It was such a novelty that the plant ran train excursions from New York for those who wanted to see for themselves.

Dr. Jesse Werner, the company's president and chief executive officer, has already assured that GAF's achievements in the future will match its past accomplishments.

At Dr. Werner's instigation, GAF has invested more than $60 million over the past twenty years in research, development and production of high-pressure acetylene chemicals, especially PVP—an unusual compound which resulted from original work by German scientists in the 1920s.

PVP (polyvinylpyrrolidone) is used in a full range of pharmaceutical and cosmetic products, as a food preservative and in plastics, paper, textiles, electrical components, adhesives, agriculture and detergents.

Often called an "alchemist's stone," it is also used in a procedure that isolates cancer cells from blood, and in the measurement of intestinal permeability of kidneys to determine various types of jaundice. In addition, the compound has been used for such purposes as localization of brain lesions and the diagnosis of injury from radiation.

For his role in developing the market uses of high-pressure acetylene chemicals, including PVP, Dr. Werner is the only man ever presented with honor awards of both the Commercial Chemical Development Association and the Chemical Marketing Research Association.

GENERAL ELECTRIC

□ □ □

Into the Barn—and a Lofty Future

One of the "great moments" in General Electric Company's history was the day a young professor of chemistry from the Massachusetts Institute of Technology walked into a barn behind the Schenectady, New York, house of Charles Proteus Steinmetz, the electrical industry's "mathematical wizard" who was then GE's chief consulting engineer.

The barn was the first home of what was probably the first industrial laboratory in the United States conceived with the specific objective of conducting basic research— looking for new knowledge about nature. The young man from MIT, Dr. Willis R. Whitney, then a part-time employee of GE, became its first Research Laboratory director.

His meeting with Mr. Steinmetz took place in the fall of 1900, but our historical records do not tell us the precise day of the "great moment." We do know that before winter was over the barn had burned to the ground. But the idea— that basic research could be done in industry—lived on, nurtured in a succession of larger and larger facilities by the genius of Dr. Whitney and by the foresight and courage of the company's chief executive officers.

Today it is a cliché to say that technology is one of the forces that most conspicuously shapes our world, and that technology springs from the discoveries of science. In 1900 the truth of these statements was not so obvious. It was

General Electric's research and development began in the early 1900s in this barn in Schenectady, New York, owned by Charles Proteus Steinmetz. Below are Steinmetz, his technician, Thomas Dempster, and Dr. Willis R. Whitney.

appropriate—perhaps inevitable—that the first industrial laboratory directed toward basic research in the United States should have been established in the young electrical industry, since that industry was so clearly built upon the scientific discoveries of the preceding decades.

Men like Faraday and Henry made possible the inventions of men like Edison, and the more farsighted leaders of the electrical industry recognized that if the flow of applications was to continue, basic scientific research in the field would have to be nourished.

General Electric found such leaders in a small group at or near the top of the company: Edwin W. Rice, vice president and technical director; Elihu Thomson, a former high school science teacher and inventor, whose arc lighting system had been the reason for the formation in Lynn, Massachusetts, of the Thomson-Houston Company, the firm that had joined with the Edison General Electric Company to form GE; A. G. Davis, manager of the Patent Department; and, of course, Steinmetz himself, who had never been without a personal laboratory of one sort or another since he had been a boy.

All were involved in the decision to establish this new kind of industrial facility.

Late in 1901 Rice told the company's shareowners: "Although our engineers have always been liberally supplied with every facility for the development of new and original designs and improvement of existing standards, it has been deemed wise during the past year to establish a laboratory to be devoted exclusively to original research. It is hoped by this means that many profitable fields may be discovered."

One of the marks of a leader is his knowledge of men— his ability to select promising young men, to work along with them and to inspire them to their best efforts. In this aspect of leadership Whitney excelled, and he soon began to attract to his staff brilliant young men whose subsequent contributions to scientific knowledge are known throughout the world.

One of Whitney's first recruits was Dr. William D. Coolidge, who came to the laboratory from MIT in the fall of 1905. He found, as had Whitney, a fertile field of exploration. With vigor and enthusiasm he embarked upon a series of researches that bore fruit both in additions to scientific knowledge and in material benefits to mankind.

Early in his career Coolidge played a major role in the development of the modern incandescent electric lamp. At that time, existing lamp filaments were brittle and short-lived. The material with which he worked was tungsten—itself a notoriously brittle metal. His goal was to make it ductile, so that it could be worked and drawn into a very fine, very tough wire.

After two years of intensive experiments Coolidge produced the first ductile tungsten. After two additional years of research large-scale production of ductile-tungsten wire was a commercial reality and, in 1911, GE marketed its first ductile-tungsten lamps. Coolidge's invention is still at the core of the billions of incandescent electric lamps sold throughout the world each year.

Coolidge's name is also inseparably linked with the X-ray tube that he invented. His "Coolidge tube," unveiled in 1913, completely revolutionized the generation of X-rays, and remains to this day the model upon which all X-ray tubes for medical applications are patterned.

Dr. Irving Langmuir joined the laboratory's staff in 1909. His brilliant analytical mind, keen observation and amazing powers of concentration promptly established him as a leader in research. Langmuir typified to an extraordinary degree the two most essential characteristics of a research scientist—originality and an insatiable curiosity. His curiosity led him to explore a great variety of fields, and his basic researches in thermionic emission, heat conduction in gases, chemical valence, molecular films and surface chemistry are now classic. His work brought him many scientific awards and honors, including the Nobel Prize for Chemistry in 1932.

Whitney, Coolidge and Langmuir helped to establish the

pattern for performing scientific research in industry. They showed that it was possible for industry to attract and keep the very best technical people, giving them freedom to pursue their own ideas in an atmosphere conducive to truly first-rate work.

Perhaps the most widely known achievement of the General Electric Research Laboratory was the invention—announced in 1955—of the first reproducible process for converting graphite, an abundant and inexpensive substance, into diamond, nature's hardest material. This climaxed a worldwide scientific effort that had begun 125 years earlier, when diamond was first shown to be a form of carbon.

In 1957 GE began to manufacture and market its famous Man-Made™ industrial diamond crystals, and the company today is one of the world's major producers of industrial diamond abrasives. This has freed U.S. industry from total dependence upon foreign sources of supply for this critically needed industrial material.

GE's diamonds are produced by subjecting graphite to extreme pressures and temperatures in a special apparatus. Another major milestone resulting from this work was announced in 1970, when GE scientists reported that they had made clear, gem-quality diamonds, some of them weighing more than a carat. However, these carat-sized crystals are currently many times more costly than those dug from the ground, and it is still not known whether synthesized diamonds will ever be able to compete economically in the gem market.

The independence of thought and the freedom of choice that are inherent in the concept of basic research are not very compatible with a narrowly limited technical horizon, so it is not surprising that the spirit that led to the establishment of the Research Laboratory led, in succeeding years, to technical activities that span a very wide spectrum.

GENERAL FOODS

□ □ □

The Decision That Built Managers

Company management generally can be described by one of four words: autocratic, centralized, collective or decentralized. Normally classifications leave out too many realities necessary for an understanding of a living organism. But these four terms do fairly well cover the management spectrum, from the single concentration of power at one end to its radical dispersal at the other.

They also define the directions in which General Foods Corporation could have chosen to move following World War II, when the company made the decision that had perhaps a greater influence than any others in recent years on the business. Specifically, General Foods' management felt that its managerial system at the time restricted the strengths of its top leadership. Also, it did not encourage the development of the additional strong leadership that management knew the company must have to achieve its goals.

Until 1946 General Foods was operated under a basically centralized management. Manufacturing, sales, marketing, research, personnel and other key functions were administered by corporate headquarters. But there were many signs that this system was out of phase with the company's actual needs in the postwar era.

The corporation had widely diversified its production by a number of acquisitions since the Postum Cereal Company began to expand by acquiring Jell-O in 1925. General Foods was processing and distributing cereals, flour, coconut, chocolate, syrup, coffee, desserts, dog food and a growing line of frozen foods. GF's top management found themselves more and more snarled in scores of daily decisions that were frequently unrelated to each other, sometimes in actual conflict, and certainly exhausting in their multiplicity and repetition.

Consider one example: General Foods had a single sales force for all dry grocery products. This made little sense when you considered that these products could be as different in nature, use and sales potential as coffee and coconut. It was evidently time to rearrange the company's managerial resources. GF's many plants, products and markets called for decisions to be made closer to the firing line. Authority belonged where the action was.

This sounds like a cue to decentralize. GF management

C. W. Post had less than $100 worth of materials and equipment when he began making Postum in this barn—shown against a battery of modern silos—in Battle Creek, Michigan.

didn't hear it that way. They felt the company had to have something better than a simple distribution of authority. The goal was management that could act with greater independence and agility but without losing its sense of the corporate whole or the advantages of corporate strength.

What General Foods' top management did, briefly, was to lodge authentic managerial responsibility at the operations level—that is, with the presidents of its divisions. At the same time, the responsibility for company policy, objectives and coordination was retained at the corporate level. Divisional presidents were supported with staff offices in special fields of expertise, such as finance, law, manufacturing and engineering services, public relations, advertising services, purchasing and traffic.

As so often happens with a new idea, enthusiasm went too far. By 1949 sixteen divisions had been established. It soon became evident that a division must be substantial enough in production and profitability to stand alone. Many of the sixteen divisions weren't. Over a period of years the number of operating divisions in the United States was reduced to the present five.

It was in 1972 that senior management began a study which led to the current organization—an organization that once again underscores GF's mid-1940s decision that authority belongs where the action is.

Traditionally, General Foods' many products had been divided on a brand, rather than on a consumer market or menu segment, basis. Top management recognized that the way products were divided among operating divisions was not achieving optimum continued growth. The self-imposed constraint of marketing brands in families often made it difficult to both see and deal with the interaction of these brands with one another—and with competition. There was agreement that not being structured to view GF's various businesses in the context of total consumer markets was somewhat shortsighted and could mean some opportunities for new products were being passed by.

The desirability of grouping GF's products along consumer market segments had been recognized for some years. The 1972 study, however, pointed up the need for even more effective management of the company's franchises, and this precipitated a reorganization that now permits General Foods to bring its resources to bear on the growth of the business in the most focused way possible.

Fundamental to the reorganization of General Foods' domestic grocery business is the concept of the Strategic Business Unit. In such a unit a group of brands are held together by their natural interrelationship on the consumer's menu, rather than—as formerly—by their common technology, family brand name or method of distribution.

The company had an excellent precedent for adopting this concept throughout its U.S. grocery business. General Foods' coffee business had, in effect, been organized for decades along Strategic Business Unit lines. Those managing the coffee business had been able to make decisions and allocate resources in the light of the whole coffee market, not just a portion of it. And this had paid off.

General Foods formed five Strategic Business Units representing the distinct segments, in addition to coffee, in which the corporation does its domestic grocery business: desserts, main-meal dishes, breakfast foods, beverages and pet foods. These five SBU's were grouped into three divisions—one responsible for main-meal and dessert items, another for beverages and breakfast foods, the third for pet foods.

Under the new organization, division presidents participate in deciding overall U.S. grocery strategy and share responsibility for achieving an adequate return on directly invested capital. Importantly, they are responsible for the best possible use of resources within their divisions, and for approving the strategies recommended by the Strategic Business Unit Managers who, in turn, are responsible for the health, competitive standing and ongoing profit contribution of their businesses.

Clearly, under this reorganization the major focus of management attention has shifted from the divisional level to the strategic business categories—the new operational level. The

Strategic Business Unit manager is charged with achieving agreed-upon results for his category, and he has both the authority and the professional resources to meet this responsibility.

Although the new grocery organization is still young, it represents a further step toward precise pinpointing of authority at the action level. At the same time that serious, autonomous authority has been given to divisional and Strategic Business Unit chiefs, senior corporate management has made certain it shares with them an intense, continuing knowledge of the corporation's overall goals and needs—in order to deepen and broaden their understanding and perspective. Managers are thus able to act independently, yet with maximum insight into the company's total plan. This gives their decisions a force and effectiveness they would not otherwise have had.

Corporate management receives valuable feedback, too. Its decisions are supported by and based on the hard, factual realism of line experience. Managerial development moves in both directions, corporate and divisional.

Two advantages stand out among the many that this management system has brought to General Foods:

1. The managerial load is better distributed. There is less waste of individual ability, less misdirection of managerial energies.

2. A special kind of manager has developed. He has an independent viewpoint. He is open to better ideas than his own. He is resourceful and flexible. He fears caution above risk. Such men have risen to the new levels opened to them.

This type of management builds men, and they build the business.

Organization tends to frustrate people. This is part of the basic conflict that exists between the individual and the system he is a part of. General Foods' management organization substantially reduces the conflict, giving maximum room to individual creativity. It unites two forces—the spirit of freedom and the spirit of collaboration—in the pursuit of the corporation's goals.

GENERAL MOTORS

□ □ □

"Boss" Kettering's Decision:
Build a Better Diesel

"For a century, as you know, steam has been the principal railroad motive power. It still is and, in my view, will continue to be. . . . Yes, gentlemen, steam marches on!"

That confident assertion was made in a 1938 speech by the president of one of the country's largest railroad locomotive builders.

Only nine years later a subsequent president of that same company sadly reported that it had ceased steam locomotive production. A company spokesman told the press that "all orders and inquiries for new motive power from domestic railroads are for diesel-electrics."

The story of why the 1938 prediction turned out to be completely wrong is a powerful testimonial to the vitality of innovative competitive enterprise and to its indispensable role in American progress. It is the story of a transportation revolution.

It was the new and then little known GM Electro-Motive Division at La Grange, Illinois, that led the way to what the locomotive "establishment" had proclaimed impossible— the overthrow of steam by diesel power on the nation's railroads. No one could have foreseen the tremendous change in store for rail transportation when the legendary Charles K. Kettering, then General Motors' research director, began trying to develop a two-cycle diesel engine in the 1920s. His

79

*The Chicago, Burlington & Quincy's crack "Zephyr"
pioneered the use of the new lightweight two-cycle diesel
engine.*

work was a natural extension of internal combustion power studies, one of the principal activities of the General Motors research operation at the time.

The four-cycle diesels of the period were heavy and sluggish. Most designers assumed that these characteristics were inherent in the diesel concept. "Boss Ket" thought otherwise. It was his opinion that existing diesels—to the extent that they were replacing steam engines in certain applications—were designed according to steam-engine practice. As he put it, no one was interested in seeing how a diesel wanted to be built. He set out to develop a light-weight, two-cycle diesel engine that would do twice the work at half the cost.

By 1930 he knew it could be done. No one, however, yet envisaged the full implications of the work of Kettering and his associates.

It was happenstance that first put GM's two-cycle diesel into a locomotive. Two of these engines, regarded as experimental, were installed at Chicago's Century of Progress exposition in 1933 to supply power for a Chevrolet model assembly plant exhibit. The president of the Chicago, Burlington & Quincy Railroad Company saw them there and persuaded GM to build a modified version for a new stream-lined train that was to become famous as the Burlington Zephyr. On May 26, 1934, the new diesel-powered stream-liner made its run from Chicago to Denver at an average speed of 77.6 miles per hour.

The event occurred at a significant time in railroad history. The Great Depression had driven fifty-five railroads into receivership, and all roads were trying strenuously to stimulate traffic and reduce costs. Naturally they watched the Burlington experiment with great interest.

GM produced diesel engines for other trains, and in 1935 —taking one of those considered risks that are the source of progress under American competitive enterprise—GM decided to build a plant at La Grange for the production of complete locomotives. The first locomotive was delivered from the La Grange plant in 1936. Now the revolution was truly under way.

The odds against GM were long. The locomotive business of the era was shared principally by three large and well-established companies whose executives had been closely associated with the leaders of American railroads for many years. Historically railroads had bought custom-built locomotives, each with different and distinctive components—a practice that was in direct conflict with the principle of standardization espoused by GM. Finally, the diesel was unproven as a locomotive engine; indeed, GM's engines had their problems in early railroad use.

In its favor at the start, GM had the inherent superiority of diesel-electric power over steam for locomotive use—plus the attitude of its chief competitors. Kettering once said that GM's main advantage in the battle was its competitors' belief "that we were crazy." There was nothing to prevent those companies from building and selling diesel-electrics; their manufacturing facilities were many times greater than those of the La Grange plant; yet they remained stubbornly wedded to steam too long.

To overcome the railroads' understandable partiality toward the steam locomotive, which had served them for a century, Electro-Motive developed a now familiar sales tool called an economic study. Based on the performance record of diesel-electric locomotives, it was possible to project the economies and return on investment of replacing all steam power with diesel-electric equipment. A return on investment of upwards of 30 percent a year could be shown in comparison with steam operations.

Another factor in Electro-Motive's success was its firm insistence on standardization in the face of a railroad tradition that no two locomotives should be exactly alike. Through experience the railroads learned the economic wisdom of the Electro-Motive policy. Electro-Motive's components, wherever possible, were interchangeable. Moreover, even as components were improved, they retained the same physical configuration and exterior dimensions as their predecessors. Thus GM locomotives built in 1939 can be repaired today with current production parts—and improved in the process.

"Boss Ket" lived to see the complete triumph of his idea. By the time of his death in 1958 at the age of eighty-two, steam locomotives were becoming a rarity. Today the few that are left are maintained for their historic value.

But the triumph is not necessarily permanent. General Motors and others long have been investigating other forms of transportation power. The diesel-electric may itself fall to a revolution some day. That is the way our American competitive system works.

General Motors likes it that way.

GILLETTE

□ □ □

Changing the Faces of the Earth

One hot summer morning in 1895 a forty-year-old traveling salesman struggled in his Brookline, Massachusetts, home to shave with a dull straight razor. His thoughts turned, as they often had in the past, to the idea of developing a product that could be used by the public and then be discarded and inexpensively replaced. On that particular morning, he thought of the answer.

"As I stood there with my razor in my hand," said King C. Gillette describing his inspiration, "my eyes resting on it as lightly as a bird settling down on its nest—the Gillette razor was born. I saw it all in a moment, and in that moment many unvoiced questions were asked and answered more with the rapidity of a dream than by the slow process of reasoning. . . ."

According to Gillette, his concept for a razor came to him full blown: ". . . it seemed as though I could see the way the blade could be held in a holder; then came the idea of sharpening opposite edges on the thin piece of steel that was uniform in thickness throughout, thus doubling its services; and following in sequence came the clamping plates for the blades and a handle easily disposed between the two edges of the blade. All this came more in pictures than in thought as though the razor were a finished thing and held before my eyes. Fool that I was, I knew little about razors and

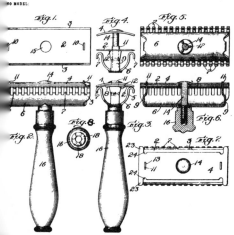

No. 775,134.

PATENTED NOV. 15, 1904.

K. C. GILLETTE.
RAZOR.
APPLICATION FILED DEC. 3, 1901.

NO MODEL.

The patent application drawings for the original Gillette safety razor.

practically nothing about steel, and I could not foresee the trials and tribulations that I was to pass through before the razor was a success."

"I have got it, our fortune is made," Gillette wrote to his wife, who was away on a visit. He described what he'd thought of and, to make sure she understood, drew sketches. It was a safety razor that used disposable blades.

Gillette wasted no time in pursuing his dream. The same day he envisioned its design and function he went to a Boston hardware store where he purchased "pieces of brass, some steel ribbon used for clock springs, a small hand vise, some files and with these materials made the first razor."

Mr. Gillette's razor was needed, for men were still plagued with the age-old problem of what to do about facial hair. It has been a concern of kings and poets, of statesmen and generals.

Beards have been, depending on the historical moment, a stamp of uncouthness—even insanity; a danger to warriors (Alexander the Great ordered his Macedonian troops to remove their whiskers, which, he said, were a too-convenient handle by which enemies could seize them); a conclusive sign of manliness; a mark of dignity.

The last attitude was particularly prevalent in the period of the safety razor's advent. For example, there was a serious strike in Paris at the turn of the century against a rule of hotels that waiters must be clean-shaven. In the United States, however, beards went somewhat out of fashion following the Civil War, and by 1880 or 1890 most men chose to be clean-shaven. Well over half of those who shaved depended upon barbers and Gillette commented that in 1900 barber shops were "as thick as saloons."

Now, after thousands of years, a slow, painful, even dangerous operation—shaving—was to be changed to one that could be performed with speed, ease and comfort. But it wasn't until a host of technical and financial problems were solved that King C. Gillette and several associates formed a company and began operations over a South Boston store in 1901.

In seeking to develop his razor, Gillette visited every cutler and machine shop in Boston and some in New York and Newark. He even worked with the Massachusetts Institute of Technology, which failed to solve Gillette's key problem of making a razor blade from sheet steel that would harden and temper suitably for holding a sharp edge. Gillette was told by all the metal experts of the time that it was not possible to put a sharp edge on sheet steel. "The razor was looked upon as a joke by all my friends," said Gillette.

With the expertise of William E. Nickerson, a highly regarded mechanical engineer, Gillette found solutions to the sharpening, hardening and tempering problems that appeared to block successful development of the safety razor. The solution to these problems required the "invention" of special machines and processes to sharpen and harden the steel—these mechanical innovations, in themselves, were considered major inventions and advanced the state of the art of metal treating.

In 1903 Gillette put his first razor on the market—and by the end of the year he had succeeded in selling exactly 51 razors and 168 blades!

Then the new shaving instrument caught on, and an international multimillion-dollar business was launched. By 1905 manufacturing operations had to be moved to larger quarters. A suitable building was found on West First (now Gillette Park), near Dorchester Avenue in South Boston. That same year the company's first overseas branch opened in London.

A driving force in Gillette's obsession to invent was his strong belief in the necessity for devices that would save time and give more freedom for other activities, and that would increase comfort. He also realized that such products must be inexpensively priced to realize the benefits of mass distribution. Although other companies were tinkering with and developing safety razors at the time Gillette invented his, all other versions were simply a section of a straight razor placed in a holder, enabling the individual to shave himself safely. But these razors required frequent stropping and honing of lifetime blades—which sold for $1.50 apiece. Gillette's first razor was offered to the public for $5 with a set of twenty blades. A replacement set of twenty blades sold for $1. The price of the razor and blades came down in ensuing years, making the new safety razor more accessible to men.

The freedom the safety razor gave to men was expressed again and again in early Gillette advertisements. One, printed in 1906, stressed the theme under a picture of George Washington. It said:

"George Washington Gave an Era of Liberty to the Colonies. The Gillette Gives an Era of Personal Liberty to All Men."

The advertisement continued:

"If the time, money, energy and brain power which were wasted in barber shops of America were applied in direct effort, the Panama Canal could be dug in four hours." (Just where Gillette got the documentation for this statement remains unknown.)

In late 1917 the campany got its biggest boost when the U.S. government bought 4.2 million safety razors for World War I servicemen. This wholesale exposure to the product by millions of men encouraged tremendous growth of the self-shaving habit in America.

Cartoons of the day showing a man shaving invariably had him doing so with the safety razor. Sinclair Lewis began his novel *Babbitt* with his hero raking "his plump cheeks with a safety razor." The revolt against the straight razor was so complete that new Pullman cars had a slot in the men's washrooms for used blades. By 1926 over 140 million razors and six billion blades had been sold.

Gillette's new razor not only changed the shaving habits of millions of men through the world, but it also had a dramatic effect on the world's straight-razor industry at the time, which was centered in Sheffield, England, and Solingen, Germany. Although the United States produced straight razors of its own, the market was hindered by limited domestic capacity. As a result, in 1907 the United States was importing more straight razors than it produced. The arrival of the safety razor altered the situation. Almost overnight the United States went from being a large-scale importer of straight razors to a large-scale exporter of the new safety razors.

As innovation followed innovation through the years the company's South Boston location earned the title of "World Shaving Headquarters." In 1948 the Gillette Company took its first step toward becoming what it is today—a diversified consumer products company—by acquiring the Toni Company, a small Midwestern firm with one major product: kits for women's home permanents.

An advertising campaign was launched featuring sets of twins with new permanents, one given at home and the other by a professional in a beauty shop, and asking readers: "Which twin has the Toni?" Toni soon became a major factor in the women's grooming market. It, too, has diversified, and is now Gillette's personal care division. It still makes the "home perm," but its product line also includes hair sprays, personal care appliances, shampoos and—the most recent addition—Hosiery Guard, a laundering product that gives strength and elasticity to women's hose.

Gillette continued to seek new products, but ones that had marketing and/or manufacturing similarities to its major line. In 1955 the company acquired Paper Mate, a small West Coast firm that made ballpoint pens. Though the ballpoint pen had entered the market after World War II, it fell into disrepute because of smearing, poor writing qualities and the fading of its ink. Paper Mate turned the entire market around by offering the first guaranteed ballpoint pen, and it won acceptability from bankers and educators, who had scorned other models.

In the sixties another major step was taken. The company that had started men on the daily habit of shaving started another trend—the aerosol spray deodorant. Launched with strong marketing campaigns, such as "nothing touches you but the spray itself," and followed by a family-oriented approach—"Don't leave your family defenseless"—the Right Guard family of deodorants was born.

Again, a nation's daily habits were affected. Right Guard soon became so successful that it, along with Foamy aerosol shave cream, formed the foundation for an entirely new Gillette operation—the Toiletries Division. Since its establishment in 1968 the division has become one of the company's most successful. The Dry Look aerosol hair groom for men and other family toiletries products have been added.

While its product line has expanded, shaving products have remained a major factor in the business of The Gillette Company. In 1967 it made another acquisition, Braun AG, a West German maker of electric razors sold internationally.

The company has continued to make great strides in easing the chore of shaving for men and women throughout the world. Carbon steel blades were followed by plastic-coated ones and stainless steel in the 1960s, platinum-alloy blades at the end of the decade and the TRAC II twin blade razor in 1971—all inventions of Gillette researchers.

The company employs more than 1,000 research and technical people—all seeking products that help to make life more enjoyable.

Last year Gillette's sales reached $870 million. Its products were sold to more than one billion consumers in 170 nations and territories around the world.

Gillette is a company with strong resources—skilled people and marketing and technical expertise. The capable management of these resources has made Gillette what it is today.

GOODRICH

□ □ □

The Doctor's Prescription:
Invention and Quality

It was 1888. Dr. Benjamin Franklin Goodrich was speaking to managers of the rubber company he had founded eighteen years earlier. He was thin from illness, but his voice had a touch of steel.

"The only anxiety I have—the things that might break up this concern—are just what I have always talked about . . . whether the discipline is kept up, whether the repairs are kept up, and whether the standard of quality is kept high.

"If these are done as well as they have been done in the past, there is no question about the success of this concern.

"But if it fails in any of these particulars, it will go to the devil in one-fourth the time it has taken to build it up."

Failing health was forcing Dr. Goodrich to leave Akron, Ohio, for Colorado. As in the past, his spirit masked the seriousness of his sickness. In three weeks he was dead of tuberculosis.

Only forty-six when he died, Dr. Goodrich had overcome poverty and poor health to become a physician (he was an Army surgeon during the Civil War), and later a businessman and industrialist. He was one of those rare men of conviction who impress their ideas on others with such force that the ideas live long after the men are gone. His great conviction was that industry must make quality products that serve human needs.

91

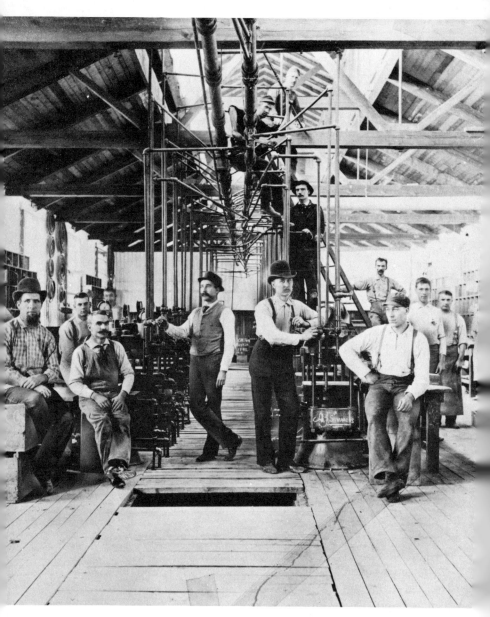

The B. F. Goodrich press room in Akron, Ohio, in September, 1890.

When the B. F. Goodrich Company started in Akron, Ohio, in 1870, there were few known uses for rubber, and many of the rubber items being made were of poor quality. Goodrich saw the need for product development and product quality and was determined to make his firm outstanding in these. The ideals and innovative drive that led him to found the first rubber company west of the Allegheny Mountains and keep it growing in the face of incalculable problems are still evident in the B. F. Goodrich Company today. Perhaps nowhere in American industry has the philosophy of a company founder endured within the enterprise so long and with such good results. B. F. Goodrich is currently one of America's 100 largest corporations, with 40 manufacturing plants in the United States and Canada. It has more than 40 foreign subsidiary and associate companies and manufacturers and sells rubber and chemical products in more than 100 countries. Its employees total more than 50,000.

From the time Dr. Goodrich and a business partner made loans to the floundering Hudson River Rubber Company of Hastings-on-the-Hudson, New York, in 1868, he was convinced that rubber would become an increasingly useful material. Even though Hudson River Rubber Company failed after he took it over, Goodrich did not lose faith in rubber's potential. Earlier, as a struggling physician, he had seen a friend's house destroyed by fire because a leather hose burst. He believed rubber would make a better fire hose. In the early oil fields of Pennsylvania he had seen the need for hose to move oil and he knew rubber could be used for that. He knew rubber could be used in surgery and therapy, and he wanted to develop products for these uses.

He also saw the growing use of leather transmission belts for harnessing the power of steam engines, and he knew rubber could be used for that.

The financial condition of Hudson River Rubber Company would not permit product development, so he decided to establish a new firm in the Midwest where production costs were lower. He wanted a location where there was abundant power transportation and labor, as well as the opportunity to grow with a fast-developing area. He found such a site in Akron, Ohio, then a town of 10,000 with two canals, two railroads, a coal mine and a large number of skilled craftsmen from Central Europe.

Akron businessmen agreed to invest in the company and it was organized on December 31, 1870. By May a newly erected and equipped factory building was turning out hose, gasket rubber, bottle stoppers, jar rings and rolls for the handwringers used by housewives and laundresses of that era. Before the end of the firm's first year Goodrich had developed the world's first cotton-covered rubber fire hose, which quickly became the firm's main product.

But success was not instantaneous for the company. More than once, when faced with the probability of a shutdown, Goodrich packed his bags and went on a hunt for new business. His enthusiasm and his strong belief in the quality of his products enabled him to obtain enough orders to keep his one-building factory in operation. When he returned from these trips, he would spend long hours supervising the making of products which were to make his name respected throughout the world. For eighteen years following the 1870 founding of the company, Dr. Goodrich ran it on a close, personal basis.

By the nineties it had become general practice for anyone having a manufacturing problem involving rubber to take it to B. F. Goodrich. The most significant of all such visitors was Alexander Winton, a bicycle manufacturer from Cleveland, who came to the factory one day in the latter part of the decade. Winton explained that he had built a "horseless carriage" and wanted some pneumatic tires made for it. They would have to be considerably larger than bicycle tires, he said. As Inventor Winton told the story years later, the B. F. Goodrich man replied: "I guess we can make them, although we never have."

Thus BFG evolved and produced the tires used on the first gasoline-powered car made for sale in the United States. The tires were so good that not only Winton but other automobile manufacturers came to BFG for their tires.

Within ten years after making its first automobile tire, sales of this product accounted for the major part of the company's earnings.

The inseparable relationship between B. F. Goodrich, automobiles, tires and the motoring public began with that first visit from Alexander Winton. Modern examples of the company's creativity in the tire field include development of the first puncture-sealing tubeless tire and the first American-made radial tire for American automobiles.

The innovative spirit that has characterized B. F. Goodrich from its inception led Charles Cross Goodrich, one of the founder's two sons, to establish America's first rubber research laboratory. The laboratory that he founded in Akron in 1895 has grown into one of the most highly regarded rubber research facilities in the world.

An early BFG discovery of major significance occurred in 1880 when the first practical method for reclaiming rubber was developed. The method is still widely used. In 1904 a company chemist discovered the first organic accelerators. These reduced the time needed for vulcanization of rubber by up to 75 percent and greatly increased the durability and tensile strength of rubber products. This development is generally regarded as one of the most vital advances in the history of rubber processing.

Another important discovery changed for all time the appearance of automobile tires. Carbon black had been used for a number of years as a coloring pigment in rubber products. Up to 1912, however, tires were generally white, containing no carbon black. It was found that the use of carbon black in substantial quantity added greatly to the abrasion-resisting properties of rubber, and if used in the proper proportion in automobile tires, would add many thousands of miles of service.

Today B. F. Goodrich has hundreds of important "firsts" to its credit. Many of them not only represented significant technical achievements but also proved to be giant steps in man's progress toward achieving a better life. One of these was the first commercial manufacture of butadiene-copolymer synthetic rubber in the United States in 1939. Two years later the company introduced the first passenger car tires containing man-made rubber ever sold to the public.

No achievement of B. F. Goodrich exemplifies better the broad benefits of creativity in industry than the company's pioneer work in synthetic rubber down through the years. The highlight of this involvement was the company's spearheading of the cooperative industry–federal government synthetic rubber program that was instrumental in helping the Allies win World War II. Today the company, through its chemical division, is one of the world's largest producers of man-made rubbers.

A goal of world scientists for generations was achieved in 1954 when a team of B. F. Goodrich scientists succeeded in duplicating the true molecule of natural rubber, a major scientific achievement.

B. F. Goodrich research also led to the birth of the nation's multimillion-dollar vinyl industry in 1926 when one of its scientists discovered the first rubberlike polyvinyl material. Today the company is the world's largest producer of vinyl raw materials that are used to make thousands of different plastic products for industrial and consumer use.

From the day he opened the doors of the B. F. Goodrich Company until he died, Dr. Goodrich pursued a relentless campaign of product development and improvement. His devotion to this objective and the sincerity of his commitment to "make goods destined for service" inspired his early associates and established a strong sense of mission as a tradition for those who followed in his footsteps.

Dr. Goodrich made quality and invention the hallmarks of his company and, in doing so, raised the standards of the entire rubber industry, which contributes materially to our economic and social progress.

GREYHOUND

□ □ □

With Several Ways to Go, He Chose Up

Fortunately a bit of misfortune can turn into an advantage for an individual and, in some instances, for the entire population.

Such was the case for Orville S. Caesar, who was president of Greyhound Lines, now the world's largest intercity bus company, from 1946 to 1956, and later served as its board chairman.

Back in 1918 Caesar and his partner in a Superior, Wisconsin, truck agency were stuck with two high-priced trucks they couldn't sell. To salvage their investment they had coach bodies built for the trucks' chassis and began a small bus operation between Duluth, Minnesota, and Superior.

Seven years later Caesar sold his interest in the operation, joined Greyhound as assistant general manager and was on his way.

During forty years of service with Greyhound, one of his important contributions to its success was his effort in developing the dual-level Super Scenicruiser—the most radical bus design for its time and the most popular ever to go on the highway. It was introduced in the mid-fifties.

But why a dual-level bus?

The need for more space for Greyhound's growing package express service was one of the major factors behind its

Today's transcontinental Greyhound giants have their ancestors in coaches like this one, whose routes in the early years of the century were much more limited indeed.

development. With several ways to go, Caesar chose up. Not only to provide more space for package express, but to give the traveling public a better and safer view of the country.

Caesar decided on a streamlined design, a far cry from the "boxy" look of previous buses, and improved upon or, when necessary, invented bus equipment.

Greyhound's Super Scenicruiser—voted one of the 100 best-designed products in history—contained many important innovations for passengers, and drew patronage from a broader market than had ever been attracted to bus travel.

In addition to nearly doubling the baggage space, the Super Scenicruiser brought recognition to Greyhound for developments such as—

- On-board restroom.
- Improved bus air conditioning—change of air in the bus every forty seconds.
- Individually controlled air vents above each seat to enable passengers to smoke without annoying others.
- Air-suspension ride, which was introduced by Greyhound in an earlier model and became standard equipment on the Super Scenicruiser and all future models. Passenger comfort was greatly increased since the coach body was held constantly level on curves, despite variation in load distribution.
- Spacious rear passenger deck, elevated above the forward seating area, which provided unequaled sightseeing opportunities.
- A wide windshield, which curved around the entire forward section of the upper level to give an unobstructed view of the road ahead.
- Six-foot-long "panoramic" windows of glare-resistant glass, which made up more than 90 percent of the side structure above the seats.
- Skylights installed in the roof for sightseeing in mountain areas.
- Twin diesel engines mounted side by side at the rear of the bus, which eliminated a separate engine for air conditioning units. The engines' location and design also allowed maintenance personnel to remove and replace them in a matter of minutes.
- Tandem rear axles, which provided greater riding ease and more even distribution of weight.
- Colorful interior decoration.
- Power steering.
- An electric eye headlight dimmer.

Not only had Caesar seen to it that the Super Scenicruiser had the qualities passengers would find attractive, but he had also taken into consideration the problems of the drivers and maintenance operations.

In fact, all today's vehicle owners owe him something: He invented the automobile hot-water heating system in the

1920s and—later—gradual shading of windows (he personally hand-dipped the first pieces of glass used in the prototype of the Super Scenicruiser).

The Scenicruiser's forty-foot length and capacity for forty-three passengers made it possible for Greyhound to reduce the number of second sections it added on many of its runs and to achieve higher revenue per bus mile.

Caesar's baggage space innovations have taken Greyhound into one of its fastest-growing operations.

Following introduction of the Super Scenicruiser, Greyhound was operating more than 5,000 buses over 90,000 miles of routes in every state and Canada. And ownership of The Greyhound Corporation had increased to more than 50,000 stockholders. In 1961, just three years before Caesar's death, Greyhound began to diversify. The Greyhound Corporation today is a multi-industry company with more than 130 active subsidiaries, employing some 55,000 persons in worldwide operations. It has more than 165,000 stockholders.

The company nurtured by Caesar today ranks as one of the country's thirty-five largest industrial firms. With transportation as the continuing backbone of the organization, diversification has flourished. Greyhoud's activities are far-ranging and specialized. Generally they can be categorized into six major groups:

Transportation: The world's largest intercity bus company, operating the safest, most modern equipment on the highways. It also provides sightseeing services, tour planning and wholesaling services, international travel services and bus manufacturing. Motor Coach Industries, a Greyhound subsidiary, ranks as the largest builder of intercity buses in North America. It manufactures all buses going into the Greyhound fleet and sells its products to other bus lines as well.

Leasing and Financial: Greyhound has the world's largest general equipment leasing company, Greyhound Leasing & Financial Corporation. Equipment leased ranges from machine tools to oceangoing vessels, from railroad locomotives and cars to jet aircraft. Greyhound Computer Corporation is a pioneer computer leasing company with more than 300 computer systems under lease in the United States, Canada and the United Kingdom. They also provide facilities management, data processing service centers and software services.

Services: A wide range of service companies make up this group. Aircraft Services International and Dispatch Services provide aircraft ground-handling and into-plane fueling at twenty-six major foreign and domestic airports. Border Brokers is Canada's number-one customs brokerage firm. General Fire and Casualty Company writes various lines of insurance including casualty, workmen's compensation, fire and burglary and travel accident insurance for Greyhound bus passengers and travel agents' clients. Travelers Express is the nation's second largest money order firm. Technical design and personnel services are offered by Consultants & Designers. Duty-free shops and export service are provided by the Florida Export Group. Manncraft Exhibitors Service provides decorations and exhibitors services for trade shows and conventions. Greyhound Rent-a-Car leases cars on a daily, weekly or monthly basis.

Food Service: Greyhound Food Management provides centralized management and coordinates Greyhound's food service operations. Greyhound food service companies serve more than two million meals a day. Post House operates 108 restaurants coast to coast, primarily in bus terminals. Prophet Foods Company is a food service company serving industry, banks and other commercial establishments, colleges, schools, hospitals and nursing homes. It also operates route vending in selected cities.

Food: Armour and Company manufactures and distributes a broad range of fresh, processed and portion-control meats and poultry products for consumer and institutional use. It ranks as the nation's second largest meat packer producing Armour bacon, hot dogs, fresh meats, canned meats, self-basting turkeys and other foods. Armour food service products are used widely by airlines, hospitals, restaurants, industrial plants, schools and other institutions.

Consumer Products and Pharmaceuticals: Armour-Dial,

Inc., manufactures and distributes a wide variety of grocery, personal care and household products for the consumer. Dial, the nation's number-one toilet soap, is produced at the world's largest and most modern soap factory at Aurora, Illinois. Armour-Dial produces more than 300 million cans annually of more than thirty varieties and sizes of shelf-stable convenience foods, and now has the world's largest, most modern sterile-canned meats plant in operation at Fort Madison, Iowa. Armour Pharmaceutical has worldwide operations for manufacturing and distributing a variety of ethical pharmaceuticals and diagnostic chemicals and animal health products.

Did Orville Caesar know that his one small venture into the bus transportation could lead so far? Probably not, but he was a man of vision, engrossed in developing a great corporation.

HALLMARK

□ □ □

What's a Nice Firm Like Yours
Doing in a Place Like This?

One overcast January morning in 1967 a group of greeting card executives entered the Kansas City, Missouri, City Hall. Amid TV lights and cameras, they presented to the mayor, Ilus Davis, nearly 50 pounds of carefully drafted documents.

Collectively, the affidavits, maps, exhibits, surveys and photographs made up a proposal for the redevelopment of some twenty-five city blocks on the edge of the central business district.

More than a decade of study and decision had preceded that morning call. More than $200 million in private funds was budgeted toward land purchase and construction.

The intent of the visit was to win official blessing for a noble experiment: Let private industry take a crack at urban renewal—let one firm, Hallmark Cards, Inc., replace 85 acres of blight with a model urban community to be called Crown Center.

Let private financing, instead of public money, erect a million square feet of office space, a thousand guest rooms, 2,500 apartments for 9,000 people, 7,000 concealed parking spots, and an innovative retail-cultural center—all in a parklike downtown section.

In the years since then, the most frequently asked question the president of Hallmark Cards hears is: "Mr. Hall, what's a greeting card firm doing in urban renewal?"

If Hallmark made steel, gypsum or aluminum, there would be an obvious explanation. But they are designers and pub-

Joyce C. Hall, founder of Hallmark, with a model of Crown Center.

lishers—people who market candles, playing cards, books, stationery, writing instruments, calendars, paper party dishes. After all, what does sentiment have to do with environment? What does a social custom have to do with social consciousness?

The decision to move boldly into urban renewal, to attack the crisis of our cities by building a model city-within-a-city, may have surprised the man on the street, but not those close to Hallmark.

Unusual methods have marked Hallmark's rise to the top of its industry ever since Joyce C. Hall, founder and current chairman, came from Nebraska to Kansas City in 1910. He set up shop as a postcard jobber, but when the picture postcard fad began to ebb, he made the cards a social custom by adding "from me to you" sentiments.

Hall Brothers, Inc. (as the firm was called until 1954), began to compete seriously with the Eastern manufacturers who dominated the business prior to 1930.

To get national distribution, two uncommon stratagems were adopted. First, eight trailers with model greeting card departments were outfitted. They were manned by salesmen drivers, and for six years, in town after town, the men sold merchandising systems.

Next, in the mid-1930s, the message was carried over network radio. Experts disapproved; they said only art and words sold cards, and people would not buy them because of a brand name. But a Chicago radio "philosopher" named Tony Wons read greeting card poetry and urged listeners to look for the hallmark and crown on the back of cards when they bought them.

Later sponsoring of award-winning television dramas such as *Hamlet* and *Macbeth* continued the campaign. This national advertising has done much to identify Hallmark with quality—and greeting cards with Hallmark.

As the business grew, popular figures were brought to greeting cards. Writers such as Dr. Norman Vincent Peale, Pearl Buck, Edgar Guest, Father James Keller, Bishop Fulton Sheen and Ogden Nash; painters such as Grandma Moses, Norman Rockwell, Sir Winston Churchill; and the Disney characters and Charles Schulz' Peanuts troupe.

Joyce Hall built Hallmark Cards with bold programs.

Neighborhood redevelopment was another bold idea that had long intrigued him. For the first decade Hallmark was in business, its quarters were in a cubbyhole downtown. When the time came to build its own building, the company's employees were offered a choice of four locations. "They are the ones who have to get to work from their homes—and they should be proud of where they work and it should be convenient for them," the public was told.

The 122 women and 88 men opted for the "Penn Valley Park location," just twelve blocks south of downtown and adjacent to more than 200 acres of rolling, wooded parkland. The building topped out in 1923 and Hallmark Cards has been the neighborhood showplace ever since.

The company underwent a major expansion in 1936, and in 1956 moved into its present contemporary headquarters facility. The new nine-story building is a handsome inverted pyramid built into the side of an unwanted hill. It offers street-level entrances on every floor, and natural north light for the world's leading design and art studios.

By the late 1950s, however, the neighborhood had deteriorated severely: to the north were surface parking and used car lots, fifty-year-old brick eyesores, unpalatable restaurants and aging low-rise warehouses; to the south were nineteen substandard dwellings and an uneven collection of small businesses, warehouses and abandoned blight. Only to the east and west could one look with pride. The sylvan Penn Valley Park lay west, and on the east Hospital Hill bustled, with its spacious lawns and nearly $100 million in future construction.

At first there was talk, mind-stretching brain sessions with old friend Walt Disney ("Get plenty of land, don't crowd yourself as we did in Anaheim"); with architect Ed Stone, who was designing the Hallmark Gallery for Fifth Avenue in New York; with James Rouse, who pioneered the "new city" approach with his Columbia, Maryland, project; and with Hallmark executives such as Lynn Bauer, now president of Crown Center.

Then there were land use studies by Victor Gruen, feasibility studies by Seattle's Larry Smith. What was to become Crown Center grew, shrank and changed in concept almost weekly.

First and last Hallmark's executives are businessmen. They believe in business and always seek a reasonable profit in their endeavors.

Would Crown Center be good for Hallmark? Yes.

Would it be good for Kansas City? Yes. Would it inspire private industry to get into the urban problem? Hopefully, yes.

Because the company believes in downtown, Crown Center has been designed to complement the central business district rather than compete with it—especially in retailing.

Crown Center is programmed to attract new businesses to Kansas City, not just relocate existing local offices. And it is designed to be fun, educational and culturally stimulating. Museum-quality sculpture in a 10-acre central square will be on public display, with an 18-foot metal sculpture by David Smith the initial acquisition.

Art, music, crafts and exhibits will create a things-to-do-and-see-and-learn environment.

Crown Center is now nearing completion of its first phase —a vast undertaking which occupies more than one-third of its 85 acres and nearly one-half of the estimated total cost. Sometimes slowly, sometimes with remarkable dispatch, it is remodeling Kansas City's profile. The five interconnected office buildings are completed and more than half are occupied. New York's Ed Barnes has given it remarkable strength in architecture, a 660,000-square-foot skyscraper on its side. The vast structure, with its terraces and fountain, is over one of the largest underground garages in the world.

The Harry Weese–designed hotel opened in May, 1973, and already this 738-room facility is contributing to the growth of Kansas City as well as to the neighborhood. It has been termed an architectural masterwork. But most of all, it gives the Kansas City visitor and the Kansas City conventioneer a new option on where to stay. Kansas City, like so many others, has been sorely lacking first-class hotel space for the business world of the 1970s and beyond.

Soon the first-phase 400,000-square-foot retail-restaurant-entertainment structure, another Ed Barnes building, will open. This edifice, along with vital community programs —which involve everything from kite flying to chamber music—will bring the public to the neighborhood, for there is no question that people are the secret. They supply the retail traffic and rent the offices and occupy the guest rooms. Most important, they provide vitality and humanity. They furnish the spirit and they, more than the developer, are the eventual catalyst that revives declining neighborhoods.

Finally, under construction are the first of what will be 2,500 residential units, both apartments and condominiums. These quality "homes" will convert a once-neglected area into a permanent address for some 9,000 people.

Urbanologists, sociologists, architects and businessmen have been very kind in their critique of what Hallmark is doing at Crown Center. This pleases the company. Besides being a sound business venture for Hallmark Cards, Inc., it wants the development to be good for people and a potent stimulus for the community.

But most pleasing, to all concerned, is Hallmark's pioneer role in showing the nation's troubled cities just what the private sector of the business community can accomplish with careful planning, sound management, superb design and patience. It is unthinkable that public monies alone can rectify the blight of our inner cities, disperse the degrading density of our older cities or centralize the senseless sprawl of some newer ones. Only private capital—directly, privately —can accomplish certain goals.

We read of real estate developments of commendable quality and purpose announced for other cities and we like to think that some of these may have been prompted by Crown Center, though we do not believe that Crown Center should be copied. What is right for Hallmark Cards and Kansas City may not be appropriate for another firm in another place. But the idea of utilizing the skills of private businessmen toward the solution of public problems in such a way that both benefit has proven to be a powerful and rewarding landmark in the history and health of Hallmark Cards, Inc.

HART SCHAFFNER & MARX

□ □ □

Good Things Come to a Firm Whose Name Is in Three

A season or two ago a West Coast football coach was deluged with an irate fan's cup of beer. Inspecting his soaked garment, someone asked him, "What kind of suit are you wearing?"

The coach replied, according to a sports columnist, "A Hart Schaffner & Schlitz."

The story points up just how well known the Hart Schaffner & Marx name is.

"The name caught on because of its rhythm," declared Edward L. Bernays, veteran public relations counsel, in his memoirs. It also caught on with writers—and headline writers—because it affords quick, recognizable puns and references. For example, the headline of a story about a man who urged that all dogs be clothed: "Hart Schaffner & Barks."

When a typographical error in a newspaper advertisement made it "Hart Schaffner & Mary," a columnist wrote that the firm was to be commended for "making the seamstress a full partner."

A fashion writer, decrying sloppy attire, decided such dress would cause Hart Schaffner & Marx "to commit triple harakiri." So it goes!

In the fast-moving business that America's male apparel industry has become in recent decades, Hart Schaffner & Marx is, according to consumer surveys, far and away the

Hart, Schaffner & Marx fashions of 1899.

best-known name. The firm is also one of the oldest and largest.

Its beginnings go back to 1872, just six months after the Great Chicago Fire, when twenty-one-year-old Harry Hart and his eighteen-year-old brother Max opened "Harry Hart and Brother," a retail clothing store on Chicago's State Street. Later brothers-in-law Levi Abt and Marcus Marx joined them, and the partnership was called Hart Abt & Marx. In 1887 Joseph Schaffner replaced Abt, and the present name was adopted.

The move into manufacturing as well as retail operations evolved by chance. A downstate Illinois merchant saw clothing the young firm had made to sell in its own stores, and liked it so much that he ordered several garments for his own customers. The partners decided to find out if other merchants might be interested in buying their clothing.

Orders came in, and the wholesale business gradually overshadowed retailing operations. As the company grew, larger production facilities were needed. The firm provided the nucleus for Chicago's men's wear industry by being the first to build garment factories in that city.

Soon Hart Schaffner & Marx salesmen—with silk toppers, spats and walking sticks—were "on the road," showing finished garments from as many as twenty wardrobe trunks. Later the company introduced the then-revolutionary idea of selling from more convenient "swatches," or small fabric samples. This innovation was widely adopted by the rest of the industry.

The firm has grown to the point where it has nine manufacturing divisions operationg 38 factories in 12 states and a network of 258 men's and women's apparel stores in 73 U.S. metropolitan areas. Sales last year were $423 million, more than double those of a decade ago.

Under the slogan "America's First Name in Men's Clothing"—its registered trademark—Hart Schaffner & Marx produced what is generally conceded to be the most comprehensive selection of men's apparel of any manufacturer. Its divisions make everything from suits to slacks, sport coats to country casuals, weathercoats to jeans, at a wide range of price levels and qualities.

The Hart Schaffner & Marx Clothes Division manufactures and distributes clothing under its own label as well as under the Graham & Gunn, Ltd., Sterling & Hunt, Jack Nicklaus and Fashionaire (career wear) labels. Other separate manufacturing divisions market their clothing under Hickey-Freeman, Walter-Morton, Society Brand, Ltd., Austin Reed of Regent Street, Gleneagles, Great Western, Jaymar-Ruby, Johnny Carson, Blue Jeans, Californian and Stuart Nelson (the latter two are sportswear).

The Johnny Carson line of men's clothing has been tremendously successful for Hart Schaffner & Marx since it was introduced in January, 1970. Johnny Carson appears in print and television advertisements, and makes promotional appearances throughout the country for the line.

Hart Schaffner & Marx marketing strategy also features Bob Hope and Jack Nicklaus in advertisements.

The firm has entered the international market through recent investments in Austin Reed Group, Ltd., which operates forty-seven men's stores throughout Great Britain, and in Robert's, the leading manufacturer and retailer of men's quality clothing in Mexico. Hart Schaffner & Marx currently is exploring the possibility of manufacturing and marketing apparel in Japan.

In its eighty-six years under its present name the clothier has evolved as a trend-setter, not only in fashion but in business ethics as well.

At the end of the nineteenth century, when a huge wave of immigration from Europe took place, there was no protective labor legislation and ill-ventilated upper-floor lofts and tenement factories were the rule. Seething unrest created by difficult working conditions, long hours and low wages erupted into Chicago's disastrous four-month industry strike.

From these events Joseph Schaffner emerged as a leader and humanitarian. His sense of strong, personal responsibility caused him to adopt improved working conditions in an agreement with the union. This agreement became a working model for the men's garment industry, and later for the women's.

In the years since, the firm has never had a strike or a lockout, a milestone honored by the U.S. Labor Department in 1964 when it named Hart Schaffner & Marx and the Amalgamated Clothing Workers of America as the first two organizations admitted to its Hall of Honor.

The company has had many "firsts."

It was America's first volume clothing manufacturer to adopt standard pricing ("one just price and just one price"). This was a startling move in a day when prices to individual retailers were in proportion to the size of their orders.

HS&M also was the first to introduce an "all-wool" policy— a courageous move in the early 1900s. Prior to Federal Trade Commission labeling standards, many garments were labeled "all-wool" even though they contained as much as 80 percent cotton, flax or other fibers. HS&M's truthful labeling, and the backing of the label by national advertising, eventually forced the entire industry to follow suit.

HS&M ran the first national clothing advertising campaign in 1897. Within a few years such famous illustrators as Leyendecker, Abbott and Penfield—famed for their *Saturday Evening Post* covers—painted illustrations for these ads. HS&M national campaigns have been running uninterrupted ever since.

Another first was the introduction in 1953 of the original Dacron polyester and wool suit. Hart Schaffner & Marx was also the first to use nylon-wool and Orlon acrylic-and-wool blends to produce the lightest-weight clothing possible. In 1917 HS&M also tailored the first tropical-weight suit—the famous Dixie Weave which was a forerunner of today's light-weight garments.

Heading up Hart Schaffner & Marx today are John D. Gray, chairman and chief executive officer, and Jerome S. Gore, president. Mr. Gray joined the firm in 1945 as president of its Baskin retail stores in Chicago, and was named president of its Wallachs retail stores in the East in 1948. He joined the parent firm in 1952 as vice president, was promoted to executive vice president in 1960 and president later the same year. He became chairman in 1970.

When Mr. Gray assumed the chairmanship, Mr. Gore became president. Mr. Gore has spent his entire career at Hart Schaffner & Marx, joining the firm in 1941 and rising through the ranks: a vice president in 1960, group vice president six years later, executive vice president in 1967.

Keeping abreast or ahead of new fashion trends has been vital to the company's success from the beginning. But fit receives equal emphasis. HS&M was the first to offer proportioned fit. As a result of extensive studies begun in 1906, the company pinpointed the basic body types among American males and translated these types into a wide variety of specialty sizes and shapes to fit all men. Thus individuality was achieved as a combination of quantity production and quality.

Designing to fit these many variations is an involved, complex task, as is the subsequent manufacturing. At drafting tables designers express their ideas in patterns. It is not uncommon for designers to draft and redraft models many times and make dozens of experimental garments.

Other factors must be considered too: If shoulders are broadened, will the hang of the back be spoiled? If collars are widened, will this affect coats at the shoulders?

Finally, through painstaking effort, skill and knowledge a model emerges that meets specifications. Once the model for a so-called regular figure is achieved, patterns are developed for other sizes and shapes.

Then come the other major steps: processing of raw materials, cutting, tailoring.

The average suit contains 72 pieces of fabric in the coat, 39 in the pants and 36 in the vest (if one is included). These comprise 7,074 square inches of fabric, 8,000 square inches of varied inner fabrics, 16 buttons, 565 yards of thread of 19 different types and 150,000 stitches.

While this adds up to an impressive total, its value and usefulness would be relatively small without the vital flair of the design as well as meticulous attention to processing and hand-detailed tailoring.

The assembling, stitching, shaping, steaming, pressing and inspecting of the components of a suit require innumerable operations by scores of skilled craftsmen.

In reviewing the company's record over the years, it seems the Hart Schaffner & Marx name will continue to be popular not only with consumers but with writers as well.

Such as the West Coast writer who reported that a baseball manager had questioned a fashionable third baseman who appeared for a road trip carrying a suit carrier slung over a shoulder. Was it necessary to carry so many suits?

"Well," the player told the manager, "I heard you were looking for a fourth infielder to go along with Hart Schaffner & Marx."

HERTZ

□ □ □

From the Back Street to the Front

The Hertz Corporation is always interested in entry into new markets for its services. But it just isn't true yet that it is planning to open a station on the moon—despite the fact that not too long ago *The New York Times* printed a map of the place that identified one of the locations merely with the word "Hertz" (in honor of a German scientist).

Nowadays, however, you're never too far from the ubiquitous yellow-and-black Hertz emblem, whether you're in the wilds of Uganda, the streets of Moscow or the canyons of Manhattan. The familiar insignia can be found in over a hundred countries around the world, usually in busy airports and business districts.

Today Hertz and its licensees operate a fleet of 160,000 vehicles domestically and internationally. A half-century ago, however, when the Hertz business started, you could only find the emblem in one city, Chicago, and on only one back-street garage at that.

What happened to the company that became number one in the rent-a-car industry it virtually created is not just an example of getting there first with the most. The annals of American business are filled with forgotten names of pioneering concerns that just never made it. But Hertz made it big and today is a diversified equipment rental company, generating well over $600 million in annual revenues.

116

Hertz had its beginnings in 1918 when Walter L. Jacobs opened a small rental business with a dozen used Model T Fords. The business grew, and in 1923 was purchased by John Hertz and became part of his Yellow Truck and Coach Manufacturing Company. In 1925 the Hertz Drive-Ur-Self System was purchased by General Motors Corporation, which primarily wanted the truck manufacturing facilities. These plants subsequently formed the nucleus of today's GMC Truck Division.

The Hertz properties operated as a GM subsidiary until 1953, when they were sold to the Omnibus Corporation, which up to that time had been a holding company for bus

A Hertz rental car lot in Miami at the time of the Florida land boom of the twenties.

operations. Omnibus divested itself of the bus interests to concentrate on vehicle renting and leasing. It changed its name to The Hertz Corporation. In May of 1967 Hertz became a subsidiary of RCA Corporation, operating with its own board of directors and officers.

Hertz' greatest period of growth began after World War II, with a substantial extension of its activities both in the United States and abroad.

In the early twenties, the renting and leasing business wasn't yet booming. There were a small number of car rental concerns here and there, offering economy cars. But in those days most people didn't want anybody to know they were driving a rented car. They'd slink into a back-street garage and ask for "that black Model T with the banged-up right front fender I rented last week."

Around this time Hertz began to phase out the back-street image. Soon its offices were located in high-rent business and residential districts, at train depots and even at the fledgling airports of the thirties. Then, despite the ravages of the Great Depression and, later, the shortages and priorities of World War II, the Hertz enterprise began to turn around the public's ideas about renting cars.

Nothing is stronger than an idea whose time has come—and Hertz began to cash in on the fact that its services were decidedly in tune with a nation whose mobility needs were rapidly expanding. The idea of using a car without having to own it—of paying for it only when you needed wheels—was beginning to appeal more and more to the automotive-oriented, convenience-minded public of the postwar era.

With the coming of high-speed transcontinental and trans-atlantic air travel, the car rental business got a tremendous boost from the new "fly-drive" travel mode. Businessmen, and then vacationers, began to use planes for long-distance hops with rental cars waiting at destination airports for on-the-scene mobility.

Over these years the Hertz organization consolidated its leadership position and pioneered innovations that motorists today take quite for granted. For example:

• Hertz was the first to introduce what amounts to a "wardrobe" of vehicles to suit any purpose, offering for rent late-model cars in many sizes and models.

• "Rent it here . . . Leave it there" service—on a broad nationwide basis—was strongly promoted by Hertz.

• Service at airports made "fly-drive" feasible, as earlier depot service had made "rail-drive" a reality.

• As early as 1926 Hertz took the bold step of introducing a rudimentary charge-card service. Today Hertz service can be charged by more than 25 million motorists in the United States alone.

• Hertz' Number One Club—a major step in bringing automation directly to customers of a service industry—was launched in 1972. Under this system car rental information on hundreds of thousands of regular and high-volume car renters, both individual and corporate, is fed into a computer data bank for instant retrieval, eliminating the need for frequent customers to repeat routine information each time they rent a vehicle.

Though Hertz is best known for its rent-a-car activity, which represents about one-third of its business and is the oldest company "arm," other divisions have contributed greatly through the years to the world's largest renting and leasing company.

Truck renting and leasing is Hertz's second most senior business. From the 1920s onward Hertz provided trucks on short-term and long-term leases. In 1953, before the Rent A Car Division started its phenomenal growth, revenues from the Truck Division's rentals actually exceeded those of car rentals by about 50 percent. It was not until 1958 that the truck business was surpassed by Rent A Car.

This business grew steadily along two lines: leasing and short-term rental. The lease activity provided to various companies trucks of virtually any size or model, which Hertz painted and lettered to the customer's specifications. These trucks could be leased singly or in fleets as large as required.

The rental part of the truck business has always appealed primarily to individuals who require large vehicles for short periods of time, and to business concerns that need to fill gaps in an established leased or owned fleet for peak periods of use or one-time jobs.

In 1955 Hertz entered the long-term auto leasing field through establishment of the Car Leasing Division. This service appeals to firms whose needs vary from five cars to hundreds on a nationwide basis—for generally two years. Under a full-maintenance lease, Hertz provides all services, including registration and insurance, except fuel and lubrication. Under a finance lease, Hertz buys the vehicle and, at the end of the lease, disposes of it. The lessee handles all other matters himself and absorbs the gain or loss on disposition of the car.

Hertz International, Ltd., provides car and truck rental services in more than a hundred countries outside the United States. This operation conducts corporate activities in about thirty nations and territories, and handles licensee operations in the remainder. This division primarily rents locally manufactured cars and employs local citizens of the countries it serves.

Hertz International, Ltd., does do some truck renting, but the bulk of its revenue is derived from self-drive car rentals. Like the domestic rent-a-car business, many Hertz International rentals take place at airports.

Hertz Equipment Rental Corporation rents construction-type equipment to building contractors and industrial firms. Begun in 1965, this subsidiary rents a wide variety of tools, ranging from hand-operated power devices to air compressors and large cranes. This service is provided through more than forty locations in the United States, and is expanding rapidly.

In 1967 Hertz embarked on yet another service activity. Its subsidiary, United Exposition Service Company, provides trade shows, conventions and expositions with three types of service: drayage, delivering exhibitors' equipment to the site and personnel to install and dismantle exhibits. The company also designs and builds displays. Its combined activities use seven locations in this country.

In 1968 Hertz unveiled an unusual service for air travelers

with the official opening of its first Skycenter at the Huntsville, Alabama, jetport. Regarded as a model for airport centers of the future, this Skycenter features a "city-within-a-city" plan—transportation facilities, lodging, business, banking and recreation all under one roof.

Through its subsidiary, Hertz Skycenter, Inc., the company runs all terminal service facilities (other than those related to air traffic control).

In 1972 a second Skycenter was opened at Jacksonville International Airport in Jacksonville, Florida.

Companies in forty-six states and Puerto Rico are currently using machinery or equipment leased from another subsidiary, Hertz Commercial Leasing Corporation. Hertz buys the equipment and leases it to the user on a three-year basis or longer. The customer can renew the lease or buy the equipment, if he chooses, at the end of the lease period. The user pays insurance, maintenance, operating and other costs during the lease.

As the leading and most diversified of the firms in the renting and leasing industry, Hertz has benefited from the significant trends toward increased use of its industry's services. The same forces in society—mobility, convenience and effective utilization—that shaped the broad expansion in use of renting and leasing services to date, remain strongly in effect. This holds true both for domestic and international markets for Hertz services.

As with other burgeoning service industries, all signs in the field of renting and leasing point to further healthy development in the years ahead. The outlook is bright for the continued growth of Hertz, for expanded opportunities for its people and for greater service to its many customers in the United States and abroad.

HEUBLEIN

□ □ □

Riding High on a "Moscow Mule"

America showed little taste for whiskey in the 1930s. This may seem strange, considering that the country had been legally dry for fourteen years—1920 through 1933. Yet it was a fact of life at the time.

The men at Heublein, who had endured the Prohibition period on the sales strength of A.1. Sauce, were wondering how they were going to make a go of the liquor business again. The same apprehension applied to almost everybody else in the field, too, for it was very difficult to sell whiskey to Americans then. Maybe there were other reasons, but probably the main one was the Depression. People just didn't have the money to spend. The company had all kinds of whiskey—Heublein Private Stock, Old Waverly, Powerhorn, Forest Park—but it just couldn't sell it.

Then, about 1939, came a stroke of good luck. Heublein got a chance to compete in the liquor business with a new product: Smirnoff Vodka.

While Smirnoff was new to this country in those days, its tradition dated back to 1818, when the Smirnoff family started making vodka in Russia. They did pretty well at it for about a hundred years—until the Russian Revolution of 1917.

In 1933 Rudolph Kunett, a Russian who had escaped after the Revolution and settled in the United States, recalled that his family had been friends with the Smirnoff family in Russia

The Heublein factory and restaurant were housed in these quarters in Hartford, Connecticut, for thirty-three years beginning in 1901.

in the pre-Revolution days. He went to Paris and persuaded Vladimir Smirnoff, the only surviving member of that family, to give him the American franchise for Smirnoff Vodka.

Kunett set up a little factory in Bethel, Connecticut, in 1934. Those were hard times for everybody, of course, and Kunett's Smirnoff Company didn't do very well. Soon he wanted out. He approached several big distillers, but nobody wanted to gamble on a spirit that was all but unknown in this country.

Heublein gambled and offered Kunett $14,000. It also offered him a royalty on each bottle of Smirnoff it sold for a certain period of time, and gave him a job with Heublein.

When Heublein took over Smirnoff in 1939 it was selling only 6,000 cases a year. Even the Russians in this country weren't drinking vodka then. The problem was to make the product known. In a way, you could say the problem solved itself—in quite an unusual manner.

Heublein had ordered 2,000 cases of Smirnoff put up so that there would be no hurry moving what little equipment there was from Bethel to Hartford, Connecticut, the company's home. Heublein thought the 2,000 cases would provide a six-month inventory.

However, Kunett's people had run out of "Smirnoff Vodka" bottle corks. They did have some around that said "Smirnoff Whiskey"—leftovers from an ill-fated attempt at the whiskey business—and these corks were used on the vodka.

The first sale of Smirnoff Vodka—with the whiskey corks —was made to a distributor in Columbia, South Carolina. He bought 25 cases on good faith. Pretty soon, Heublein got an order for 50 more cases of Smirnoff, then an order for 500. John G. Martin, chairman of the executive committee, decided to go down to South Carolina to investigate.

It turned out that one of the distributor salesmen had tasted the first batch of Smirnoff and noticed it didn't have a taste or a smell. He'd noticed the whiskey cap, too, so he had come up with a rather ingenious, but totally illegal, scheme. He'd had streamers made that said, "Smirnoff's White Whiskey

. . . No Taste, No Smell." The idea caught on and people started buying Smirnoff.

When the war came along Heublein couldn't make any Smirnoff for four years because alcohol was restricted. It made only Heublein Cocktails—martinis and manhattans.

Before the war Martin had got together with a friend, Jack Morgan, who owned the Cock 'n Bull Restaurant in Hollywood, and with a friend of his. Jack had Cock 'n Bull Ginger Beer, which he could not sell. Martin had Smirnoff Vodka, which he couldn't sell. The friend was in the business of making copper mugs and couldn't sell those either. So the three devised a drink and called it the "Moscow Mule," which is Smirnoff Vodka and Cock 'n Bull Ginger Beer served in a copper mug. The war prevented them from getting that drink going. But right after the war it really took off in Southern California.

About this time the Polaroid people came out with a camera that took pictures and, in a minute, self-developed them. Martin bought one of those cameras and went from bar to bar with a Moscow Mule mug and the Smirnoff bottles. He would tell the bartender he'd take his picture and give it to him if he'd take a sip of the Moscow Mule.

Usually the bartender was so intrigued by the Polaroid camera that he would agree. Martin took two pictures, actually. One he gave to the bartender and the other he showed to his next customer as proof that everyone was switching to Smirnoff.

That was one of the ways that Smirnoff was launched in California. A device of this kind is always helpful in getting attention for a new product, of course, but what really got the job done was hard work and lots of it. It's the old story of genius being 2 percent inspiration and 98 percent perspiration.

There were several people who deserve recognition, but none more than a man named Eli Shapiro, who is now dead. Eli was hired as the Smirnoff salesman in California after World War II, and by the results, you'd think Heublein had hired five or six men instead of *one* man with a singular dedication to his job.

Eli's persistence and fortitude in selling what was then an unknown brand was unforgettable. Because he didn't represent a big company or a popular brand, Eli usually had a difficult time just getting in to talk with restaurant operators, package store owners, liquor wholesalers and other potential customers. Oftentimes he'd sit in someone's waiting room for hours, only to be told at the end of the day that the prospective buyer wouldn't be able to see him. But Eli would be back the next day, and the next and the next, if necessary. Like water wearing down rock, his persistence would finally prevail and the buyer would order a few cases of Smirnoff.

Repeat that story a few thousand times and you begin to understand Mr. Shapiro's role in making Smirnoff a big seller in California. From there the popularity of Smirnoff spread eastward, and today it's the second largest-selling liquor brand in the United States and number one in the international market. Smirnoff now is made by Heublein licensees in thirty-four countries abroad and has sales of about seven million cases a year. That's a long way from the 6,000 cases sold in 1939.

Perhaps one of the most amazing things about the phenomenal Smirnoff story is that the brand is still growing at a rapid rate. In 1972, for example, Smirnoff sales in this country were up about 11 percent, while the increase abroad was even greater, due in great part to the rapidly growing popularity of white liquors.

One other factor was critical in this success story, the quality of the product. Repeat sales are the basis for long-term success in the liquor industry, and you don't get such sales unless the quality is in the bottle. Fortunately for Heublein, this has always been true of Smirnoff.

After World War II Heublein thought it would be wise to also obtain the international rights to Smirnoff. By then Vladimir Smirnoff had died, so Martin went to Paris to see his partner, a man by the name of Harry Zarris.

Zarris was a very devout fellow, and one of the conditions

he laid down before he'd sell the business was that Heublein would have to rebuild the Greek Orthodox Church in Paris. The company did so, and it was a very handsome structure. This was the start of the international Smirnoff business, which seems to have virtually unlimited potential.

Today Heublein is no longer a one-brand company. Besides Smirnoff it has such products as Kentucky Fried Chicken, Harvey's Bristol Cream Sherry, Lancers wine from Portugal, Italian Swiss Colony Wine, Arrow Cordials, Black Velvet Canadian Whiskey and many, many more.

But it was Smirnoff that made all this possible. It provided the financial resources to expand the company. Just as important, the marketing job done with Smirnoff attracted the other companies as partners in the major mergers made in recent years. People like to be associated with success.

Smirnoff is still the backbone of the Heublein business. When it acquired Smirnoff in 1939, the value of the Heublein company was less than $5 million. Today the market value is something close to $1 billion. So you can see this little vodka has done very well.

HOOVER

□ □ □

One Man's Theory Opens a New Door

In 1907 the W. H. Hoover Company was a thriving business making saddles, harnesses and other leather goods as well as accessories for the automobile industry in North Canton (then New Berlin), Ohio. The growing popularity of the automobile was soon felt in the dwindling demand for harnesses. The Hoover family wisely began looking around for other new promising investments. Within their own community they came across a crude but new invention made of tin and wood which showed promise of relieving the American housewife of endless hours of dusting and sweeping. They agreed to begin the manufacture of this device, the forerunner of the modern Hoover Cleaner, in a corner of the leather goods factory.

Through a simple but practical sales approach a number of interested dealers were contacted and persuaded to market this new and revolutionary device. The company gradually phased out its leather goods business and expanded the more profitable manufacture of electric cleaners under the name of the Electric Suction Sweeper Company in 1908. The name was later to be changed to The Hoover Company. Thus began a business that was to lighten the day-to-day chores of housewives around the world.

It became apparent early in the company's history that although the dealer was the keystone in the success of Hoover sales, training and personal demonstration were equally

One of the Hoover Company's early sales training classes for dealers.

important. That principle has resulted in today's nationwide network of Hoover sales personnel and dealers thoroughly trained in the features and advantages of all Hoover products.

The Hoover Company might have remained a small, respected manufacturer and marketer of vacuum cleaners in North Canton, Ohio. Instead, it has become an international organization making a wide range of household appliances in eleven countries, selling them in more than one hundred and constantly seeking new ways to expand. One recent expansion was the acquisition of Knapp-Monarch, a manufacturer of small electric appliances in St. Louis, Missouri.

Although many men and women have had a share in this over the years, much of the credit for the achievement belongs to the broad-shouldered young Norwegian who joined the company as a service salesman in Green Bay, Wisconsin, more than forty years ago. He is now a widely traveled international businessman and the company's president and chairman—Felix Norman Mansager.

Reared on a farm in South Dakota, Felix Mansager was the son of a Norwegian immigrant mother and a first generation Norwegian-American father. Hard work and long hours were the daily routine on the South Dakota farm. He learned early in life to analyze problems and find solutions to make routine operations easier and more productive for all concerned. His decision to join The Hoover Company was a serious one but one he would never regret.

Felix Mansager guided the company through the rapids of a momentous transition—the shift from selling a single product, the vacuum cleaner, basically door-to-door, to selling more than a score of products through dealers.

To say he had a dream is perhaps being too poetic. Call it a theory that evolved into a plan that gave the company global stature.

To say the decision to change over came sharply and suddenly is being overdramatic. The move took form gradually, as do many important alterations in corporate concept and policy.

From its birth in 1908 The Hoover Company had worked closely with dealers. Early advertisements, notably in the now-defunct *Saturday Evening Post*, directed prospects to them. Company salesmen furnished them leads. Every sale, in effect, was a dealer sale. But Hoover management placed top reliance for increased sales upon those who rang the doorbells. They were the men hired and trained by the company. They were the men who fully understood the product and thoroughly believed in it. They had incentive instilled in them.

Felix Mansager went to Sioux Falls, South Dakota, not far from his home in Colton, as a door-to-door salesman in 1935. During the forties he was district manager there. Somewhere along this passage of time the dream, or the theory, began to take clearer shape.

The young manager said to himself: "My men and I can call on just so many housewives a day; at least three or four times that number will visit dealer stores in town. If the dealers understood the product as we do, they could help us sell. What they need for that understanding is training."

Slowly the theory was put into practice. Dealer meetings were held whenever possible. The dealers were shown through training how to sell a product in the home or in the store. They were persuaded to place orders for cleaners and actively display and promote them. They were told Hoover men would help in every way they could. The results were fantastic.

In 1950 the home office sent Mr. Mansager to Milwaukee as district manager. He requested permission to do what he had done in Sioux Falls: meet with dealers and train them when not making sales rounds of his own.

Some of his managers were openly skeptical. A few recalled that dealers had returned their stocks to North Canton when a minor depression ensued just after World War I. The Doubting Thomases thought this could—and probably would—happen again. Furthermore, they argued, Milwaukee was a whole lot larger and more sophisticated. Who knew whether big-city dealers would be as responsive? But

Mr. Mansager persisted and finally got the permission he needed for this more exacting test. His theory proved successful again—and when he went to Chicago as division manager three years later, it proved successful once more but on a larger scale.

The changing times were on his side. Young men were showing less interest in door-to-door sales employment. Turnover in the sales force was cresting at a height of 600 percent. The company's management had to spend more and more time training new salesmen. Commissions had to be increased to get them interested at all. Rising costs were adversely affecting product price.

Except for smaller items that can easily be brought to the door, house-to-house canvassing was growing less popular—and less profitable. It was getting harder to find housewives at home in a buying mood. The lady of the house was more likely out patronizing the shopping center. Or visiting a dealer's store, after television, radio, magazine and newspaper advertising had called attention to the attractive offerings she might find there. She was growing accustomed to buying away from home.

Steadily the Dealer Plan gained ground. The dealer was becoming the sole point of sale throughout the United States. Trained and assisted by the company, he and his staff were not only selling more cleaners than ever before, but also were prepared to handle increasing numbers of products wearing the red circle of quality. Diversification Day for the company was not far off.

When Felix Mansager became general sales manager at North Canton in 1959 he found some faint stirrings of diversification. Hoover had started making a few irons and some floor polishers. These were being marketed to distributors by a special products department, quite apart from the sales effort expended on the cleaner. Now they were all placed under one roof, so to speak, and the campaign for diversification began in earnest. To cite one measure of the success of the change, the recently completed warehouse close to the main plant currently handles 35 products and over 300 models.

In 1963, when he was made executive vice president of the Hoover Group, Mr. Mansager installed the plan first in the United Kingdom and then in all the other company-related factories and offices around the world.

Proof of his leadership in the marketing field in the United Kingdom was that he was the first American named Marketing Man of the Year by the prestigious British Institute of Marketing in 1971. Hoover employs over 24,000 people in factories and offices around the world. Finding ways to improve quality and save time are all part of the Hoover tradition reinforced by Felix Mansager's leadership. The plan Felix Mansager dreamed about more than forty years ago is now flourishing universally.

A final assessment of this attainment and its architect seems fitting: In the years since 1963 the company's consolidated sales worldwide rose from $241,802,548 to $458,-415,022 in 1972. During the same period U.S. sales increased more than 160 percent.

JACK DANIEL'S

□ □ □

The "Little Ole Still" a Lot
of People Came to Know

If you have never heard of Jack Daniel's Whiskey, so
much the better. Its relative obscurity is part of its
charm. Little knots of Jack Daniel fanatics are to be
encountered in all parts of the country and in all walks
of life. They pluck at one's sleeve and whisper: 'Try
some of this. It's made in a little ole still way off somewhere in the hills of Tennessee. The same family has
been making it by the same secret process for nearly
100 years. It's expensive and hard to get, but no other
whiskey in the world tastes quite like it.' The enchant-
ing thing about this legend is that it is largely true.

This is how a business magazine described the beginnings of
a phenomenal word-of-mouth campaign about Jack Daniel's
in early 1951. Phenomenal, because now, after more than two
decades, the legend still persists, and the whispered word-of-
mouth campaign continues to expand and grow. The "little
ole still" now occupies an enviable position in a most difficult
and demanding manufacturing and marketing arena. This is
due, in no small measure, to the astute and far-seeing leadership of one man in particular: Winton E. Smith.

Jack Daniel's Whiskey is considered unique by many. It
has a distinctive taste, though it is made, as most good
Bourbons are, of no blessed thing except grain and water.
The brand's difference stems from an ancient Tennessee
practice of seeping the just-made whiskey through 12 feet of
finely-ground hard sugar maple charcoal. The result is an
unusually smooth and mellow potable, so distinctive in taste

134

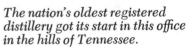

The nation's oldest registered distillery got its start in this office in the hills of Tennessee.

Jack Daniel

that the federal government insisted in 1942 that Jack Daniel's could not properly be called a Bourbon, but must be labeled instead "Tennessee Whiskey."

The distillery was founded in the early 1860s by a precocious Tennessee teenager named Jack Daniel, and located in a small hollow near his hometown of Lynchburg. The site was selected because of the spring-fed limestone cave which offered a constant stream of cool, iron-free water. The distillery still stands and operates at the mouth of that Cave Spring. It has been in constant operation longer than any other distillery in the country. Though not the oldest in years, it was first under the wire when the registration law was enacted after the Civil War, which makes it the oldest registered distillery in the United States.

For years Jack Daniel operated, with the help of his nephew, Lem Motlow, at a maximum production of only ten barrels a day. When he died in 1911 he had already seen his whiskey awarded the coveted Gold Medal at the St. Louis World's Fair, the first of several such international recognitions.

After the repeal of Prohibition Lem Motlow reopened his inherited distillery. Upon his death in 1947 his four sons became the proprietors. Soon the remarkable word-of-mouth buildup began about Jack Daniel's Whiskey, and while the Motlow brothers still declare they did nothing to foster or promote it, they felt its effects and recognized that they needed a professional sales manager.

Winton E. Smith was their selection. In January, 1953, he set about expanding Jack Daniel's sales beyond the Southern states. While he was aware that Jack Daniel's had among its devotees such notables as John Nance Garner, William Faulkner and Humphrey Bogart, he also knew that his roster of rooters lacked in quantity what it evidenced in quality. Expansion to national distribution would require a carefully planned strategy.

His analysis of the marketing problem was at first discouraging. Taste patterns of the American consumer were changing in the postwar period. Premium-priced bonded whiskeys (100 proof) were losing their market share. The lower-priced, lower-proof straight whiskeys, along with Scotch and Canadian potables, were curving upward. Jack Daniel's price was high, though for a good reason: its exclusive charcoal-mellowing process more than doubled its cost of manufacture. Thus it was aligned with the sagging premium-priced Bonds. But Smith was convinced that the slipping 100-proof Bonds were ailing because of high proof rather than high price. He sensed the trend to lightness in taste, and reasoned that Jack Daniel's, at the lower 90 proof, and strengthened by its distinctive taste and mellowness, could possibly exploit this change in consumer preference. With the help of the Motlow brothers, Smith set his goals and outlined the company's first long-term marketing strategy. It was a three-pronged program: (1) to get Jack Daniel's recognized as one of the world's most distinguished whiskeys, a product of great rarity; (2) to strive for near perfect distribution, based on a strongly developed nationwide consumer franchise; (3) to achieve recognition in the liquor trade as the ultimate in a highly-profitable quality product—worthy of being accorded showcase positions on the dealers' shelves.

Ambitious goals, and admirable. Reaching them would be difficult. But Winton Smith was up to it. It is interesting to note that the marketing strategy laid out in those early days of 1953 is still vital and valid to company executives in today's marketplace—strong testament to the advanced thinking that developed it and the enlightened consistency of the management team that implemented it: (1) the company will never compromise the product's quality or change the method of charcoal-mellowing that produced its unique taste; (2) Jack Daniel's will hold to the high unit price and stubbornly guard against discounting to either wholesaler or retailer; (3) advertising should always reflect the distillery's uniqueness, and be calculated to create an emotional involvement between consumer and product; (4) continuous efforts will be made to closely coordinate the thrust of the company's advertising with its sales effort; (5) come what may, the company will maintain a consistency in its total marketing effort.

Smith moved quickly and decisively. By early 1954 the company had spread its distributor network and set the stage for its first national advertising campaign. That the advertising plan was well conceived and consistently followed is evidenced by comparing an ad today with this sketch of product character and personality written in 1954:

> Every drop of our whiskey is lovingly crafted to a rare flavor not to be found anywhere else.
> Our language will be homey, but never quaint.
> We will speak distinctly and directly—with the quiet conviction that we have much to offer.
> We will use pictures that make our advertising look like it sounds.
> Photography shall center around those things inherent to how and where Jack Daniel's is made—the symbols at the heart of the difference that makes Jack Daniel's unique.
> Pictures, like copy, must never appear slick or tricky. While our photography will picture the down-to-earth, grassroots personality of Jack Daniel's, it must do so with dignity and importance—never a hint of shoddyness or oafishness.

Homey, direct, and consistent . . . establishing a comfortable emotional involvement between consumer and product, such as one would have with a trusted and respected friend. A constant weaving of the story and the picturesque image of the quiet, unhurried pace and unabashed reality of the Hollow, its inhabitants and its "lovingly crafted" product.

The results were explosive. Jack Daniel's sales soared far beyond the expectations of its owners. All available inventories were stripped, and the small company faced a consumer demand far greater than its ability to supply. The imbalance—while heady—was hazardous; the alternatives were few.

Whiskey, unlike most products, requires many years of aging before its maturity allows it to be marketed. For Jack Daniel's Black Label, this means five years; for the Green Label, four years. To short-cut is to compromise product quality—an anathema to Winton Smith and the Motlows. They chose to gamble their new-found acceptance and popularity by candidly asking their customers and dealers to sweat it out with them. Late in 1956 Jack Daniel's ads appeared under the headline: "We'd rather ask your patience than lose your respect for Jack Daniel's."

To be fair to retailers Smith established a firm policy of allocating the existing Jack Daniel's on the basis of previous purchases. This garnered the healthy, though grudging, respect of the nation's liquor trade.

For the consumer, the shortage served to enhance the brand's image of rarity, to dramatize further the mystique developing around the backwoods distillery and the unique product it produced. Today consumer demand for Jack Daniel's still exceeds supply, though the company has more than quadrupled its availability. Trade estimates of Jack Daniel's sales range from 650,000 to 1,000,000 cases, far above the 100,000 cases being sold when Winton Smith came to Tennessee.

In September, 1956, Jack Daniel's was sold to Brown-Forman Distillers of Louisville. Brown-Forman, a family company like Jack Daniel's, wisely insisted that its new acquisition be run autonomously. It recognized that the marketing strategies and advertising format were as unique as the company itself, and so maintained the Motlows and Winton Smith in their positions of leadership. In the mid-sixties Smith was elected president and chief executive officer of Jack Daniel's, and in January, 1973, he was elevated to chairman of the board. He described the move as "the first step in the gradual and orderly transfer of top management responsibilities to a group of younger men."

Meanwhile the mystique and legend of Jack Daniel's continues to spread. During 1972 Jack Daniel's was marketed in over ninety countries throughout the world, where more ". . . little knots of Jack Daniel's fanatics, like Prince Rainier of Monaco, pluck at one's sleeve and whisper: 'Try some of this. It's made in a little ole still way off somewhere in the hills of Tennessee. The same family has been making it by the same secret process for over 100 years. It's expensive, hard to get. . . .' "

KELLY

□ □ □

A Distress Call Changed the
Temporary Help Industry

Kelly Services, the pioneer of the temporary help industry, is entering its second quarter-century. The company currently serves over 100,000 business, industry, government and academic institutions. As the largest supplier of temporary white-collar office help, Kelly employs more than 150,000 people annually—offering income and increased mobility to those who find temporary work best suited to their needs.

Chairman of the Board Russell Kelly, who was forty when he founded the company in 1946, has guided its growth from a one-room office staffed by two girls into a corporation of more than 300 offices throughout the United States, Canada and Europe with annual sales of over $85 million.

Ironically, founder Kelly never evisioned himself as a pioneer of today's multimillion-dollar temporary help industry. But a frantic call from an accountant one afternoon during his first year of operation opened the way for a dramatic switch in his approach to the service business.

His premise for launching what was then called Russell Kelly Office Service was that office needs in booming postwar America would be enormous. He had rightly judged the economy. Mature companies expanded, new companies cropped up and products entered the market at an increasing rate, bringing with them an onslaught of sophisticated office equipment and the need for trained people to process the paper work.

*The reception area of the Russell Kelly Office Services in
Detroit in the early years of the business.*

Russell Kelly's military experience in World War II helped prepare him to move the bottleneck of paper work he knew business firms would face. He had served as a fiscal management analyst in the Army's Quartermasters Corps, a position he found to be "a marvelous course in how to cut red tape." He established a centralized system for speeding up food delivery and prompter invoice payment. (Notes an associate of those days, "Russ moved food the way General Patton rolled his tanks.")

Mr. Kelly, whose lifetime ambition had been to own and successfully run a business, had fortuitously gambled that the Motor City was the ideal location for his new enterprise. Detroit was a well-established manufacturing center, and he sensed the great market potential for a service business.

In his early years he had studied business administration at the University of Pittsburgh. Later, as a salesman, he gained practical knowledge about people and their needs, and devised ways of serving those needs in his new venture.

He made the rounds of Detroit firms, offering to help them with their typing, duplicating, addressing and almost any kind of office service a business might require.

Mr. Kelly's intention was to bring the work he obtained into his office, but other businessmen saw things differently. Although businesses sought his services eagerly, many were purchasing their own office equipment in hopes of eventually solving their dilemmas internally. The problem was they had few people trained to operate the machines.

The urgent call from an accountant needing a typist that afternoon in 1946 vocalized this critical need of industry for a different kind of service—skilled assistance supplied to firms on an as-needed basis.

Mr. Kelly sent over one of his employees to get the typing done. Although he had originally offered the service as a courtesy to a particular customer in distress, he soon realized this was to be the trend of the future. He gradually shifted the emphasis in his operations from service bureau to temporary help as industry increasingly demanded "those Kelly Girls."

It was this ability to be flexible enough to change that assured the success of the business. Mr. Kelly was offering a new service concept which complemented the needs of business. Using temporary help on an as-needed basis, companies could avoid overloading payrolls to meet occasional peak work loads—and thus avoid paying for nonproductive employee time. And Kelly Girl employees could also be sent out to fill in for regular staff members in their absence. This concept gained increasing favor with the business world as costs continued to rise.

One of Mr. Kelly's problems was that his success soon used up his available personnel, which consisted of carefully trained, white-collar office workers. So Kelly himself went out into the field and talked to all sorts of organizations— PTA groups, civic groups and church groups. He soon discovered that there were many women interested in part-time work who had had previous office experience and whose children were now in school. Trained older women, who often found their age a disadvantage when they attempted to reenter the business world, were also a hidden source of talent.

Right from the beginning Mr. Kelly backed his attractively-packaged temporary assistance offer with a 100 percent guarantee. Unique in the service industry, this unconditional guarantee was a significant factor in his company's growth, especially during the early days when it was used to reassure customers who were skeptical about the performance of temporary help.

The Kelly Girl idea caught on rapidly in Detroit, and during his first full year of operation Kelly's sales totaled $92,000. By the year 1954 sales had climbed to $1.5 million. Russell Kelly's brother Richard joined the firm at this time and started an expansion program to open offices in other cities.

Russell Kelly's ability to change when the times called for it kept his business growing. The name Kelly Girl quickly became the company's trademark, and in 1959 he officially changed its name to Kelly Girl Service, Inc.

Always aware of employment and marketing trends, he

could see that businesses needed other temporary services in addition to his by now well-established office-clerical assistance. He therefore carefully test-marketed and added three other divisions: Kelly Marketing in 1962, and Kelly Labor and Kelly Technical in 1964.

Each broadened the spectrum of the company's services, giving its operations an overall approach to business needs in the temporary help field. To better reflect the range of services offered, the company name was modified again in 1966, this time to Kelly Services, Inc.

But those famous "Kelly Girls" are still the company's largest operation, and account for the majority of Kelly's working pool. Female and male, they range in age from eighteen to eighty, and come from all walks of life—housewives, students and teachers, moonlighters, people between jobs and those who prefer the variety and flexibility of temporary assignments.

Today Kelly Services is international. The company entered the Canadian marketplace in 1968 and began expansion abroad in 1972 with the opening of the first European Kelly office in Paris.

You might say change has been William Russell Kelly's forte for over twenty-five years. True, he never envisioned himself as a pioneer of the temporary help industry, but keen knowledge of his customers' staffing needs coupled with the sensitivity to interpret business trends led him to modify his original service concept. He became a pioneer and innovator in this industry because he was willing to be flexibile in his approach to the service business.

The only thing Mr. Kelly has never changed is his unconditional guarantee of service.

ELI LILLY

□ □ □

The Train Trip That Was a Turning Point

On Christmas Day, 1921, George Henry Alexander Clowes, Ph.D., a young chemist from England, skipped the traditional family festivities at his home in Indianapolis. Early that morning he packed a suitcase, said goodbye to his family and boarded a train for New Haven, Connecticut.

His trip was to be a turning point for Eli Lilly and Company, the pharmaceutical firm that Colonel Eli Lilly had founded in 1876.

Dr. Clowes, director of the Lilly Research Laboratories, had heard a few months before that insulin had been isolated at the University of Toronto by Dr. Frederick G. Banting and Charles H. Best. Dr. Clowes had been evaluating many current theories about the causes and treatment of diabetes, and had come to the conclusion that this pancreatic hormone might be the most promising approach to complete control of the disease.

A starvation diet was then the only medically acceptable treatment for severe diabetes. Something less stressful for the patient was needed.

With the words "Go to it!" Vice President Eli Lilly (grandson of the company's founder) gave his approval to Dr. Clowes' idea of contacting the Toronto scientists, who were in New Haven presenting a paper on their work.

For the diabetic, eating carbohydrates leads to overpro-

Colonel Eli Lilly, founder and president of the firm until 1898.

Packing insulin at the Lilly plant in 1923, the first year of the drug's large-scale production.

duction of sugar, which the body is unable to use for energy because little or no insulin is available to facilitate its utilization. Dr. Banting and Mr. Best hypothesized that diabetes would be controlled if insulin could be supplied from another source, animal pancreas. But a way to manufacture a stable, standardized insulin product in large quantities would have to be found.

Dr. Clowes convinced the Canadians that Eli Lilly and Company had the capability to develop a large-scale production method. Scientists worked day and night. Soon procedures for isolating insulin and purifying it in large quantities were discovered.

The purchasing department worked out a supply system with meat packers so animal pancreas glands that slaughterhouses had always discarded would be brought frozen to Indianapolis. Manufacturing facilities were designed and ready for use by the following year. Lilly insulin was marketed in 1923.

The Canadian scientists' discovery of insulin therapy, and its development, constituted one of the great landmarks in medicine, ushering in a new era of cooperation between pharmaceutical industry researchers and university scientists. Years later, in 1941, Josiah K. Lilly, Sr., son of the founder and at that time chairman of the board, wrote: "Insulin revolutionized our place in the industry."

Insulin was to be followed by many other outstanding products developed in the Lilly Research Laboratories. In the 1920s the company discovered the first in a series of barbiturate sedatives and hypnotics and, in association with Dr. George Minot and Dr. William Murphy, developed the first liver extract for control of pernicious anemia, a condition invariably fatal if it is untreated.

Another was poliomyelitis vaccine. Not long ago an eleven-year-old Boston boy was asked if he knew who discovered the vaccine that has virtually wiped out polio. The boy replied: "What's polio?"

His response was typical of the generation now growing up, which has never heard of what was once one of the most feared childhood diseases. Polio killed or crippled millions from as early as 3,700 B.C. until the discovery, development and widespread availability of a vaccine. The answer to the disease, of course, was provided by Dr. Jonas Salk, with whom the company worked closely in the development of a killed-virus poliomyelitis vaccine.

Since the vaccine's discovery and development, polio has almost disappeared from the United States. In 1955—not a particularly severe polio year—29,270 Americans were stricken with polio. Nearly half of those—13,850—suffered paralysis. That same year the polio vaccine was made available in large quantities. In 1971 only seventeen cases of polio were reported in the United States.

Among other contributions were the discovery and development of erythromycin, one of the first of a new class of antibiotics; and the development of the cephalosporins, a new family of broad-spectrum antibiotics, following a chemical breakthrough that permitted synthesis of a large number of derivatives of the original cephalosporin.

Through the development of the cephalosporins particularly one can readily see the company's emerging world approach to today's scientific problems. The cephalosporin products came from an organism discovered in Sardinia by Professor Giuseppe Brotzu of the Institute of Hygiene of the University of Cagliari. Further laboratory work at Oxford University in England by Professor E. P. Abraham and the late Dr. G. G. F. Newton proved the organism had antibiotic activity that was scientifically interesting. It was Lilly research and development that unlocked the door to the full potential of the cephalosporins and made them into commerical realities.

Early in the 1950s the company began to seek new areas where its research experience in the life sciences could be used. Eli Lilly and Company entered the agricultural market in 1954. Today Lilly agricultural products, marketed by its Elanco division, include herbicides, fungicides and growth regulators for plants; lawn and garden products; and veterinary medicines and other animal health products.

With the acquisition of Elizabeth Arden in 1971 the company has moved into the world of cosmetics and fashions. In Elizabeth Arden the company found a business that it felt to be closely related to its interests.

Since the first export order for a Lilly product was recrived in 1884, Eli.Lilly and Company has grown into a worldwide enterprise. Lilly, Elanco and Elizabeth Arden products are sold in approximately 150 countries outside the United States.

Throughout its ninety-seven years the company has made every effort to see that its products reflect the emphasis on quality set by its founder, who turned his back on the popular patent medicines of the day to produce quality products, honestly labeled, for physicians. At the time Colonel Lilly made the choice to take the "ethical" path, it appeared far less remunerative. He could not foresee that the slow results of education and pure food and drug legislaton would eventually make it surer as well as more satisfactory.

Colonel Lilly was a remarkable man whose concern for people was evidenced by his community leadership and service. His view of human worth was reflected in corporate policies that attracted people of talent to his organization at all levels of responsibility.

J. K. Lilly, Sr., who followed his father as president, put the Lilly philosophy into words when he said: "The people who make up this company are its most important assets."

That also was the credo of the colonel's grandsons, Eli (now honorary chairman of the board) and J. K., Jr. (who was chairman when he died in 1966), and it remains company philosophy today.

The present "Mr. Eli" has been exposed to the affairs of Eli Lilly and Company longer than anyone who has served it, past or present. In his words: "Indeed, I suspect that I was baptized with some of Grandpa Lilly's crystal clear elixirs!"

At the age of ten the colonel's oldest grandson began washing bottles. Later, during high school and college vacations, he worked in practically all parts of the company. Frequently his were the dirtiest and most disagreeable jobs in the plant, such as grinding green pokerroot or washing calves' stomachs for the essence of pepsin. He was paid at the going rate of ten cents an hour. From his earliest associations with the company to the present, Eli Lilly maintained the human touch with employees at all levels.

Soon after he joined the company permanently in 1907, he displayed a talent for innovation. He designed machinery, developed new production methods and outlined employee benefit programs.

In 1914 his brother Joe joined the company. Immediately, young J. K., Jr., was assigned to study the establishment of a personnel department. Two years later, in a 154-page typewritten report to his father, J. K. Jr., recommended a personnel policy that was far ahead of the times:

"The greatest business problem of today is the human problem of labor and the wise handling of employees. . . . Fair wages, reasonable hours, working quarters and conditions of average comfort and healthfulness, and a measure of protection against accident are now no more than primary requirements in every factory."

In 1916 the company's first employment office was established. An industrial medicine department for employees was added the following year. In 1920 the company adopted a pension plan and paid the entire cost for employees. A company cafeteria was started in 1924. Three years later a health insurance program was arranged.

Under the leadership of the Lillys and their successors, the company has grown from its original four employees to more than 23,500 associates worldwide. From an 18-by-40-foot building, once described by Colonel Lilly as "not big enough to swing a cat in," Eli Lilly and Company has grown to a large complex of manufacturing plants in the United States and seventeen countries abroad. It is a world enterprise that takes a global approach to everything it does— research, production and marketing.

Its medicinal products have changed from "pills, fluid extracts, elixirs, and cordials" to the broadest line of pharmaceuticals and biologicals in the industry. It also has become established in the fields of agriculture, industrial products and cosmetics.

In the last decade annual sales of Lilly products have risen from $241.9 million to $819.7 million. Such progress fulfills the prediction of J. K. Lilly, Sr., in 1946 that if the company followed the principles on which it was founded and built, "There are no limits to where we can go."

MACY'S

□ □ □

The "Value Store" That Grew and Grew

At thirty-six, Rowland Hussey Macy was a failure.

Born on Massachusetts' Nantucket Island in 1822, he had gone off at fifteen on a four-year whaling voyage, returned to some in-and-out jobs and finally settled down in retailing. At twenty-two he had opened dry goods stores in Boston and Haverhill, Massachusetts, and in Marysville, California. All had floundered, even the one at Marysville, where the discovery of gold and the influx of the Forty-niners might have been thought to assure the success of any store.

But in 1858 Rowland Macy, an obstinate and quick-tempered Yankee, was determined to try again, this time in New York. Two months after his thirty-sixth birthday he started a small, fancy dry goods store near the corner of Fourteenth Street and Sixth Avenue. Over the next twenty years this shop grow spectacularly. It became one of the first real department stores in the world and was the start of an organization that today consists of sixty-five stores throughout the country. Last year R. H. Macy & Company, Inc., recorded more than a billion dollars in sales.

What did Rowland Macy do so differently in New York to succeed so well? The answer, surprisingly, is very little. All through his retail career he had held to certain policies, which, if not original, were distinctively combined and pursued: He bought and sold for cash (even his family could not buy on credit). He charged the same price to everyone.

Rowland Macy set up his "fancy dry goods" store in this building on New York's Sixth Avenue in 1858. It was one of the world's first true department stores.

He sold at the cheapest prices possible. And he advertised and promoted his stock aggressively.

Macy altered none of these policies in the Fourteenth Street store, but obviously, he here found at last the right place and time to apply them. Competitive, bustling Manhattan on the eve of the Civil War was ready for his "value store," just as he was ready for Manhattan.

Macy's death in 1877 brought outside owners to R. H. Macy & Company—and eventually two brothers whose family name was to be linked with the store almost as closely as his.

Nathan and Isidor Straus had owned the china and glassware department at Macy's for years, and had made it the driving center of the store. In 1888 they became partners of the company and eight years later took complete control. Although Macy's converted to a public corporation in 1922, Strauses have remained in its management hierarchy ever since.

The Strauses brought many changes to Macy's, but none more important than its change in location. By the late 1800s the city's main shopping district had nosed northward, making Fourteenth Street its lower, rather than upper, end. In addition, the Macy store had grown about as much as it could on its old site. Spreading left and right into other buildings, it had become an architectural scramble of levels and elevations that made shopping complicated and further expansion almost inconceivable.

What the Strauses decided was to build an entirely new Macy's. And build it well uptown. The site they picked was at Thirty-fourth Street and Broadway. In 1902 the new store opened. How right they were in their choice was proved a few years later when the Pennsylvania Station was erected just blocks away, bringing thousands of people almost to the store's doorstep.

By the mid-twenties Macy's was doing so much business that the decision was made to break ground for a second building, which eventually filled the entire block and created what is still the biggest department store in the world.

While Macy's is a different store today, and a national organization operating through six merchandise divisions, there is still much about it that Rowland Macy would recognize. True, his cherished cash-only policy is gone, the victim of changed consumer demands and rising income levels. And the customers are different, for Macy's no longer caters only to the middle class, but to the style and quality tastes of all income groups. Yet the central concept that Macy established—a value store offering a wide assortment of goods —remains very much intact and, indeed, has been strengthened with time.

Long before consumerism became a national movement, for instance, Macy's established a Bureau of Standards, probably the first in any retail store in the country. Since 1927 it has been testing merchandise at the rate of over 1,000 analyses a month, all with an eye to improving the technical quality of products and assuring the consumer maximum value for his dollar.

In 1927 the first Macy-Own brand was also developed—for sheets and pillow cases. Today Own brands run the full gamut from aspirin to vacuum cleaners, and are always priced to give customers unusually good value for their money.

Similarly, Macy's has consistently stressed the value concept in its executive training programs. Beginning in 1919, these programs have groomed hundreds of managers for the company's stores and, as luck would have it, for some of its competitors.

Over the years Macy's has pioneered many concepts and much merchandise that we now take for granted. As far back as the late 1860s the store had a woman executive, Margaret Getchell LaForge. She was probably the first woman in a managerial position in a department store in the country. Other Macy firsts range from the tea bag to the introduction of color in white goods. Until a Macy buyer had a manufacturer dye towels in pastel colors, all domestics for bedroom and bath were white.

From the beginning Macy's made a practice of searching out merchandise all over the world wherever interesting and unusual things were being made. Working closely with foreign producers, and often their governments, Macy's had this merchandise resized and often restyled for the American market.

This effort to bring its customers what the world had to offer led to another Macy innovation, the foreign festival. The first of these was a Latin American fiesta as far back as 1942. In 1951, when Europe had started to emerge from the devastation of World War II, the Macy New York division ran a tremendous Italian Fair, often cited as the first look Americans had at the products of modern Italy. Other fairs and festivals followed in subsequent years, in all the Macy divisions, each saluting a country or area, from Britain to the Far East.

No description of Macy's would be complete, of course, without mention of its best-known tradition, the annual Thanksgiving Day Parade that heralds the start of the holiday season. Beginning in 1924, it has grown from a New York institution to a national event, carried on NBC and CBS networks to the whole country. In 1972, for example, in addition to over a million men, women and children who lined the parade route to see the gigantic balloons and colorful floats that are the hallmark of the Macy Parade, an estimated 70 million also watched it on TV from coast to coast. This occasional entry into show business, however, has never deflected Macy's from its basic concern, which is the customer and what the customer wants.

Some years ago Macy's received a letter that proves how much people still look to Macy's to solve their shopping problems. A man in Maine requested a dead horse. When Macy's wrote back to ask what he could possibly want with such a thing, he confessed that he was a fisherman and he thought that he might sink the animal in a lake so that, come spring, he would know where the fish were. He had figured that Macy's, with 400,000 items in one store alone, just might have an extinct horse around.

Macy's doesn't often fail its customers, but they had to concede defeat on that one.

MASONITE

□ □ □

That Wonderful Leaky Valve

William H. Mason, an engineer and inventor who worked with Thomas A. Edison, was trying to find new and useful products from sawmill wastes.

With financial backing from a group of Wisconsin lumbermen, he had already discovered a system for producing wood fiber economically. Working on the theory that wood chips could be exploded into separate fibers, he had developed, at a cost of $37.50, a small "gun"—a hollow steel cylinder permanently sealed at one end. He filled it with wood chips and water and closed it with a tapered steel plug, then raised the pressure inside by applying heat with a blowtorch. When the plug was released, wood chips exploded from the gun in the form of individual wood fibers.

Soon Mason was working on the development of a salable product from the fibers, and was having some success producing an insulation board on a small experimental press. However, the real breakthrough came when a small steam valve picked just the right time to spring a small leak.

Pausing for lunch during an experiment, Mason closed the valve used in the pressing of "wetlap"—a thick slurry created from exploded wood fibers and water. While he was gone, the valve failed. When he returned from lunch Mason found he had just invented what he called "pressed wood."

Steam, pressure and time had transformed the fibers into a dense, hard, grainless solid.

The machinery shown in these pictures taken in the mid-twenties improved on nature by exploding wood and forming from the resulting fibers a material that would not split, splinter, or crack. Above: An experimental wood-fiber gun installation; Below: the first experimental hardboard press.

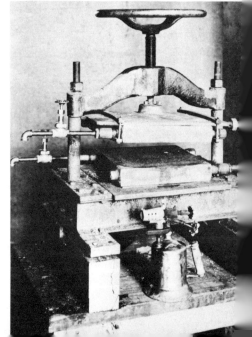

The Wisconsin lumbermen recognized the potential of this "wood made better" that would not split, splinter or crack, and increased their investment to finance a larger venture. The invention of hardboard, as it came to be called, led to formation of the Mason Fiber Company in Laurel, Mississippi, in that year—1924—and four years later, the company became Masonite Corporation.

Construction of the first factory, designed to produce both insulation board and hardboard, was started in Laurel, in October, 1925. It began operations in 1926, using machinery designed by Mason and constructed to his specifications.

Under his brilliant technical direction, both the quality and quantity of production increased rapidly during the late twenties. Mason achieved a smooth attractive surface finish on the hardboard by chrome-plating the platens, and eliminated water-spotting by placing the wetlap on thin wire screens that allowed water to escape from the presses.

A way to increase the strength of the board even more came when he discovered how to impregnate the product with thermal-setting liquids, then baking it. He called this process tempering.

Both the insulation board and the hardboard products found a rapidly expanding market. So great was the demand that the directors voted to double the plant capacity in 1927.

When the name of the company was changed to Masonite Corporation a year later, its management was reorganized, with Mason concentrating on research and technical development while others took up the general management and merchandising duties that were expanding rapidly in the growing firm. In his research capacity he worked hard and successfully until his death in 1940, earning a stream of patents for the corporation.

By 1939 production at the Laurel plant had been expanded to 30 million square feet of board per month. In addition to the mill at Laurel, other plants were producing Masonite's hardboard under license in Sweden, Italy, Australia and Canada. Five years later Masonite's corporate assets were in excess of $16 million and annual sales were more than $18 million.

Masonite's headquarters were moved to Chicago in 1935, and the company moved to the Masonite Building on Wacker Drive in 1962.

Recently the corporation announced a series of expansions that will have increased capacity to 2.75 billion square feet annually by mid-1974. This includes doubling the size of the plant at Towanda, Pennsylvania, major additions to the original plant at Laurel, Mississippi, and increases in the capacity of existing production units at these plants, plus the Ukiah, California, plant, through process efficiency improvements and equipment additions.

In addition to its three hardboard plants, Masonite Corporation now has properties that include two plants for producing plastic finished hardboard, a particleboard plant, a medium-density hardboard plant, four fabricating plants, a simulated masonry panel plant, nine sawmills, ten regional distribution centers, thirty sales offices, a research center, interest in eighty oil wells and more than 500,000 acres of timberland.

Research, the genesis of Masonite Corporation and the hardboard industry, has been centralized at a constantly growing Research and Development Center at St. Charles, Illinois. Masonite's scientists and engineers specializing in wood technology, finishes, glues, production processes and basic research join with product development specialists to improve hardboard and extend its applications in home building, remodeling, construction for commercial purposes and in industrial uses.

Originally inspired by the desire to make useful products from the wasted raw materials of the forest products industries, Masonite continues to find valuable applications for as much of its raw materials as possible. Wood sugars, for instance, removed from the fibers in the hardboard manufacture, are sold to the livestock industry as Masonex, a molasseslike cattle feed supplement. Some of the tree bark is marketed as a decorative ground cover and mulch called Fibrex. In addition, Masonite's sawmill waste is converted to chips for use at paper mills and its own hardboard mills.

Shavings and sawdust are used by particleboard manufacturers.

Early in its history Masonite acquired its own timberlands to assure raw material supplies and the spirit of conservation has prevailed in timberland management. Company timberlands have been selectively thinned and scientific reforestation practiced to obtain a sustained yield. In addition, the company has encouraged independent wood suppliers to grow trees for market, by providing them with free professional advice and seedling trees.

More recently, in entering the lumber industry through acquisition of sawmills, Masonite has continued its spirit of conservation and the mills have been equipped with "thin" saws and precision equipment that conserve natural resources by reducing waste in the mill and increasing the lumber yield from each log processed.

The hardboard industry, founded on the invention of William H. Mason, is an excellent example of the American way of life, showing how the incentive of private gain, the profit motive, can channel resources of inventors, investors, machinery makers, managers and workmen into profitable growing industries. This is how the profit motive works in America.

MAX FACTOR

□ □ □

Women Are the Same the World Over

On a gray, misty morning in December, 1935, a young American business executive walked briskly down the ramp from a twin-engine plane and set foot on French soil for the first time.

Inside the airport terminal he stood in line for the usual immigration processing. Quickly satisfying the official that his passport was in order, he moved across the hall for customs inspection.

There an official wasted no time in passing on the contents of all but the last piece of luggage. His experienced hands pulled out several bottles and jars bearing foreign labels.

"What are these?" he asked.

The American smiled. "Cosmetics," he said. "Cosmetics?" the officer repeated, looking more closely at one of the labels. He turned the bottle around and placed it on the counter beside the others.

"What is your name?" he asked.

"Factor. Davis Factor," the young man said. "My father is Max Factor. We manufacture cosmetics in the United States and I am here to open a branch of our company in Paris. We intend to sell our cosmetics in France."

A look of disbelief and utter amazement came over the customs official's face. He studied the American for a moment, then started to laugh.

Max Factor, left, with his sons Davis and Max Jr. in his shop in downtown Los Angeles in the early 1900s. Below, the shop's exterior.

"Sell American cosmetics in France!" he exclaimed. "Why, that's preposterous. France is virtually the birthplace of cosmetics. You won't stand a chance." The young man shrugged. "You may be right," he said, "but I don't think so. Women are the same the world over and we have something every woman wants. Women in the United States want it and so will the women of France."

Another man might have been more easily discouraged, but Davis Factor, the then administrative head of Max Factor & Company, had been doing unpredictable things in business ever since he began working with his father after school and on Saturdays.

Many astute businessmen had tried to dissuade him from his plan to have the relatively unknown American cosmetics company open a branch in France. He did not heed their advice in the mid-thirties Depression, and he was not about to be influenced in any way by the customs official.

As the former chairman of the board of his company, which has been manufacturing aids to feminine beauty since 1909, he often thinks back to that December morning in Paris and smiles.

The phenomenal success of Max Factor—not only in France, but throughout the world—is legendary. It is one of the best-known and most respected business names in the 144 countries where its products are sold. In 20 of these countries there are company-owned branches or subsidiaries, such as in France.

Today, Max Factor & Company operates as a self-contained, wholly-owned subsidiary of Norton Simon, Inc., a consumer products marketing firm with annual sales of over $1.1 billion.

The company's greatest achievements have been in creating fashion makeups and fragrances for the beauty and glamor enhancement of women throughout the world. When it first started over a half-century ago, the average woman used little, if any, makeup. "Society actually frowned upon it," Davis Factor explains. "But now, the average woman wouldn't appear in public, or even her own home, without it."

Max Factor sales of $192.4 million and earnings of $17.3 million in 1971 established new records for the fifteenth consecutive year. Almost half this volume and profits came from countries outside the United States. Growth abroad has an even greater potential than in the United States.

And it all began because of the vision and persistence of the young man who looked to foreign countries for expansion, just as his father before him had gone west to California to seek fame and fortune.

During the years when he was board chairman of the company Davis Factor was one of the most dynamic and respected leaders in the cosmetic industry. He was a former two-term president of the old National Toilet Goods Association (now the Cosmetics, Toiletries & Fragrance Association, Inc.), the first man outside the New York area to hold this office. He also served as the association's vice president during the four years preceding his election to its presidency.

Some of his fondest memories are of the small, early Max Factor makeup and wig shop in downtown Los Angeles. With one of his younger brothers, Max, Jr., he used to grind face powder in hand-cranked machines and look forward to such festive occasions as New Year's Eve and Halloween when they would pick up extra money for themselves by making false beards and moustaches and selling them on the streets to the holiday merrymakers' trade. "Some of our high school friends helped to sell them," he says, "but my father quickly put a stop to that when he discovered that a few of the older boys were charging fifteen cents each, or three for a half-dollar."

Davis also likes to tell of his boyhood "acting" experience in Hollywood when he and his brother worked as extras in westerns.

"When my father rented Indian wigs to the studios," he recalls, "part of the deal was that Max, Jr., and I had to be hired as bit players. At the end of each day's shooting, the whooping Indians, riding bareback on their horses, would gallop past the camera, pull off their wigs and toss them onto the nearest brush or tree. Our job was to retrieve them, and if we returned home with even one missing, my father would deduct its cost from our studio paychecks."

No reference to the great moments or great men in the history of the company would be complete without mention of its founder.

Max Factor was born in Russia on August 5, 1877. As a boy he was extremely poor. His first job was selling newspapers at the age of seven. Twenty years later, after serving his apprenticeship as a wigmaker and cosmetician, he migrated to the United States with his wife and three children.

Although he knew little English, he opened a perfume, hair goods and cosmetic shop at the St. Louis World's Fair in 1904. He moved to California in 1908 and started a small makeup and wig business in downtown Los Angeles. Almost from the beginning it was successful, and down through the years Max Factor made many notable contributions to his company and the entire cosmetics industry.

Among a long list of innovations he originated the first makeup for motion pictures and was recognized for this achievement with a special citation by the Motion Picture Academy of Arts and Sciences.

He is credited with having created the fundamental art of makeup application as women know it today. He was the first of the professional makeup artists and is acknowledged in the industry as having brought this art to its present state of perfection. Many of Hollywood's foremost makeup men received their early training from him.

As a personal tribute to Max Factor, just about every big name celebrity in the film capital turned out for the 1935 opening of his unique Hollywood makeup salon, which since has become one of the town's most famous landmarks, attracting beauty-seeking women from all parts of the world. Three thousand selected guests were invited to the opening celebration, and although more than 9,000 showed up, none were treated as gate crashers. Instead they were encouraged to join in the festivities. The resultant mob, surging in and out of the double-door entrance, created one of the biggest traffic jams

in the city's history. *The New York Times'* Hollywood correspondent in reviewing the event wrote that it was perhaps
the greatest premiere Hollywood had ever witnessed, rivaling
anything Sid Grauman had staged in his world-famous
theaters.

Max Factor created the first makeup packaged in tubes. He
originated the eybrow pencil, the face powder brush, the lip-
stick brush, lip gloss—and Erace, the first cosmetic cover-up.
He patented his creation of hair-lace wigs for women and
hairpieces for men that enabled the wearer to have a realistic, natural-looking hairline for the first time.

He coined the word "brownette" to classify those women
who have brown hair not dark enough to be called brunette.
He developed a totally new kind of beautifying product,
later to be known as pancake makeup, which was the forerunner of all present-day fashion makeup and still enjoys
widespread popularity.

These are only a few of Max Factor's personal achievements. He, with others, changed the course of the cosmetics
business, which is as dependent upon change and innovation
as the whole world of fashion it complements.

3M

□ □ □

Key to Success: A Scrub Pail

For the struggling young sandpaper company it was a crisis of life-or-death proportions—a crisis spawned in a storm at sea and solved in a scrub pail.

Twelve years after its founding Minnesota Mining and Manufacturing Company had just reached the point in 1914 where it was gaining a precarious foothold in the highly competitive coated abrasives industry. Then came a cloudburst of customer complaints. The garnet, an abrasive grit, was falling off the sandpaper; not just a batch or two—all of it. Sales declined and repeat orders became almost impossible to get. The newly won and hard-earned reputation of 3M was at stake.

All the efforts of production personnel to find the answer and correct the problem were fruitless. Then one day a worker, unknown today, noticed an oily film on water standing in a scrub pail. At the bottom of the pail were bits of garnet mineral that had been mopped up from the floor. He summoned the plant superintendent, and both pondered the discovery. The superintendent then realized that the garnet somehow had been contaminated with oil, which made it impossible for the grit to stick to adhesive on the sandpaper backing.

Foremen combed through the production process to pinpoint the contamination source, with no success. Railroads,

3M's general laboratory in 1924 boasted a staff of nine, eight of whom are shown here at work.

supply houses in New York and shipping lines were checked out. No luck. Finally, the garnet was traced all the way back to its origination point in Spain. Months before, a Spanish steamer had sailed for America with a cargo of olive oil. It was ballasted with sacks of garnet consigned to 3M. A storm broke in the Atlantic and as the ship pitched and rolled, several olive oil casks ruptured and saturated the garnet. It was a traumatic and almost fatal experience for 3M. But out of it grew a keen awareness of the need for a system that would insure greater control over raw materials and manufacture, control that would guarantee product quality and uniformity.

In 1916 the decision was made to organize a small laboratory, a giant step for the fourteen-year-old 3M Company and one taken at a time when industrial research was still in its infancy in the United States. Only about a hundred American companies had their own research laboratories then, the General Electric Company having been the first to establish such a facility in about 1900.

At a cost of $500—a princely sum for 3M in those days—its first laboratory came into existence. It was a closetlike, 5-by-7-foot room with rough, unpainted walls. In no way did this room fit the modern concept of an industrial research facility, but it was the modest start of a research and development organization that has grown to some fifty laboratories worldwide, manned by more than 4,500 technical personnel.

The initial $500 laboratory investment is a dramatic contrast to the approximately $100 million per year that 3M now channels into research and development programs. These increased expenditures have been accompanied by corporate growth at an average rate of 10 percent annually.

From the very beginning 3M's research and product development activities have been geared closely to customer wants and needs. When 3M started to enjoy even modest success in the abrasives business in the second decade of its existence, the turn-around was due in large measure to an insistence that its salesmen work directly with the factory people who used 3M products as well as the purchasing people who ordered them.

Throughout the years researchers, sales people and technical service teams within 3M have continued to work closely together. It has been said that a key factor in 3M's growth has been its success in keeping its scientists sales-minded and its sales force science-minded.

The flow of new products from 3M laboratories has been considered by some as phenomenal. More than thirty operating divisions and subsidiaries now produce thousands of products in forty-five major product lines. Translated into dollars, it is estimated that for each research dollar that has been invested since 1926, $28 in gross sales have been returned. It is also estimated that as much as a quarter of each year's sales come from products that left the labs during the preceding five years.

The basic technologies that have grown out of more than half a century of research and development are precision coating, bonding and image forming. Typical products of these technologies include the company's first—sandpaper— and subsequent products such as the internationally known lines of "Scotch" brand pressure-sensitive tapes, surgical drapes, audio and video magnetic recording tapes, presensitized lithographic printing plates, electro-mechanical communications devices, photographic films, copying and microfilm equipment, synthetic race tracks, reflective sheeting for directional signs, ceramically coated roofing granules and many, many more.

At 3M new products or processes may spring from any of three sources: central research laboratories, which probe whole sectors of science in an effort to develop entire families of new products; division laboratories, which concentrate on improving existing products and developing new related products; and the new business ventures division, which explores product ideas aimed at entirely new areas of business.

Although the various laboratories usually work in well-defined areas, they frequently overlap and contribute to each other's efforts. Playing a key role in this interaction is the free exchange of data and ideas among all 3M technical people through two internal scientific groups: Technical Forum and Technical Council.

Technical Forum is an organization of all technical people from the company's laboratories. One of its chief aims is keeping the entire technical staff abreast of current developments throughout the company. The Technical Council, comprised of technical directors and laboratory chiefs, serves as an advisory body to the vice president of research and development, and has an active policy-making function.

Another key to 3M's research success is the policy that encourages scientists to spend up to 15 percent of their time working on whatever interests them, regardless of short-term commercial prospects. Some, engaged in analytical work, use none of the 15 percent in pursuing new knowledge. Others are busy with assigned projects. But the average researcher, doing a day-to-day job, knows that if an idea captures his fancy he may go ahead and delve into it.

Its size notwithstanding, the company has managed to keep its emphasis focused on people, taking the position that money alone does not guarantee successful research and development. "Successful industrial research and development require those factors that we somewhat inadequately call creativity, ingenuity, imagination, curiosity, knowhow, brains, dedication, hard work and common sense," according to one 3M executive. "These are human traits," he emphasizes, "and they're much more difficult to measure than the dollars that go into a budget. But when a company invests in a new research project it is really betting on people and the qualities that enable them to develop new and improved ideas."

Technical excellence is not the sole criterion for giving a research project continued life. More than one product has survived and gone on to commercial success largely on the strength of one man's conviction.

Two other qualities that 3M management looks for in a technical person are vision—the ability to look ahead and see a project in terms of its future markets—and persistence. "If in the end you're right, they call you persistent. Until you succeed, you're stubborn," according to the 3M view. "But stubborn men will often have the courage of conviction and, if necessary, be willing to lay their jobs on the line because they have faith in what they are doing."

Take the development of 3M's first copying machine. Over a period of ten years 3M invested more than a million dollars of "patient money" in one man's idea before the first penny of profit was turned.

Through a "dual ladder" system the company offers two avenues of personal growth to outstanding technical men and women: management assignments or the continued pursuit of their technical interests. Whichever path is chosen, the individual is assured that it is 3M's intent that responsibility, recognition and reward for progress in either area be equivalent—even though not identical.

True to tradition, 3M continues to strike out boldly, with imagination and an open mind. The problems it faces now, as a multinational corporation with marketing or manufacturing facilities in thirty-eight countries, are far more complex and sophisticated than those posed by the contaminated garnet incident in 1914. Still, if 3M thinks that any of its problems can be solved by studying a scrub pail full of water, that is probably what you will find them doing.

MISSOURI PACIFIC

□ □ □

The Blueblood Who Brought
Rails to the Rugged West

St. Louis, bustling riverfront city of 78,000, had never witnessed a bigger celebration than the breaking of ground on July 4, 1851, for the Pacific Railroad, the first railroad west of the Mississippi and first link in what is now the Missouri Pacific System.

Nor was this ground-breaking a routine ten-minute affair for the television cameras with a politician poking at a bit of dirt with a silver-plated shovel. No indeed. It was a day-long celebration involving 25,000 people, scores of bands and smart military units as well as many flowery speeches. It opened at dawn with a hundred-gun salute shattering the quiet, and ended at dusk after each of five distinguished men had personally loaded a wheelbarrow with dirt and had deposited his burden on the virgin trackbed.

It was a warm, sultry Fourth of July and many of the participants were hot and thirsty. Bills from the day included such items as 40 gallons of brandy, 10 gallons of rum, a cask of claret, barrels of punch and several hundred pounds of ham, cheese and crackers. There was even an accounting for 15 kegs of gunpowder used in impromptu salutes that echoed across Chouteau Pond in what is now downtown St. Louis.

No one there could have enjoyed himself more than Thomas Allen, even if he was among the five men who had to push a heavy wheelbarrow through the humid air. Allen

174

Railroad construction in the 1870s south of St. Louis. This section of the line became part of the Missouri Pacific System.

The steam locomotive "Gasconade 6" chugs through a town in 1854.

was the principal organizer and first president of the Pacific Railroad. Then thirty-seven, he came from a Pittsfield, Massachusetts, family long on blue blood but short on green cash. First a journalist and then a lawyer, Allen had already achieved high status in the St. Louis business community. By the time he died at the age of sixty-nine, he had managed to parley $25 and a diploma from Union College into a personal fortune of $15 million. He also served in the Missouri State Senate, and at the time of his death was a first-term U.S. Congressman.

Even though Allen's Pacific Railroad was the first railroad in the Western United States, there already existed more than 9,000 miles of track in the East, at least twice as many miles as had then been constructed in the world. Men looked longingly at the millions upon millions of acres of largely uninhabited and undeveloped land in the West. Many recognized the great value that railroads would have in this rough country. Railroad charters were being handed out freely and big plans were continually under way. But no rail had been laid. In these pre–Civil War days leaders of the North and the South feared the advantage one side or the other would gain if an east-west railroad were constructed on either side of the Mason-Dixon line. And within the two regions local factions warred among themselves for inclusion on any proposed routes. The general public attitude blew first hot, then cold, depending upon financial conditions and such distractions as the Gold Rush of 1849.

Taking into account the troubled times and the political maneuverings, Allen astutely decided that if he could raise enough money to actually build a railroad, then all opposition would fade. He and his backers secured a charter on March 12, 1849, and quietly planned the financing of $10 million required to start the Pacific Railroad on its way to San Francisco. Meanwhile other would-be builders were busily trying to work out their differences at railroad conventions in Memphis and St. Louis.

Allen, an impressive-looking six-footer with prematurely white hair, was an indefatigable organizer and a smooth salesman. He needed all his gifts to convince his sometimes wavering incorporators that their investment would pay off. "Who, that knows anything of railroads, can doubt that its realization is perfectly within our reach," Allen told a meeting of incorporators. "The railroad is a noble and profitable work, reflecting the highest credit upon its projectors and its finishers." After the purple prose he spelled out in great detail just what the railroad would mean to the development of the West and just what it would haul at what prices.

Allen did not confine his efforts to the board rooms and plush parlors of St. Louis. Frequently he made long, solitary horseback rides through the rough country west of St. Louis. He made these rides partly to check prospective railroad routes, partly to publicize the coming of the railroad and partly to raise funds among the merchants in the backwoods communities.

Construction of the Pacific Railroad proceeded at a turtle's pace despite the enthusiasm which marked the ground-breaking ceremonies. The first run of five miles came quickly enough on December 9, 1852. But despite the best efforts of the brilliant Scottish engineer James Kirkwood, it was 1855 before the little line had stretched 100 miles to Jefferson City. Another decade passed before it finally linked St. Louis with Kansas City, less than 300 miles to the west.

The difficulties the early railroad builders ran into were enough to break the spirits of ordinary men. Luckily these were not ordinary men. First, actual construction costs ran far above the estimated costs, and money was extremely difficult to come by, especially during the financial panic of 1857. Second, few machines existed to aid the construction crews. As a result, the work was both slow and hard. Blasting was accomplished by cutting into the rock with hand drills and then packing the holes with black powder before setting it off. Ties were made by hand, using axe and adze, from trees cut down at the site with broad axes. Stone had to be crushed at the work site and the excavation of cuts and fills was accomplished largely through brute muscle power.

A worldwide cholera epidemic reached the United States

and in 1853 struck the railroad workers. At least a hundred men died and many more fled the area. Still another problem was an influx of opportunists who set up shop along the construction route to sell liquor to the workers, many of whom had no other outlet for their money. The "whiskey shanties" were a constant source of irritation.

The outbreak of the Civil War was particularly devastating to the Pacific. Missouri, a border state, was divided between allegiance to the Union and the Confederacy. As a result, armed men from both sides constantly fought skirmishes and battles through the state. The Pacific Railroad, even though still a comparative infant, was a highly strategic resource. As a result, dozens of battles were fought along its right-of-way.

To the Union, the Pacific Railroad served as a primary supply route for garrisons located in St. Louis, Sedalia and the state capital of Jefferson City. It served as a potent weapon to such a degree that the Rebel troops constantly tried to destroy as much of it as possible. The destruction wrought during the war was immense. Miles of track were torn from the ground. Bridges were burned, rebuilt and burned again.

The chief destroyer was General Sterling Price, a distinguished Missouri politician who had sided with the Confederacy. As the Civil War neared its end, General Price invaded Missouri with a force of 12,000 men, following the Pacific Railroad across the state, destroying as he went. Eventually he was defeated and driven from the state in the Battle of Westport on ground near Kansas City (which is now a golf course).

It was the spring of 1865 before construction could resume again at a normal pace, and even then laborers were frequently shot at by random bands of guerrillas. Money also remained a big problem, but the railroad's directors, drawing upon their own resources as well as outside funds, steadily pushed on undaunted.

A decade later the Pacific Railroad was to become a part of Western folklore as a result of train robberies carried out by the Missouri-based Jesse James gang. One of the James gang's earliest train robberies occurred at Gad's Hill, Missouri, where they carried away $5,000. Two years later they netted $17,000 in a train holdup near Otterville, Missouri. In 1882, after Jesse James died violently, his brother Frank boarded a Pacific Railroad train and rode to Jefferson City to surrender to authorities. After standing trial and being acquitted, he went on to lead a peaceful life.

Once construction actually began on the Pacific it seemed as if a logjam had been set free. Literally dozens of railroads began pushing south, west and southwest across the land on the unsettled side of the Mississippi. Many eventually became part of what is today the Missouri Pacific System, most of them south and southwest of St. Louis. Allen, who had relinquished the presidency of the Pacific before 1855, played a leading role in organizing some of these early railroads, most notably the Iron Mountain and the Southwest Branch of the Pacific Railroad. He was to remain active in railroad development for many years.

Among the many railroads which eventually became part of the Missouri Pacific System, one of the largest and most colorful was and is the Texas & Pacific Railway, now a subsidiary retaining its own corporate identity. The history of the T&P is studded with such names as Thomas A. Scott, Jay Gould and George Gould, giants of American business in their day. In fact, it was the Goulds who actually pulled the many components of the modern Missouri Pacific System together into a single, strong entity rather than a group of weak local roads with duplicate routes.

The T&P was actually chartered by Congress to be built as a transcontinental line to the Pacific Ocean. But it never came to pass. Two big powers, Jay Gould of the Texas & Pacific and Collis P. Huntington of the Southern Pacific, collided head-on through their railroad properties. While Gould built westward from Fort Worth, Huntington was building east toward Fort Worth. Both were following the same route. As the two construction crews neared a confrontation and court battles dragged on, Gould and Huntington resolved the dispute by signing the Gould-Huntington Agreement, one of the most famous documents in transportation history. Today, as a result, the two roads as connecting lines are a vital link in the national transportation system.

Thomas Allen would be pleased to see just what he started in motion on that warm day in St. Louis more than a hundred years ago.

Today, after many changes in corporate structure and after surviving a twenty-three-year receivership that did not end until 1956, the Missouri Pacific System is one of the nation's largest and healthiest transportation companies. It stretches from Chicago in the northeast to Pueblo, Colorado, in the northwest, from Brownsville, Texas, at the extreme southwest to New Orleans and Memphis in the southeast. It reaches such major metropolitan areas in between as St. Louis, Kansas City, Omaha, Little Rock, Tulsa, San Antonio, Dallas-Fort Worth and Houston. It includes three major railroads: the Missouri Pacific, the Texas & Pacific and the Chicago & Eastern Illinois, plus two wholly-owned trucking subsidiaries that operate more than 3,000 units over 18,000 miles of highway, as well as air and deep-sea forwarding operations. Its annual revenues surpass $600 million and its net income runs well over $20 million (both figures represent doubling in the past ten years). In 1972 it spent $100 million on modernization, nearly ten times the amount that Allen and his incorporators initially invested in the little Pacific Railroad.

But Allen would be most proud of the role the Missouri Pacific has played in opening the West and Southwest to expansion, even to this day. During the years before and after the Civil War Missouri Pacific agents combed Europe and the Eastern United States for new people to settle the new lands, even maintaining low-cost hotels and boardinghouses for the newcomers until they could get established on their own. Its agricultural agents predated the U.S. Department of Agriculture and worked vigorously to help farmers and stockmen develop new crop and livestock varieties suitable to survival in the new lands.

Today this development role continues in a different form with efforts to attract new industry to the region. During the past five years, for instance, more than 1,700 firms have spent

$3.2 billion on new and expanded industrial facilities along the Missouri Pacific's lines.

In an era in which many once proud railroads are sinking into financial difficulties, the Missouri Pacific thrives as a living memorial to a great man who had the fortitude and skill to make his dream true. The Missouri Pacific has had many fine presidents, but like the United States, it will always hold its first president in highest esteem.

MONSANTO

□ □ □

Dealing With a Disaster

The crucible of crisis affords the measure of a man and his company. And it was so with the Texas City disaster and Edgar Monsanto Queeny (1897–1968) of Monsanto Company.

Mr. Queeny was board chairman that momentous day of April 16, 1947, when word reached him on the East Coast that the company's big modern plant at Texas City had literally been blown up. Within the hour he and some of his associates were flying to the scene.

Initial news dispatches erroneously reported the massive blast had originated in the Monsanto plant, built during World War II to make ingredients for synthetic rubber. The truth was that the disaster was triggered by an explosion on the French ship *Grandcamp*, across the quay from the Monsanto plant.

Of his feeling of horror as his plane circled the holocaust, Queeny later wrote, "You have heard it described in the press and over your radio. The reporters did not exaggerate. Exaggeration would have been impossible; our language is too inadequate. . . . When the atomic bombs were exploded high above Hiroshima and Nagasaki, the blast beneath them . . . may have been less severe than that suffered by parts of our plant."

In what a reporter said was "a masterpiece of restrained

The Monsanto chemical plant in the disastrous fire of April 16, 1947. A French vessel loaded with nitrate had exploded at the waterfront, touching off the holocaust.

anguish," Queeny later wrote in a report to Monsanto stockholders, employees and friends:

As soon as we learned of the crushing misfortune that overtook Texas City, Mr. Rand [William McNear Rand, Monsanto president] and I, who were in the East, flew to the scene. . . .

Several other company officials came to Texas City to help, organize, and plan. Among the first arrivals were Dr. Emmet Kelly, our Medical Director, and some of his staff. A plane-load of nurses and medical supplies was also flown in.

Friday, Mr. Rand and I accompanied Dr. Kelly on his round of the hospitals. As we visited with our own stricken and saw the conditions of others, it was impossible for us to contain emotions. But we heard not one word of recrimination nor any attempt to fix blame. Each accepted his anguish stoically as the lot which Fate had cast for him. We attempted to solace wives sitting beside husbands whose lives were in the balance. Their manner was brave but their eyes betrayed the torment of their souls.

A young girl—shattered and barely conscious—who had been in charge of payroll records, seemed to be worried only about the loss of her records. Another girl, bandage-swathed and disfigured forever by flying glass, touched us to the quick by saying softly, "Oh, I'm so sorry for Monsanto, losing so many fine men." Many evidences of unselfishness, heroism, pluck, and courage were unveiled to us.

By Friday morning, except for the benzol storage tanks which continued to burn, most fires in our plant had subsided. We visited the ruins. Fires still ranged in both Humble and Republic Oil Companies' near-by tanks, raising a huge Bikini-like pillar of pall 3,000 feet into an otherwise clear sky, where it was joined by the gray of our own benzol. There, both plumed and stratified, forming a gloomy awning of darkness which drifted on southerly winds. Monsanto pilots flying to St. Louis that afternoon reported that these clouds stretched to Missouri's southern border. . . .

The ammonium nitrate aboard the *Grandcamp* did not originate in any Monsanto plant; Monsanto does not manufacture ammonium nitrate. Nor was it being loaded at our dock, nor was it destined for any of our plants. We do not use it.

Our Texas City plant did not use or manufacture any explosives. Several inflammable products such as benzol and propane constituted its raw materials. It manufactured monomeric styrene and polystyrene; the former is inflammable but the latter will only support combustion like wood—the distinction between an explosive and an inflammable material being that the former can be detonated on impact and the latter bursts into flame when ignited. . . .

Our plant was the first to produce styrene for the manufacture of synthetic rubber so desperately needed after Pearl Harbor. It is now gone and with it many of the men —chemists and engineers who contributed to perfecting the processes in the laboratory and in the pilot plant stages. Working literally day and night in the dark days of 1942, their ideas and designs took shape in the mass of pipes, apparatus, columns, mortar and bricks at Texas City. The physical part of the men and the plant have gone, but not the products of their minds. This will live on. Based on their contributions and that of others, we will build again at Texas City on their foundations The results of their work will continue to serve their fellow men.

I should like to pay tribute to the splendid work of those remarkable organizations, the Red Cross, the Salvation Army, the Volunteers of America, the Boy Scouts of America, the United States Army's medical staff, the staffs of the hospitals in the area, and the officials of both the State of Texas and the City of Texas City, for the way in which they responded to the challenge of the emergency. The manner in which the Monsanto staff overcame the initial shock and established an effective organization to command a most difficult situation, then immediately planned the future, was gratifying in the highest degree.

Although Queeny knew attempts to lessen the grief of victims would be ineffective, "this being within the province of time alone," he reacted in a characteristically direct way, knowing stockholders would approve. Widows were offered immediate payments of $1,000 to help with urgent needs. This was in addition to coverage under the company's group insurance plan, disbursement for which began two days after the blast. Other monetary payments were awarded as required under state law. And special hardship cases were helped liberally.

Arrangements were made for the company to bear all

costs for hospitalization and treatment of injured employees. Temporary repairs were made to the homes of 148 employees and more permanent housing assistance programs were started. Transportation was arranged, and its cost paid, for bereaved families moving to former homes in other cities. Wages of surviving employees were guaranteed.

Queeny ordered $500,000 appropriated "to provide for the cost of these payments beyond our legal liabilities, and to reward outstanding cases of heroism." The board of directors later approved the action unanimously.

"Sometimes," Queeny said, "it takes a tragedy to bring forth the better qualities of human beings. Our visit to Texas City made us proud to be Americans and especially so to belong to the exceptionally able group of them making up Monsanto."

The manner in which Board Chairman Queeny and his company met the Texas City disaster is now part of the Monsanto tradition. From the ashes of disaster rose a stronger, more modern plant at Texas City—and a stronger, more modern Monsanto.

Although Edgar Queeny is gone, much of his spirit remains to help move the company forward today.

MONTGOMERY WARD

□ □ □

A Century of "Satisfaction Guaranteed"

The consumer is first.

That simple philosophy of business, in effect at Montgomery Ward since 1872, remains its guiding corporate policy as it begins a second century of service.

Today Montgomery Ward is a fast-moving, growing organization committed to the improvement of the life-styles of American families. Its sales in 1972 passed the $2.6 billion mark and expansion is continuing—more than $92 million was invested in store expansion and capital improvements in 1972. About $80 million has been budgeted for 1973.

It wasn't always this way, however. Ten decades ago one man staked his life's savings on the radical idea that people could be persuaded to buy products through the mail, sight unseen, by pledging: "Satisfaction guaranteed or your money back."

For the first time a merchant had pronounced a philosophy designed to protect the consumer. And Aaron Montgomery Ward's assault on the historic credo of *caveat emptor* was successful.

He believed the consumer should have quality products at reasonable prices. Rural America responded.

When Ward began his business more than half the nation's population lived on farms and in farming communities, and their principal sources of goods were the general store and

MONTGOMERY WARD & CO

CATALOGUE AND BUYERS GUIDE № 73
1904   CHICAGO   1905

In the 1890s, Montgomery Ward's sales promotion efforts were mobile—salesmen carried catalogs around the country in battery-driven cars like this one.

the itinerant peddler. He provided thousands of families with another source from which they could fill their needs: buying by catalog. Thus middleman profits were eliminated and consumers could obtain products inexpensively by mail.

Business flourished and Ward noted: "The people of this country are not such fools as some merchants and manufacturers seem to think they are."

The new company expanded, and the one-page catalog sheet became a catalog book. In many homes it was the only illustrated book to be found. Children even learned to read from it. In less than a decade sales were $1.8 million. A new industry had been launched: an innovative industry that profoundly influenced the life-styles of millions of American families.

As the nation's frontiers were conquered and settled, consumer demands became more sophisticated. Calico was replaced by linens and silks and in 1897 the company opened its New York buying office to be close to the changing world of fashions.

Ward was a master at using the personal touch. In reply to a letter asking why customers in Nebraska were not buying by catalog, a Holdredge, Nebraska, housewife wrote telling of years of drought, no money and "expecting the stork to visit us soon."

Years later another letter arrived from the same woman. "I have a son twenty-five years of age who was named after your firm. We received a box of dainties such as one appreciates at such times, and a baby carriage. Hence the boy's name—Ward, the only son I have."

Development of a chain of retail stores was the next revolutionary step in the company's development.

Merchandise exhibits were opened in 1926 so buyers could see what the catalog had to offer in person—but these items in the stores were not to be sold. That is, until one day, an insistent farmer demanded he be sold a saw on display. When a company official finally gave in, a chain reaction set in, bringing in hundreds of customers who literally cleaned the shelves of merchandise, buying everything in sight.

The results of this particular incident were so encouraging that management proceeded to open new retail outlets —slowly at first, then at breakneck speed. Ward's first store was in Plymouth, Indiana. By the end of 1929 there were 517 Ward retail stores. Then came the big Depression and a halt to expansion programs.

In 1931 three out of four Ward stores were losing money. Sewell Lee Avery was brought in as chief executive officer to save the company from bankruptcy. His moves reversed a four-year declining sales trend and produced a modest profit in 1934. In 1935 he removed the brakes from expansion programs and during the next seven years opened 178 new stores.

His confidence and determination are credited with bringing the company safely through the thirties. The same grit and single-mindedness also carried him through a now historic battle with the U.S. government. When he refused to surrender the company to federal control during a World War II labor dispute, President Roosevelt ordered the company seized and National Guardsmen physically carried Avery from the building.

A decision by Avery concerning postwar economics is now a classic in business history. He had successfully predicted the great Depression of the 1930s, and he was convinced another and more devastating depression would follow World War II. As a consequence, he ordered managers to pull in their belts and canceled expansion plans.

While competitors went ahead with aggressive growth plans, Ward sat on cash and government securities reserves of over $325 million and steadily lost market position, personnel and momentum.

Ward's wealth tempted a youthful industrial figure, Louis E. Wolfson, whose interest was acquisition of vulnerable companies with sizable liquid assets. In August, 1954, he launched a proxy campaign to obtain enough shareholder votes to replace management. A nine-month battle ensued, climaxed by a stormy stockholder meeting in Chicago on April 22, 1955.

While Wolfson won three of nine seats on the board of directors, he failed to gain control of the company. The fight had exhausted Avery, however, and on May 9, 1955, he resigned. For the next five years John Barr, the attorney who had guided management's proxy battle to victory, served as chairman and chief executive officer.

The sixties are known as the "turnaround years" at the company, and the man who planned and motivated the building of a new, aggressive national retail chain was Robert E. (Tom) Brooker.

When Brooker accepted the top job at the company in 1961, he was confronted by sharply declining earnings, strained resources and sagging morale. He attracted experienced mass merchandising executives to revitalize and to rebuild the facilities, systems and management organization.

From a company with 562 obsolescent small-town stores, and a burdensome, manually operated mail order system, Montgomery Ward has transformed itself into a modern chain in which 293 new full-line department stores in urban areas account for 91 percent of retail sales and 99 percent of retail profits. In all, Ward's distribution system now includes 458 retail stores and 1,669 catalog stores and sales agencies.

Newness provides a strong base for the years ahead at Montgomery Ward. While 65 percent of its stores currently are new, this figure will rise to 83 percent by 1977. Total selling space will increase 45 percent in the next five years and sales per square foot will increase from a current $85 to $100 in 1977.

In the future look for more self-service packaging and computerized picturephone catalog shopping in the home. Yet even as we move ahead into the seventies, with all the anticipated mechanical improvements in retailing, Montgomery Ward reaffirms its hundred-year credo of "satisfaction guaranteed" as the best protection for all consumers.

At the same time, the company knows business must be prepared to be judged by immediate action, not by yesterday's performance or tomorrow's promises. It believes that its day-by-day actions document its commitment to consumerism and the protection of the rights of the consumer to be informed, to be safe, to choose and to be heard. Customers have the right to expect retailers to give them satisfaction, and this Montgomery Ward is determined to do with every product it sells and every service it offers. In the key area of satisfaction in service Ward has developed strategically located computerized spare-parts centers that assure prompt and economical service to customers, handling more than 40,000 different repair parts, many for major appliances, and mobile units in which continuing field training for repair servicemen is conducted.

Perhaps the consumer right that has been receiving the most increasing attention is the right to be heard. In this area, the company conducts professional telephone interviews with consumers on the merchandise they buy, their likes, dislikes and preferences. These interviews cover the entire range of Ward's merchandise and store operations and number approximately 50,000 interviews each year. Groups of consumers are continually gathered for tape-recorded sessions that explore new product ideas, possibilities for merchandise improvement and shopping preference. Mail customer survey programs, which are conducted without company identification, have been intensified so Ward can hear what consumers are concerned with and act in those areas requiring improvement. A new program in which prominent in-store signs urge customers to talk with the store manager about any type of dissatisfaction in getting good results.

In the final analysis a retailer's sensitivity to consumerism is measured at the store level—by *employee-customer relationships*, by courteous and knowledgeable salespeople. It is also judged by how the *merchandise satisfies demand and expectations* and *truth-in-advertising*. All three factors directly affect the success of any reputable retailer. They have a direct relationship to a firm's strength in the marketplace and ultimately to its profit performance.

MOTOROLA

□ □ □

When His Firm Was Auctioned, He Bid

Near the end of his career Paul V. Galvin, founder of Motorola Inc., said: "Do not fear mistakes. . . . You will know failure. . . . Reach out. . . ."

In 1928, at the age of thirty-three, Galvin had already failed in business twice, both times being forced out of the storage battery business by competition. The second time, however, success had been almost within reach. Convinced that he still had a marketable item, he attended the auction of his own business, and with $750 he'd managed to raise, bought back the battery eliminator portion of it. Thus began the Galvin Manufacturing Corporation, known today as Motorola Inc., the largest corporation in the United States devoted exclusively to electronics.

With the advent of AC radio sets, Galvin knew the eliminator would cease to have a market. He began to manufacture a nine-tube AC home radio. To this standard set he applied the nameplates of his twenty suppliers for their private-label sales.

The fledgling company enjoyed the economic boom of the twenties until the stock market crash nearly put Galvin out of business for a third time. But his uncanny marketing sense led him to take a bold step—the packaging of car radios on a big scale, something never done before. After

The "Motorola," the first car radio built for commercial use.

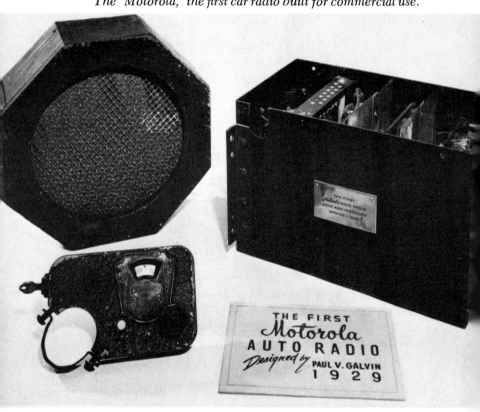

day and night work the first commercial car radio was built —the Motorola, a name suggesting both motion and radio. The name became so popular that it was later assumed as the official corporate identification.

Despite the Depression and a concentrated effort by some states to outlaw car radios on the basis that they constituted a hazardous distraction to the driver, the number of Motorola distributors grew and the market flourished. Galvin's philosophy in dealing with his distributors played a key role in this success. "Tell them the truth," he said. "First because it's right and second because they'll find out anyway."

Car and home entertainment units might have been the culmination of Motorola's success story had it not been for the growing need for two-way radio communications. For some years Galvin had been modifying standard car radios to permit police departments to receive the higher frequencies assigned to them. Their need for better communications prompted him to set up a separate Police Radio Department that concentrated on manufacturing and selling AM police radios. Today that department is the Communications Division and the world's leading manufacturer of two-way radio systems.

When Galvin heard that the Army lacked proper radio communications he sent his chief engineer to inspect the heavy, cumbersome, back-pack radios being used. Upon receiving his engineer's report, he set out to develop a lightweight portable transceiver, achieving what he knew to be an amazing unit. Several months later Pearl Harbor was bombed. Nearly 40,000 of the HANDI-TALKIE portable radios were used during World War II.

Just prior to the war Galvin became impressed by the successful development of an FM mobile communications system for police use. He persuaded the system's developer, Dan Noble, a University of Connecticut professor, to join the company on a temporary basis. Dr. Noble, still with Motorola, is now chairman of the board of directors' science committee.

The war effort channeled Motorola's effort. With Dr.

Noble's experience in FM equipment, a new, longer-range, portable two-way radio was built. The famed SCR-300 Walkie-Talkie radios gained tremendous recognition · for their contribution to the war effort. Over 50,000 of these FM units were built during the war.

Following the war, efforts were channeled back to developing FM equipment to meet the increasing demands of a fast-paced public. Better two-way radio communications were needed: police and fire response was expected to be immediate; taxicabs were impatiently awaited; farmers required a method of coordinating their farflung fields to get their products planted, harvested and to market at the best time; housewives turned to the plumber or druggist who could deliver service the fastest. The public demanded quick service. Two-way radio provided the method of furnishing it.

Paul Galvin's "reach-out" philosophy and desire to meet the needs of his customers led him to venture yet further into the field of electronics. Today his son, Robert W. Galvin, carries on the tradition of innovation and growth.

The company's story is one of two-way radio communications but it is also a story of the semiconductor, the integrated circuit and electronic microminiaturization. It is a story of consumer electronics for the home and the car, and one of space exploration. Some forty years after the first car radio a Motorola radio was relaying from the moon Neil Armstrong's historic words: "That's one small step for man . . . one giant leap for mankind."

In those forty-odd years Motorola has grown from a small Chicago-based company to a worldwide corporation with some 50,000 employees and with manufacturing facilities in the United States, Canada, Mexico, France, Germany, Malaysia, Italy, Hong Kong, Israel, Korea, Puerto Rico, Taiwan, Switzerland and the United Kingdom . . . and joint ventures and licensing arrangements for the manufacturer of its products in twenty-one other countries.

By the end of 1972 sales had reached a record of over $1 billion. Today Motorola has four equipment divisions—the

Automotive Products Division, the Communications Division, the Consumer Products Division and the Government Electronics Division—plus the Semiconductor Products Division. The Automotive Products Division is based in Franklin Park, Illinois, along with the corporate headquarters. Since pioneering the first successful commercial car radio in the early thirties, the company has never relinquished its leadership position in the automotive electronics field. The division manufacturers such products as eight-track stereo tape players for autos, alternator charging systems for car manufacturers like Chrysler, automotive instruments such as tackmeters and hour meters, and solid-state ignition systems for Chrysler and others. Motorola developed and produced the original eight-track tape player introduced by Ford in 1965 and continues as its sole supplier. The company also developed a mini eight-track cartridge and private-label unit manufactured by Alps-Motorola in Japan.

The Communications Division has its headquarters in Schaumburg, Illinois, and a second major plant in Fort Lauderdale, Florida. It has long been the world's leading supplier of sophisticated electronic communications systems for markets such as the public safety field, fire departments, forestry, farmers, commercial and professional groups, industry and transportation organizations like the airlines, truckers, taxi and railroad companies. The company that pioneered the first two-way radio system in the late thirties now distributes a broad product line that includes mobile and portable FM communications systems, radio paging systems, communications control centers, as well as visual communications systems, signaling and remote-control systems, car telephone systems and microwave communications systems. The division also makes medical emergency communications systems, precision instruments and component products. Research and development remain the cornerstone upon which the Communications Division retains its position of world leadership. The quality of its products is insured by the use of integrated circuits, hybrid transistors and the latest advances.

The Consumer Products Division, based at Franklin Park,

Illinois, is an outstanding supplier of TV and sound products for the home. The product line is headed up by the popular "Quasar" color TV set. "Quasar" electronic components are grouped in modules and can be plugged in and out of a "Works in a Drawer" chasis for easy service, usually at home. Recently the "Instamatic" color-tuning button has further enhanced this line.

The Government Electronics Division is a leader in research, development and the manufacture of a variety of communications and electronic equipment, ranging from undersea electronics through radar to deep-space tracking and spacecraft systems. This division, headquartered in Scottsdale, Arizona, produced the S-band transceivers that served as the only link in all voice and TV communications between the moon's surface and the earth in the historic Apollo lunar missions. One of the exotic electronic products of this division was the radio assembly and support equipment for the Mariner/Mars 7 Mission. Motorola products participated in every Gemini, Mercury, Apollo and Mariner shot of the past and will be in future space shots.

The headquarters and largest part of Motorola's other division, the Semiconductor Products Division, are located in Phoenix, Arizona. Its line of over 35,000 devices is the broadest in the industry and is used in virtually every type of electronic application.

Speaking of the company's future, Board Chairman Robert Galvin says: "Fundamentally, I want Motorola to be progressive, diversified and dynamic. This means an unobstructed wide-angle view. In ten years we'll probably be making products we've never heard of today, and we will have dropped out of some we're in today. Selectively and logically, we must take on more interests, new interests."

NATIONAL
CASH REGISTER

□ □ □

Self-Service Rings Up a Billion-Dollar Sale

An idea born in Memphis more than fifty years ago revolutionized the world's shopping habits—and also helped start The National Cash Register Company along the road to becoming a billion-dollar corporation.

The idea was self-service merchandising. It was the inspiration of Clarence Saunders, a Memphis businessman who founded the Piggly Wiggly food store chain. Like many great ideas, it was amazingly simple: Let the customer get close to the merchandise, pick it up and examine it carefully. Give "impulse buying" a chance to come into play and volume would increase dramatically.

There were many skeptics. Some said pilfering losses would be staggering. Others claimed the customer would never be willing to serve himself. However, NCR concluded that Piggly Wiggly was only the beginning, that customers instead of resenting self-service would like a system in which they could shop at their own pace.

Furthermore, the time was right. The typical American family now had a car in which to haul purchases home. Refrigeration permitted bulk purchases of perishable items. The daily trip to the corner grocery and meat market would no longer be necessary. Fewer but much larger food stores were clearly the wave of the future.

How would all this affect a cash register company which

*A self-service grocery store in the 1920s. This new concept
of merchandising required a fast, sturdy, itemizing cash
register—and NCR filled the bill.*

for half a century had looked to the small neighborhood store for most of its business? It could have been disastrous, but instead it provided the impetus for a dramatic new period of growth. At the same time it launched NCR on a product development course and a broader concept of marketing which eventually enabled a relatively small company to become the world's second largest producer of general business equipment.

As for product development, it was obvious what self-service demanded: an itemizing sales register completely electrified for fast checkout operation. It had to be more rugged than any yet produced in order to endure almost constant operation.

But the engineering of new equipment was only a small part of the challenge. Prior to the birth of self-service, NCR had tailored cash registers and other business machines to mechanize accounting functions. But it had scarcely touched upon such matters as how and where a merchant should display his merchandise, how customers should be routed through the store, and similar operational problems. It had done much toward "organizing the books" but hadn't yet attempted what the industrial engineer calls "organizing the work."

It soon became apparent that the self-service development would require NCR to do much more then merely market machines. Henceforth it would be promoting new merchandising techniques as well as equipment.

So parallel to development of the early checkout registers, it specialized in store organization, setting up what was then known as a Merchants Service Department. An extensive library of merchandising literature was developed. Using miniature models of store fixtures, NCR specialists designed thousands of store layouts for merchants. Strategic placement of merchandise, traffic patterns and many other factors were analyzed scientifically. Training manuals and schools were developed for checkout personnel.

This broader marketing concept also made the company more systems-conscious. Greater emphasis was placed on researching the needs of different lines of business and developing specific systems to meet those needs. This service-oriented approach permeated practically all areas of corporate activity and, much later, helped pave the way for meeting the unprecedented systems challenges of the computer era.

What eventually evolved was a "total system" philosophy which one day would enable not only sales registers but other basic business machines to communicate with computers.

After World War II NCR's pioneering efforts in self-service mass merchandising spread to Europe, Latin American and Asia. The company developed seminars on "Modern Merchandising Methods" and "Advanced Management Systems" which attracted tens of thousands of foreign participants.

These programs present new management concepts in practically every field of business. During their stay the overseas visitors combine a series of presentations given at Sugar Camp, NCR's Corporate Education Center, with visits to shopping centers, fast-food operations, discount stores, supermarkets and convenience stores. The combination of classroom activities and on-the-scene inspections gives them a broad and practical view of the state of the art of merchandising.

During the seminar the participants hear lectures on the socio-economic factors that influence business, retail gravitation, advertising and sales promotion, trends in shopping center construction and layout, the role of the independent, the discounter and the chain in food marketing, franchising, and department and discount stores in general merchandising.

The byword of the seminars is "Adopt *and* Adapt." Those attending are cautioned that they should not adopt everything they learn at the seminar without considering local conditions, customs and dislikes. For instance, shopping centers are not practical in the center of cities where everyone is an apartment dweller.

The real purpose of these seminars is to motivate people to action. NCR believes that retailing is a business of motivation, of change and ideas, and it tries to impart this idea to those who take part in these sessions.

The checkout registers the visitors see in today's retail establishments are, of course, vastly different from those used in the first Piggly Wiggly stores. Contrasting with those mechanical models of half a century ago are the new-generation electronic marvels that today have internal "intelligence" and can do such things as automatically figure sales taxes where applicable, extend prices for quantities and calculate "split-package" pricing where a customer buys less than the advertised number of units.

At the same time they are gathering more data than ever before, so that store management can watch merchandising trends and react faster, while at the same time better scheduling employees to meet peak sales periods.

NCR's family of food store registers today includes the world's first free-standing fully-electronic register and two others with even greater abilities for those stores wanting the utmost in data gathering and computing ability.

The most sophisticated of these units is actually a complete store system, tying as many as sixteen electronic registers together with an in-store minicomputer, allowing for instantaneous price look-up and credit authorization as part of the checkout process.

As a family, these new electronic registers meet the needs of virtually any type of retailer, providing more accurate sales records and speeding customer checkout. Thus over the fifty years since self-service first started at Piggly Wiggly NCR has strived to provide the most efficient means of sales recording for every type of retail business.

Although NCR's innovative founder, John H. Patterson, died before self-service stores became widespread, it is interesting to note that this development—perhaps more than any other—demonstrated the validity of his favorite NCR dictum: "We progress through change."

NEW YORK LIFE

□ □ □

The Willingness to Innovate

Singling out one development that changed the course of New York Life is almost impossible. There is, however, a spirit of innovation that runs through the 128-year history of the company that has been a major factor in the changing life of New York Life. The constant search for new and improved ways to manage more effectively and to serve policyowners more efficiently has been a driving force in the company's progress.

Before 1887, for example, the life insurance industry had little or no management organization in the field. That year New York Life pioneered the branch office system that later was widely adopted throughout the industry. Under this system, a full-time salaried branch office manager recruited and supervised the activities of individual agents. The agents' contracts were made directly with the company rather than with an intermediary general agent. The net effect was a more direct relationship between New York Life and its agents, which resulted in growing efficiencies and greater service to policyowners.

New York Life President John A. McCall was so proud of the effectiveness of the branch office system that in 1894 he took the unusual step of publicly inviting the insurance commissioners of seven states to examine the company. The commissioners were intrigued with the branch office system,

George W. Perkins, vice president for agency affairs in 1895, developed a pioneering plan for agents' compensation, thus stabilizing New York Life's sales and service force.

analyzed it carefully and noted the significant drop in the cost of placing life insurance on the company's books. In their report they concluded that: "The financial statement shows unquestionably the sound and prosperous condition of the Company, and the management, the public, and especially the policy-holders in whose interest the great trust is conducted, are to be warmly congratulated upon its solidity and security."

One of the more recent examples of the company's innovative skills was demonstrated in 1968 when New York Life played a key role in developing a new and exciting product, variable life insurance. The details of this new kind of life insurance policy were first reported in a paper presented at the annual meeting of the Society of Actuaries in Boston. The authors of the paper were three New York Life actuaries, the late Charles M. Sternhell, executive vice president, and John C. Fraser and Walter N. Miller, currently vice presidents of the company.

The new concept was widely praised throughout the life insurance industry as an actuarial breakthrough of major proportions. The plan's uniqueness lies primarily in its provision for certain variable benefits while retaining traditional-level premiums. The policyowner is guaranteed that the initial face value of his policy will never decrease, although it may rise depending on the investment performance of reserve funds, invested primarily in common stocks. The cash value of the policy, however, may fluctuate up or down depending on investment results.

Through such willingness to innovate New York Life has made many notable contributions over the years to the life insurance industry and to the financial security of its own policyowners.

New York Life was the first to originate policies with paid-up values. Before this, lapsed life insurance policies returned nothing to the insured. New York Life was the first to freely accept women for insurance at the same rates as men; the first to issue policies, on a scientifically rated basis, to people with impaired health and to those who worked in hazardous occupations; the first to issue permanent disability insurance and term insurance to cover loans. The company's detailed annual financial report for its policyowners and the public in 1896 was the first of its kind from a life insurance company.

Sparked by the recommendations of a committee of "Young Turks" appointed to chart some new directions for the company, New York Life made significant life insurance news in the early 1950s. The company initiated a series of new administrative, underwriting and marketing procedures that had far-reaching effects on both New York Life and on the life insurance business. As a result of the committee's efforts (known inside New York Life as Project 25), policy forms were vastly simplified, premium rates were lowered, medical impairment ratings were widely relaxed and the company's underwriting staff was reorganized. These departures set the stage for new sales records for the company and new trends in the industry.

As a growing company in a growing industry, in 1956 New York Life became the first life insurance company to install large-scale data-processing equipment. And today a nationwide computer network between the company's home office and its central service offices provides quicker, more accurate and more complete information for agents and policyowners than ever before. Many of the company's current products and services would not now be possible without the sophisticated technology of today's advanced computers.

In the area of social concern, New York Life was the first life insurer to join Plans for Progress in 1964, and its executives were among the architects of the life insurance industry's $2 billion Urban Investment Program launched in 1969.

These are but a few of the company's benchmarks of continuing progress. Another, one of the most far-reaching, perhaps, was a new system of compensation for agents. It was not only revolutionary in its day, seventy-eight years ago, but remains unique in the life insurance business. It has enabled the company to build a loyal, professionally-trained corps of full-time career agents, better able to serve the lifetime financial security needs of their policyowners. And this, after all, is the very essence of the life insurance business.

By 1895 the relatively young life insurance industry was thriving. Sales in that year topped the $1 billion mark and insurance in force was at an all-time high of $5.7 billion. But there were serious selling and service gaps in the industry growing out of the fact that agents worked mostly on a part-time basis and were quick to jump from one company to another. For the policyowner this resulted in constant disruption of service; for the company it meant erratic sales performance. For everyone concerned the practice was costly and wasteful.

The problems were the same for all insurance companies, but New York Life took the lead. Spurred on by its resourceful vice president in charge of agency affairs, George W. Perkins, New York Life in 1895 approved a farsighted agents' compensation plan with benefits never before proposed in the life insurance industry. New York Life agents were provided regular compensation and a lifetime monthly income after twenty years if they maintained specific sales results over that period. This monthly income accrued to an agent even though he had not retired from the company. Known as the Nylic Plan (an acronym of the company name), its elements of deferred compensation and old-age security were rare for any industry in 1895 and unprecedented in the life insurance business.

A year after the plan was started only 73 New York Life agents qualified. But within ten years the membership was over 1,100. Today, the Company has 9,000 full-time career agents. In 1972 Nylic benefits to agents, exclusive of commissions, came to a record $21 million, an increase of almost 29 percent over 1967.

Has this life insurance industry "first" been an important and significant factor in New York Life's development? New York Life thinks so and credits the plan with helping to encourage quality performance among its agents that is second to none in the life insurance business.

Today more New York Life agents are members of the

Million Dollar Round Table and the Women Leaders Round Table than agents from any other company in the world. And the number of New York Life agents who are National Quality Award winners—the industry designation for quality service and selling—has almost doubled in the past decade. In 1972, as in each of the previous six years, more than a hundred Chartered Life Underwriter designations were earned by the men and women of New York Life, bringing the company's total number of CLUs to over 1,450. The CLU designation is a symbol of the highest professional attainment and is awarded to qualified men and women only after years of intensive study.

The true measure of an agent's worth, however, is the respect and confidence he wins from his policyowners. And it is significant that most of New York Life's business in 1972 came from men and women introduced to New York Life agents by existing policyowners—and from existing policyowners themselves, who took additional life insurance.

To maintain this unique vote of confidence from its consumers New York Life continues to refine and improve its policies and practices throughout the company. Agents and indeed all employees are recruited and trained to maintain the highest possible standards of performance.

"The responsibilities of leadership in the life insurance business are very real," says R. Manning Brown, Jr., chairman of the board. "The personal nature of life insurance carries with its an implicit trust that requires the highest sense of integrity and concern for the best interests of our policyowners.

"We are proud of our agents and proud of our company. And we recognize, too, that constant improvement and constructive change must remain the order of the day in our continuing efforts to serve the growing and increasingly complex insurance needs of our policyowners."

OTIS

□ □ □

A World's Fair Stunt That Lifted Skylines

American cities in the 1850s were feeling the growing pains of the Industrial Revolution. With building heights held to the four or five stories that people could climb, space was lacking downtown to house the nation's burgeoning businesses.

Elisha Graves Otis found the way to lift that barrier to progress. In 1852 he had built a hoist for the Yonkers Bedstead Manufacturing Company, where he was master mechanic. Hoists for freight were nothing new, but few passengers would ride in them for fear of falling if the rope should break. Otis added a simple but sure automatic safety device to keep his hoist from falling.

Thus he had invented the elevator, but his vision ranged far beyond that first step. Sensing the needs of his own time and of times to come, this businessman-innovator in 1853 opened the first plant to manufacture elevators. It was the start of a company and an industry.

The next year, in a shrewd public relations move, Elisha Otis rode on his "safety hoister" at America's first World's Fair in New York. Hoisted high up in the crowded Crystal Palace, he ordered the rope cut. The platform held fast, demonstrating to thousands of fairgoers and millions of people in the world who read about it that the safe elevator had arrived.

Elisha Graves Otis

Elisha Otis riding his "safety hoister" at America's first World's Fair, held in New York in 1853.

The earliest elevators were for freight. Otis installed his first passenger elevator in the E. V. Haughwout & Company store in New York in 1857.

When Elisha Otis died of diphtheria during an 1861 epidemic, his sons Charles and Norton continued the business . . . and kept looking for new worlds to conquer. In 1868 they put the first elevators in office buildings, the New York Life, Park Bank and Equitable Life, in New York. Builders became enthusiastic about the potential offered by the elevator; it meant that the upper floors of a building could be the most valuable, instead of just so much wasted space. This reaction caused Norton Otis to write: "They act about elevators as though they were some new discovery that had just come out." Buildings rose to progressively greater heights to give the modern American city its distinctive soaring skyline.

Early elevators were powered by steam. As buildings grew taller, the Otis brothers tried many schemes to speed up elevator service. One of the more interesting was the "water balance" elevator. It consisted of a car at one end of a rope and an iron bucket at the other. When the bucket was filled with water, the car went up. When the bucket was emptied, the car went down, until the operator stopped it with a large hand brake.

In 1889 Otis introduced the electric elevator. Five years later came the start of automation with the first push-button elevator. Today computer systems with solid-state circuitry control whole groups of elevators for split-second response to passenger calls.

As elevators became faster and more automatic, taller buildings became economically feasible. Sky lobby and double-deck elevators now pack still more transportation service into a building without taking too much space for hoistways.

Sky lobby systems, which stack elevator hoistways to upper floors above those for the lower, make practical the twin 110-story Tower Buildings of the World Trade Center in New York City, where Otis is installing a record total of 239 elevators and 72 escalators.

A double-deck elevator has two cars, one above the other. Otis recently completed the first modern system of double-deck elevators in the Time-Life Building in Chicago, and is installing them in other buildings, including the 80-story Standard Oil Company (Indiana) Building, also in Chicago, which will have the largest such system.

Beginning in the early 1960s glass-bubble "look out" or observation elevators gained popularity with visitors to such attractions as the Seattle Space Needle, the Tower of the Americas at San Antonio and the Skylon Tower on the Canadian side at Niagara Falls. Since then they have proven powerful attractions at hotels and office buildings here and abroad. Observation elevators have transparent sides and are installed in the open or in glass-walled shaftways to give riders a view of their surroundings. This dramatic development transforms an ordinary elevator ride from everyday transportation into an exciting adventure. Passengers enjoy the sensation of rising through the landscaped inner court of a glamorous modern hotel, or seeing the scenic skyline of a famous city slip away below. Elevators cars are often rounded in shape and tapered top and bottom, suggesting futuristic vehicles for space travel. Otis has proposed combining the double-deck and observation elevator concepts to give more people a "ride with a view."

Massive housing needs in urban areas must be met largely by multistory construction, for which Otis has developed lines of preengineered elevators. Equipment is manufactured on an assembly-line basis and shipped off-the-shelf to the building site as needed. Specifying elevators is simplified, with production, delivery and installation scheduling under computerized control. Since it saves time in planning and construction, preengineering can speed the completion of an elevator building, holding down its cost and letting it start earning a return sooner. Improved, expanded lines of preengineered, premanufactured elevators have been developed for buildings ranging in height from two or three stories all the way up to thirty.

Escalators, which Otis introduced back in 1900, have been joined in the space age by "Trav-O-Lator" moving walks.

Carrying people horizontally or on an incline, quickly and comfortably, these continuous transporters are being installed at airline terminals and other places in the United States and abroad where large numbers of people must be moved without congestion.

Long at the forefront in moving people, Otis since 1954 has also become a major factor in material moving, with its Material Handling Operations that makes Baker, Baker-York and Moto-Truc fork lift trucks and other equipment. Established in 1969, the Diversified Systems Division concentrates on engineering automated systems for handling and warehousing products of various sizes, shapes and weights.

World wide, business from all activities reached a new high of more than $881 million in 1972, of which consolidated subsidiaries abroad contributed nearly $500 million. A pioneer in international operations, Otis was exporting elevator equipment to thirty-one countries by the 1890s and in the next decade started manufacturing outside the United States: in England and France in 1900, Canada in 1902, Germany by 1912.

Today, with global sales and earnings growing dynamically, Otis has up-to-date offices in 408 cities in 126 countries and plants in 17 countries outside the United States. Growth at home and overseas continues with internal development and purchase of selected businesses to strengthen Otis capabilities in its chosen fields.

One of these acquisitions, the Westcoaster line of electric-powered in-plant freight vehicles and personnel carriers, has been integrated into Material Handling Operations. Westcoaster vehicles, including the popular electric golf carts, are being marketed under the Otis trademark.

Exciting possibilities lie in Transportation Technology, Inc., in which Otis has a substantial interest. TTI is developing advanced transportation systems, including air-supported linear-induction motor-powered vehicles for use in city, airport and university complexes. Vehicles of unique design, using single-sided linear motors, can move sideways as well as forward and backward. This flexibility of movement, together with the light weight, quiet operation and low profile of TTI cars, permit their use in fully automated "personal rapid transit" systems that combine the privacy and direct transportation of taxicab service with mass transit's freedom from traffic congestion and air pollution.

Research and development is finding better ways to satisfy changing needs in fields where Otis excels. A major aid to improved overall efficiency, the Corporate Computer Center, serves all domestic operations with a versatile data base for a broad range of activities, from market analysis and product development through expediting deliveries. Otis engineers pioneered in using the computer to simulate the wide range of conditions a new elevator system will encounter in actual use. With computerized "models" simulating the configuration of buildings, demands of their occupants for elevator service and the response of elevators, engineers can thoroughly study a new system in the laboratory and predict its performance with confidence before its actual use.

The future in moving people and handling materials, in the United States and around the world, looks as promising today as it did to Elisha Otis when he recognized an emerging need and took those first fateful steps toward its satisfaction.

OWENS-ILLINOIS

□ □ □

An Improbable Genius Was Mike Owens

He left school when he was ten years old and never learned to read a blueprint or master the decimal system. He was always confounded by the size and complexity of machines that were evolved from his ideas. Yet Michael J. Owens revolutionized the glass industry with inventions that were the first technical advances made in 2,200 years.

Owens was as improbable a genius as Thomas A. Edison, who was remarkably like him in training and temperament. He had no concept of scientific theory. When engineers showed him detailed designs of machinery based on his rough sketches, he snapped impatiently: "Put it in iron." His brusque manner antagonized some, but his dynamic innovations transformed the ancient art of glassblowing from a handicraft to an automated mass-production operation in 1903.

The strangest paradox of Owens' career was his relationship with Edward Drummond Libbey, a polished and diplomatic glass manufacturer who was his chief supporter despite a damaging strike Owens had led against him.

Owens, the son of an Irish immigrant coal miner, left school after the fifth grade in 1869 to stoke furnaces in a glass factory at Wheeling, West Virginia, for thirty cents a day. At fifteen he was a glassblower, but he had a more formidable local reputation as a union leader. A forceful, if somewhat ungrammatical speaker, he was one of the agitators sent to foment a strike against Libbey's New England Glass Com-

The man and the machine that revolutionized the glass industry: Michael J. Owens stands beside a 1910 model of his automatic bottle-making machine.

pany in Cambridge, Massachusetts, in 1888. The dispute was partially responsible for Libbey's moving to Toledo, with its cheaper sources of fuel. Among the new men he hired was Owens.

Three months later the young firebrand had bombarded Libbey with so many suggestions for improvements that he was appointed foreman of the glassblowing department. Within two years he was the superintendent of the plant.

In 1898, with funds furnished by Libbey, Owens began experimenting with a machine to produce glass bottles and tumblers, which had been made by hand ever since glass was discovered by the Phoenicians. Men dipped into a furnace for a "gather" of molten glass, formed it by blowing through a pipe, then finished the shaping with crude tools. It was such a slow, expensive process that a skilled worker and four assistants could make only eighteen dozen bottles a day. Labor costs accounted for 75 percent of a water tumbler's retail price.

Owens had no knowledge of chemistry or physics, but practical experience had taught him the properties of molten glass. His chief asset, though, was an instinct for sensing how the limitations of glass could be reconciled with the limitations of machinery. There is no other explanation for his success in a field that had frustrated generations of scientists.

The device that raised glassmaking from a handicraft to an industry was a series of steel molds mounted on a wheel that rotated around a pot of molten glass. A pump sucked up measured gobs into the molds, then wafted a precise puff of air into them to shape the glass. Skeptics dismissed Owens' first crude machine, but he soon perfected it. Today's models of the Owens machine turn out 300,000 bottles a day.

Until Mike Owens' machine revolutionized the industry glassmakers had helped offset the high cost of labor by employing thousands of children. In 1880 one-fourth of the labor force in the industry were boys who should have been in school or at play but who, like Mike Owens, were forced by poverty to put in twelve- and fourteen-hour days at thirty cents a day. Owens' machine effectively eliminated child labor in the glass container industry by making it uneconomical to employ children, but that was only one side of the many-faceted revolution he touched off.

His machine made possible for the first time the production of bottles of uniform weight, height and capacity, something that even the most skilled hand craftsmen could not do. This uniformity, in turn, permitted the establishment of the first high-speed filling and packing lines, thereby bringing a corollary revolution in the food, drug, chemical, beverage and soft drink industries. More important, it permitted the government for the first time to set up and insist upon certain standards, specifications and tolerances in containers to enforce its pure food and drug laws.

But there was even more than this to Mike Owens' invention: It caused a tremendous displacement among the hand craftsmen who were no longer necessary, forcing the union to insist on the eight-hour day to spread out the work. It brought the first mass production of interchangeable parts for machinery—the Owens engineers were doing this before Detroit dreamed of it. It brought special jigs and tools for making these parts, another first in industry. Finally, the Owens bottle machine placed the glass container on the shelf of every kitchen pantry in the world, assuring the buyer that what was inside would be as fresh, pure and healthful as the day it was packed. The full significance of Mike Owens' development of the first automatic bottlemaking machine is not fully known even today by millions who take for granted the machine-made glass container.

After the success of his bottle machine, Owens turned his attention to flat glass, which still was hand-made by workers who blew huge bubbles into beds of molten material, then tried to level the lumps. More often than not, the glass was marred by flaws and distortions when it cooled. Owens perfected a system for drawing glass from a furnace in sheet form. As early as 1917 he, Libbey and associates built a plant at Charleston, West Virginia, that was completely automated —from the introduction of raw materials to the emergence of a continuous sheet of glass from the annealing oven, ready for cutting. That plant is still operated by the Libbey-Owens-Ford Company.

Colleagues constantly were alienated by Owens' abrasive personality. Libbey was embroiled in most of the conflicts, but he recognized the truculent Irishman's unique talents and authorized the then unprecedented sum of $4 million for his experiments over a twenty-year period. This year Owens-Illinois—successor to Owens Bottle Company, formed in 1903 to make Owens' revolutionary bottle-making machine—will spend $40 million for research and development to maintain the technological leadership and excitement brought to it by Mike Owens.

Glassmaking today is a $5 billion industry, a far cry from the $21 million total sales of glassware in the United States in 1880. Even this comparison, however, is an ineffectual yardstick against which to measure Michael J. Owens' technological revolution. Because glass plays such an important role in American life and is essential to so many U.S. industries, his effect upon modern America is almost incalculable. One has but to glance at the shelves of the supermarket or the drugstore to see the importance of the glass container. One need only look out the window of home, car or office to realize what flat glass means.

But the bottle and the flat sheet of glass were only the beginning. Refinements of the machines that made them and developments growing out of them give us today our light bulbs and optical lenses, our X-ray and electronic tubes, our tableware and reflectors, our mirrors and cooking ware, our scientific laboratory glassware, our glass yarn and fabrics, and thousands of other things.

Few outside of the glass industry and Toledo, Ohio, where he lived and worked most of his life, are aware of the real contribution Mike Owens made to the American standard of living. He died in 1923 and Libbey in 1925. Four years after Libbey's death, Owens Bottle Company merged with the Illinois Glass Company to form the corporation that is now Owens-Illinois, Inc. With that merger the company acquired the services of two other remarkable men—William E. Levis and J. Preston Levis—cousins who guided the company for more than three decades.

PITNEY BOWES

□ □ □

Life Begins at Forty—for a Corporation

In 1958 Pitney Bowes was a profitable one-product-line company enjoying a steady annual increase in business. Gross sales were $51 million and net profit was rising at a comfortable rate. By early 1959 the maturing corporation, then approaching its fortieth year, had taken a hard look at its prospects for continued growth—and found both some worries and a new direction.

Pitney Bowes management had known for some time that the company's single product line—postage meters and related mailing equipment—left it with all its corporate eggs in a single basket. But good profitability and steady growth had not provided Pitney Bowes with the sense of urgency to get the company moving on a more positive course toward diversification. "We needed a catalyst, and early in 1959 it came—not from within the organization, but from the outside," relates John O. Nicklis, then vice president of finance, who is now chairman of the company's board. The catalyst he refered to was the consent decree settlement of antitrust charges brought against the company because of the gradual lapse of competition in the postage meter field. Under the decree Pitney Bowes was required to give technical information and the royalty-free use of its patents to qualified competitors.

"We recognized that the restoration of competition was in

the public interest and would probably stimulate the postage meter market as a whole," Nicklis said. "We felt confident we could meet the competition. At the same time, the existence of the decrees underscored our vulnerability as a one-product-line company and brought us face to face with one of the hard facts of corporate life: Diversification, with all its risks, often is essential to dynamic growth, to security and, sometimes, to survival."

Having decided both to grow profitably and to strengthen

The introduction of smaller, desk-top postage meters for small offices over forty years ago helped to popularize the use of metered mail. Today there are more than 500,000 meters in use in the United States.

its position, Pitney Bowes began to make plans to move into new fields and to increase its existing business. This aggressive new direction was keynoted at the beginning of the company's 1959 report to stockholders, which said: "In 1959, Pitney Bowes accented preparation for the future. . . . New and improved products have been introduced, and more are in development, to enlarge our markets."

Among the first steps taken was the establishment of an international division to coordinate and expand business outside the United States. Market research studies were made and the company worked to strengthen its foreign subsidiaries and dealerships. New facilities and a push on production abroad were also in Pitney Bowes' plans for the international division. At home, the company was just completing a plant expansion and modernization program, and research and development expenditures were boosted by 50 percent.

All this, the company knew, would increase costs substantially and limit its increase in net profit for some time to come. "We were convinced, however, that such steps were fundamental to the acceleration of our growth, and that the investment would pay off. It took a while, but it indeed paid off—in our improved international operations, and in development and production of new products here and abroad," Nicklis relates.

Two years later Pitney Bowes took its first big step away from the postage meter and mailing equipment field by acquiring Adrema of West Germany, a leading manufacturer of addressing equipment in Europe. It introduced Adrema products in the United States in 1963. Then, in 1966, the company added collating equipment to its product line with the acquisition of Thomas Collators.

After these acquisitions Pitney Bowes continued investing substantially in the future. It built a new manufacturing plant for Adrema, a new manufacturing plant for Thomas Collators and an addition to its British company's plant in Harlow, England. In 1968 Pitney Bowes acquired Monarch Marking Systems of Dayton, Ohio, the leading manufacturer of preprinted firm-name tags and labels used in retail price marking, industrial product identification and inplant control systems. Monarch also makes machines for imprinting and attaching the tags and labels. Later that year the company acquired Malco Plastics, a manufacturer of printed plastic cards for credit and identification systems.

Acquisitions were an important part of the growth and change that reshaped Pitney Bowes during the sixties, but the greater part of the growth actually came through internal new-product development.

In December, 1965, the company acquired a license to manufacture an electrostatic office copier. It developed a prototype and entered the copier market the following year. There were sizable initial costs for the new copier products division, including a new plant and headquarters. But its copier business recorded an excellent increase in 1968, and as the company has introduced new models over the past several years, copier products have become an increasingly important part of its business, accounting for 13 percent of total revenues in 1972.

Through all this diversification Pitney Bowes did not neglect the postage meter. In 1969 the company brought out a new model, the Touchmatic postage meter. Aimed primarily at small- and medium-sized businesses, this keyboard-operated model operates much like the latest telephones, a concept new to the meter. It has become the company's most popular model. More recently Pitney Bowes introduced the model 6300, a low-cost international meter that promptly set new records for overseas sales of a new product. Postage meter revenues have continued to grow, despite the new competition that followed the consent decree. In 1972 they accounted for 71 percent of total revenues.

Pitney Bowes is now organized for still further growth. It has three product lines—mailing equipment, copier products and retail systems.

The last is an area on which Pitney Bowes has placed considerable emphasis since its acquisition of its Monarch Marking Systems and Malco Plastics subsidiaries. A major step was taken in 1970 when Pitney Bowes joined with Alpex

Computer Corporation to create Pitney Bowes–Alpex for the purpose of manufacturing and marketing electronic point-of-sale register systems.

Pitney Bowes saw in the Alpex-developed SPICE (Sales Point Information Computing Equipment) register system an opportunity to capitalize on the large market anticipated for such systems as replacements for conventional cash registers. SPICE systems can be operated by way of simple self-teaching keyboards, or sales can be rung up automatically via scanning of encoded price tags with a penlike scanner called PEPPER (Photo-Electric Portable Probe/Reader). These computerized systems enable retailers to improve customer service through faster, error-free sales ring-ups, and improve store efficiency by providing a means for the continuous automatic updating of sales and inventory control information, as well as performing customer credit verification and other functions beyond the capabilities of conventional cash registers.

Pitney Bowes-Alpex also offers a version of the SPICE system, called SUPER/SPICE, specially designed for the supermarket segment of the retail industry.

The products of Pitney Bowes–Alpex, manufactured in Danbury, Connecticut, are sold by that company in the United States, Canada, Puerto Rico and the Virgin Islands. Indicative of the rapid growth of this new business, Pitney Bowes–Alpex in early 1973 reported that it had installed approximately 4,000 SPICE registers in some 200 retail outlets.

Prospects for continuing sales of electronic register systems such as the Pitney Bowes–Alpex SPICE system appear good. Industry forecasts indicate that during the next several years, when the major conversion from conventional cash registers is expected to take place, the aggregate U.S. market for electronic point-of-sale systems and peripheral equipment will be in the order of $1 billion to $1.5 billion. It is estimated that the continuing market for these systems, after the major conversion has taken place, will approximate $250–$350 million annually.

The market for electronic retail systems in Europe, where SPICE systems are manufactured and marketed by Pitney Bowes under an exclusive license from Pitney Bowes–Alpex, is conservatively estimated at approximately $500 million over the next five years. Pitney Bowes, in a move to position itself for growth in this overseas market, in early 1973 formed a new subsidiary, Pitney Bowes Data Systems, Ltd., to market SPICE systems abroad.

The research, development and marketing activities of Pitney Bowes' Monarch and Malco subsidiaries have been closely coordinated with those of Pitney Bowes–Alpex. Monarch, a leading manufacturer of merchandise information, inventory control and price-marking systems and supplies, makes equipment that produces and captures machine-readable data on tags and labels. The company's encoding and reading systems can be used in conjunction with the products of Pitney Bowes–Alpex. Malco, the leading producer of plastic credit and identification cards, recently announced plans to offer bar-coded cards that can be read automatically by the scanning devices of Monarch and Pitney Bowes–Alpex. Revenues from retail systems products, excluding the sales of Pitney Bowes–Alpex, accounted for 16 percent of total revenues, which reached $342 million in 1972.

Thus Pitney Bowes has built its business substantially in promising new directions while it has continued to expand its traditional business in the postage meter and mailing equipment field. As summarized by Nicklis, the company feels that its position in domestic and international markets, and in both the established and newer areas of its business, "gives us a good combination for the balance we seek between security and a potential for profitable growth."

What one 1959 observer called Pitney Bowes' "competitive spunk" has served the company well. "As we see continued growth in revenues from each of the three lines of products that now bear the Pitney Bowes label," observes Nicklis, "the events and decisions of 1959 and the changes they sparked remind us that, even for corporations, life really can begin at forty."

PPG INDUSTRIES

□ □ □

The Unlikely Alliance That
Produced Success

Before 1883 virtually all the plate glass used in the United States was supplied by European glassmakers. Twelve American corporations, the first formed as early as 1850, had attempted to manufacture plate glass for the growing market. All failed—some because of technological inexperience, others because of inability to compete with lower-priced glass from Europe.

The Pittsburgh Plate Glass Company was the thirteenth to attempt to establish a plate glass industry in America. And it was a technological and financial success from its incorporation in 1883, due to the talents of two diverse personalities— John Pitcairn, a conservative Pennsylvania Railroad official, and Captain John B. Ford, a freewheeling entrepreneur.

Volatile and flamboyant, Ford was a speculator with a penchant for large construction schemes. Formerly the builder and owner of a successful fleet of riverboats, he had twice tried and twice failed in plate glass manufacturing schemes. Pitcairn, on the other hand, was prudent and astute —a no-nonsense organizer with a passion for detail, order and stability.

This unlikely alliance founded and guided Pittsburgh Plate Glass to success. A mechanic at heart, Ford imported modern machinery and skilled workers for the company's plant at Creighton, Pennsylvania, an Allegheny River town twenty

A ground and polished "jumbo" sheet of plate glass as manu-factured by Pittsburgh Plate Glass in 1893.

John Pitcairn, one of the founders of Pittsburgh Plate Glass.

miles northeast of Pittsburgh. A manager without peer, Pitcairn kept a careful eye on production costs and marketing. Despite stiff price competition from imported glass and total dependence on distribution of its only product through independently-owned outlets, PPG prospered.

With the Creighton plant in operation, Ford—who was more interested in construction than management—left his sons to look after his PPG interests and, with Pitcairn's financial support, built a plate glass plant at nearby Tarentum, Pennsylvania. When this plant was in full operation, he supervised construction of two more production facilities— and founded the town of Ford City, Pennsylvania. By 1890 PPG was producing plate glass at four Ford-built plants.

Despite its growing share of the American plate glass market, PPG was plagued by fluctuating manufacturing profits and irregular production scheduling. With his passion for stability, Pitcairn began to search for ways to remedy the situation.

At this time nearly all plate glass was marketed through the powerful National Plate Glass Jobbers Association, which fixed the price members would pay manufacturers and controlled distribution of the product. Alarmed by the degree of control this group had over PPG distribution, Pitcairn began studying new methods to market plate glass.

It was William L. Clause, PPG's sales manager, who suggested the company open its own warehouse and distribution system. In this way, Clause reasoned, PPG could assure permanent distribution of its plate glass and a degree of direct access to a secondary glass market. Pitcairn enthusiastically endorsed his proposal. Ford, however, thought the proposal was "unsound and impractical"—and predicted financial ruin for Pittsburgh Plate Glass if it was put into effect.

At an impasse, unable to agree with Pitcairn on business philosophy, Ford sold his interests and left the company. His sons, one of whom was president, followed and they formed the Edward Ford Plate Glass Company (now the Ford in Libbey-Owens-Ford Company).

With the Fords gone, Pitcairn put Clause's idea into operation, forming a commercial department and opening company-owned distribution centers in New York, Chicago, Boston, Detroit, St. Louis, Cincinnati and Minneapolis in 1896. The following year outlets in Philadelphia, Cleveland, St. Paul and Brooklyn were opened.

The commercial department was immediately successful. Three years after its inception PPG began paying regular dividends on its stock. It has not missed a payment since 1899.

In 1916 Pitcairn died, ending a distinguished business career. Born in 1841, he was the commercial genius behind the success of the Pittsburgh Plate Glass Company. Beginning with a one-product corporation, he steered it through economic panics, foreign competition and restrictive distribution channels to become the nation's largest plate glass manufacturer. He also was the force behind diversification of the company's product lines as well as the development of raw material sources and expansion of marketing outlets for its many products. By 1920, four years after Pitcairn's death, PPG's annual report described the company as a "diversified business" in which sales of paints and chemical products yielded a significant portion of the net return for the year.

To meet the new demands for plate and sheet glass, PPG made three notable technological advances in the 1920s.

Prior to 1924 plate glass was produced in melting furnaces by the "batch" method. Each batch required individual attention from the mixing of raw materials to the final polishing and grinding operations—which was a relatively slow, expensive method. In 1924 PPG switched to the continuous ribbon method to manufacture plate glass at its Creighton, Pennsylvania, plant. Molten glass from a constantly replenished melting tank flowed horizontally between water-cooled forming rolls, which shaped and smoothed the glass. Glass then moved over rolls into an annealing lehr, where it gradually was cooled and then cut into sheets. Grinding and polishing still were custom operations, but producing plate glass in a continuous ribbon enabled PPG to meet demands for plate glass efficiently.

Four years later PPG first mass-produced sheet glass via the Pittsburgh Process, which improved quality, speeded production—and for the first time made PPG a major supplier of window glass. In this process a continuous sheet of molten glass from a melting furnace is drawn vertically up a four-story-high forming and cooling line. This process minimized the waves and imperfections previously found in sheet glass. Glass produced by this method is known as Pennvernon glass. Licensed to manufacturers around the world, the Pittsburgh Process is still the standard manufacturing method for quality sheet glass.

Another advance was the Creighton Process, a 1928 breakthrough in economical lamination of glass plies and cellulose acetate into automobile windshields. Called Duplate laminated safety glass, the glass-plastic unit helped make automobiles safer—an important consideration as the automobile population climbed. At the end of the 1920s most automobile manufacturers offered safety glass as standard equipment, doubling the amount of glass used in each windshield.

Nearly 70 percent of the glass industry's output in 1929—a year when 5.4 million automobiles were manufactured—was consumed by Detroit. "If all the cars in the United States were placed end to end, it would be Sunday," said folk humorist Will Rogers in describing car-crazy America's ritual of the Sunday drive and its 1929 population of 23 million automobiles.

A revolution in glass technology announced in 1934 affects architectural design even today. PPG developed its first "environmental" glass—Solex heat-absorbing glass, a revolutionary green-blue tinted glass that absorbed solar heat and reduced by 47 percent the amount of heat transmitted through it. As a result, architects for the first time could design buildings featuring large expanses of glass without turning them into hothouses. Although produced in limited quantities until after World War II, heat-absorbing glass was the first step toward the glass buildings of the 1950s, 1960s and 1970s.

In 1934 PPG publicized a glass fabricating technique that

still influences automobile styling today. The company perfected a high-speed glass bending technique, making fabrication of curved windshields practical. Windshields remained flat until the late 1940s, but perfecting windshield-bending technology emphasized again PPG's reputation for glass pioneering.

PPG's first third-generation architectural glass was developed in 1963. LHR glass, a light- and heat-reflective tempered glass, introduced a new "glass conditioning" principle—achieving visual and thermal comfort by reflection rather than by absorption of solar heat. A microscopically thin metallic oxide coating fused to the outside surface of the tinted glass reflected heat and light, thus permitting buildings with smaller mechanical cooling units, lower operating costs and greater occupant comfort. In addition, since the surface of the glass was reflective, images of the sky and surrounding buildings were mirrored on it. This first reflective glass captured the imagination of architects, who believed a building should be integrated with its environment rather than competing with it.

As the Glass Division improved the performance of architectural glasses, it also began producing flat glass products by a more efficient method.

Plate glass, with its brightly polished and perfectly parallel surfaces, was a fine—but expensive—product to manufacture, even after more than eight decades of process improvements. PPG constantly searched for ways to produce a glass with the characteristics of plate glass but at lower cost. In 1963 it became the first American company to manufacture float glass. PPG now is America's largest float glass producer, with an annual production potential of more than 750 million square feet. Float glass meets requirements for architectural applications that less than a decade ago could be met only by plate glass.

In producing float glass molten glass is formed on a bath of liquid tin, and remains untouched until it hardens. The process results in glass with the fire-finished surface brilliance of sheet glass and the parallel surfaces and high optical quality of plate glass without expensive, time-consuming grinding and polishing operations.

Since PPG opened its first float line at Cumberland, Maryland, in 1963, the company has built lines at Crystal City, Missouri, and at Meadville and Carlisle, Pennsylvania. The Carlisle plant alone, put into operation in mid-1972, is capable of producing more than 300 million square feet of float glass yearly on its two float lines, and is the world's largest facility designed exclusively for float glass production. With the completion of the Carlisle plant, a decade of conversion from plate to float glass production was virtually completed by the company.

In the 1960s the company's Fiber Glass, Chemical, and Coatings and Resins divisions have also developed new products and improved technology. With this expanded product mix Pittsburgh Plate Glass Company proved to be too limiting a name for a corporation in which sales of all glass products accounted for only one-third of income. In 1968, when the corporation's sales topped the $1 billion mark, the company became PPG Industries, Inc. Sales in 1972 topped $1.4 billion.

Today PPG ranks among the top one hundred industrial corporations in sales in the United States and is busily expanding in the fields it knows best. The corporation ranks in the top twenty-five chemical producers. PPG's largest capital investment project, a $150-million-plus chemical complex in Puerto Rico, went into production in 1972. The complex includes the Puerto Rico Olefins Company, jointly owned with Commonwealth Oil Refining Company (CORCO). This company's olefins plant at Penuelas, one of the world's largest, produces ethylene, propylene and butadiene. A wholly PPG-owned three-plant complex at nearby Guayanilla produces vinyl chloride monomer, ethylene glycol, caustic soda and chlorine. PPG also is the nation's third largest coatings manufacturer and a major producer of fiber glass products.

With forty-five domestic and thirty-one foreign production facilities, PPG is proof that "unsound and impractical" ideas sometimes can lead to success rather than financial ruin.

RALSTON PURINA

□ □ □

The Tall Orders at Checkerboard Square

"Get into a business that fills a need for lots of people, something they need all year around in good times and bad." This was the sage advice William H. Danforth received from his father as he set out to launch his career in business. The year was 1893 and a financial panic gripped the country. Yet Danforth, a recent graduate of Washington University in St. Louis, reasoned it was a time of opportunity.

America at the turn of the century was basically a horsepower economy. Feed stores dotted every corner in much the same fashion as gas stations do today. Danforth and two associates decided the horse and mule feed business offered much promise.

Outside of hay, only two kinds of horse and mule feed were known, corn and oats. Oats were costly, and every year thousands of horses died from colic caused by bad corn. These facts convinced young Danforth to manufacture feed, and thus the Robinson-Danforth Commission Company was formed in 1894 near the St. Louis levee with a capital of $12,000.

"Cheaper than oats and safer than corn" was the slogan for the company's product, which was a new blend of feed grains, mixed with shovels on the floor of a back room. The feed was packaged into 175-pound sacks which were then sewn shut by hand.

The St. Louis plant of Purina Mills, clearly displaying the famous checkerboard design.

Although Danforth began as a bookkeeper, he quickly demonstrated considerable ability as a salesman. He soon became a familiar sight, traveling by horse or train through neighboring farm areas, buying ingredients and selling feed.

Several years passed and the young company grew and prospered, and Danforth eventually purchased control. In 1896 a tragic event occurred which was to have a profound influence on the fledgling business that was to become Ralston Purina Company. May 27 dawned clear and warm. The sun shone till about 4:30 P.M. Then heavy winds began to blow, accompanied by ominous clouds. At 5 P.M. the worst tornado in St. Louis history struck. The mill was completely destroyed; workmen fled the building and clung to the iron supports of a railroad viaduct to save their lives. The fire that followed burned for three days.

The disaster left Will Danforth as president and majority stockholder of nothing. His company had been obliterated in a matter of minutes. This cataclysmic event served perhaps to propel him to aspire to even greater heights. Regrouping his forces, he demonstrated his zest for challenge and managed to obtain a basically unsecured loan from a local banker. Soon the mill was rebuilt several blocks west of the original site, at Eighth and Gratiot streets, which is the present location of Ralston Purina Company's world headquarters.

Characteristic of his genius for sales promotion, Danforth scored several coups that were to have lasting effect on his business.

In 1898 he began to package a whole wheat cereal that was highly nutritious. He later won for it the endorsement of Dr. Ralston, a prominent health club president, and the product was renamed Ralston Wheat Cereal. As the name's popularity grew and it became widely know, Danforth changed the name of his firm to Ralston Purina Company. The "Purina" was coined from an early company slogan: "Where Purity is Paramount."

By 1904 word was spreading about the quality of his company's feed, but Danforth felt that it needed further identification. As he searched for distinctive packaging for his products, he remembered a family from his boyhood days. Mrs. Brown had always made the family's clothes from the same bolt of distinctive red and white checkerboard cloth, and you could always tell a Brown kid by his checkerboard clothes. Danforth figured checkerboard would identify his products as boldly as it had the Brown family. His reasoning was sound and the famous Ralston Purina checkerboard trademark was born. It has been used ever since with almost unique effectiveness. Even the company's world headquarters in St. Louis is known today as Checkerboard Square.

A remarkably persistent and resourceful man, Danforth more than once turned apparent failure to astonishing success. When in 1904 he found his company saddled with a delivery of thousands of wrong-sized paper flour sacks, he ordered that a handle be attached to each sack and then had them distributed free as shopping bags to visitors to the World's Fair which was then being held in St. Louis. Many visitors to the fair found themselves carrying red and white Checkerboard bags advertising Purina feeds.

During World War I Danforth went to France to serve as a YMCA executive for the troops of the Third Army Division. Characteristically, he did not allow his nonmilitary status to prevent him from winning four battle stars. And although his business was out of his sight, it was not out of his mind. He noted the enthusiasm with which American doughboys responded to the word "chow." Shortly after his return to the business the word "feed" was quickly replaced with "chow" on all Purina feed products. Purina Chows for animals and poultry are now known the world over.

Through the early 1900's the animal feed industry was based on fairly casual mixtures of various ingredients. From his earliest dealings in the feed business, however, Danforth recognized the importance of maintaining uniform quality in his company's products and in 1916 he established an analytical laboratory as part of the company facilities.

The discovery of vitamins and subsequent expansion of knowledge of animal nutrition in the early 1920s revolutionized the feed industry. Ralston Purina's already operating laboratory allowed the company to immediately begin producing the more nutritionally formulated feeds that were to propel the company to its present position of leadership in its field. Today the company's research laboratories continue to develop new products to meet future needs. Current research projects include work with soy protein and other restructured protein products, potentially as a basis for great advances in human nutrition.

Health and nutrition were more than business matters for Danforth. Weak and sickly as a boy, he was once dared by a teacher to become the healthiest boy in his class. In taking up the teacher's dare, Will Danforth began what became a lifelong concern with good health for himself and others. He walked at least a mile every day and would proudly claim that he had never missed a day of work because of illness. In Ralston Purina's early days company employees were led in daily exercises by the vigorous Danforth.

A deeply individualistic and religious man, Danforth lived by a code of ethics which eventually was transcribed, characteristically, to fit the four basic segments of the company's Checkerboard trademark. In later years he referred to the obstacles he and his company had endured, and dared his employees and associates to assume his "four-square" philosophy for living: Stand tall, think tall, smile tall and live tall.

Indicative of the company's driving quest for challenge, Ralston Purnia people operate today from a strong base in agricultural products while diversifying rapidly into the consumer industries. The company is the nation's leading producer of pet foods.

Ralston Purina Company's other activities cover a very broad range which includes sea food processing, production of cereals and snack foods, operation of more than 700 quick-service and specialty restaurants, running a ski resort in Colorado, industrial real estate development, mushroom cultivation and mariculture. In addition, Ralston Purina International has expanded to include operations in some twenty-six countries. A number of developing countries have greatly benefited from agricultural systems which Ralston

Purina International has helped them to build. On a world-wide basis, the company's sales and earnings have increased almost two and one-half times in the last decade, reaching about $60 million in net income in fiscal 1972 on sales of $1.8 billion.

Not a man to forget those who helped him, Danforth felt a lifelong commitment to the city of St. Louis, in which his company had grown and prospered. Today that commitment continues through Ralston Purina's LaSalle Park Redevelopment project. LaSalle Park is an area immediately to the south of Checkerboard Square, the company's world head-quarters. The area has long been declining and is presently in a totally blighted state. The LaSalle Park Redevelopment Project will transform this area, replacing slums with an at-tractive parklike community of low-rise housing, light indus-try and commercial services. Ralston Purina has committed up to $2 million to the renewal project which is considered to be the first project of its type and magnitude undertaken by private industry. This type of involvement indicates the sense of obligation the company feels to the city that has been its home for nearly eighty years.

Ralston Purina today would no doubt dwarf even William Danforth's vision and highest expectations. Although the company conducts its business on five continents and employs some 36,000 people, its basic emphasis remains on food—and food-related businesses. This thread of continuity winding through the company's history no doubt reflects and bears strong resemblance to the admonition which inspired a young man to start a business near the turn of the century: "Get into a business that fills a need for lots of people . . . in good times and bad."

REYNOLDS METALS

□ □ □

The "Alarmist" Whose Thinking
Was Sound

A lot has been written about the American dream of taking
an idea, establishing a business on a shoestring and making a
big success of it. If Reynolds Metals Company had a shoestring in the days it was entering into the primary aluminum
business, it would have been immediately mortgaged.

The company is the outgrowth of the U. S. Foil Company,
founded by R. S. Reynolds, Sr., in 1919 to roll tin and lead
foil packaging materials, primarily for cigarettes and candy.
The company began rolling aluminum foil in the middle
twenties, and in the late twenties, Reynolds Metals Company
was founded. Throughout the thirties Reynolds was a relatively small fabricator of aluminum, buying all of its aluminum ingot outside. The company's great moment, entry into
the primary business as the second American producer of
aluminum ingot, came in the forties.

R. S. Reynolds, Sr., in a radio address years ago, told the
background of the story:

"Some time before the fateful September of 1939, one of
the officials of the French Aluminum Company visited me in
Virginia. I asked him if, under present world conditions,
France could afford to ship aluminum metal to America and
bauxite to Germany.

"On the very threshold of war this great Frenchman said,
'We do not need the aluminum.'

240

R. S. Reynolds, Sr., founder of the firm, watches the pouring of the first aluminum ingot in 1941.

"I then said to him, 'What is Germany doing with all the aluminum it is manufacturing?'

"He replied, 'Germany is short of other metals and is using aluminum for door knobs, truck bodies, window frames, boats and a thousand other products.'

"I replied that I thought Germany was using aluminum for the manufacture of airplanes to bomb France. He laughed and said, 'Don't be alarmed. France has drilled an army every year for twenty years and has nothing to fear from Germany.'"

This conversation and a visit he had made to Europe to search for metal convinced Reynolds that the United States would badly need more aluminum.

He went to Washington and camped on the doorsteps of many Congressmen to tell his story to anybody who would listen. One of the kinder things he was called was a "alarmist." But he was finally introduced to Senator Lister Hill of Alabama by Marion Caskie, vice president of Reynolds and a friend of the Senator. Senator Hill was responsive and arranged a meeting with Jesse Jones, administrator of the Reconstruction Finance Corporation.

Despite opposition, Reynolds Metals was granted a loan for $15.8 million. The interest rate was 4 percent—low by today's standards, but not very advantageous in 1940. To secure the loan the RFC took a first mortgage on all of Reynolds existing eighteen plants, which had never been mortgaged and were worth $24 million. It also took a first mortgage on all new plants to be built. Furthermore, when the company's earnings reached over three times the amount of the mortgage being paid off in any one year, all extra profit had to be turned over to the RFC to pay off more of the mortgage.

The terms put a heavy burden on the company, but the government's strictly-business attitude was based in part on a realistic awareness of the overwhelming odds against Reynolds' success. Since 1888 there had been but one company making aluminum in the United States. They were the only people in the country with aluminum-making know-how. No lesser men than Henry Ford and J. B. Duke had considered going into aluminum production. On second thought, they had backed out.

Less than four months after the RFC loan was granted Reynolds found a plant site and broke ground in a cotton field near Sheffield, Alabama. A government official had predicted it would take a newcomer five years to get started. Five months and twenty-eight days after ground was broken Reynolds poured its first aluminum ingot in May, 1941. It was a record for aluminum plant construction.

Reynolds quickly started building more plants—two aluminum fabricating mills, an alumina plant, a second primary ingot facility in the Northwest—and started mining bauxite in Arkansas.

By the time of the attack on Pearl Harbor, Reynolds Metals had facilities to produce 100 million pounds of aluminum ingot annually, and construction under way on a 60-million-pound-per-year expansion.

Shortly after Reynolds was granted the RFC loan one of the opponents, the chairman of the National Defense Advisory Commission, told the press, in effect, that aluminum production during the next two years would be adequate to take care of military and civilian requirements and leave a surplus. But three months later the aluminum shortage was officially recognized and aluminum was the first metal to be put under mandatory priorities.

R. S. Reynolds, Jr., son of the company's founder and present chairman of the board and president, recalls that war's end brought the problem of absorbing in a peacetime economy the production capacity of additional aluminum plants built by the government during the war. Experts in both government and industry felt that these plants should be canibalized.

"My father and I went to Washington to testify before the Senate. He put forward the radical notion that not only could the nation absorb the output of all these plants, but that within five years it would be necessary to build new ones. He foresaw all sorts of uses of aluminum—in housing, transportation, in packaging and other areas—which would require all the metal we could produce.

"History, of course, proved him right. It was only three years until new plants had to be built.

"In support of his confidence, we leased—and later bought—six government plants that were up for disposal. This was in January of 1946. By April we had the plants back in production.

"The peak war production, in 1943, by the entire U.S. aluminum industry was 920,000 tons. Today our company alone has a yearly capacity larger than that."

During World War II Reynolds had changed from a small packaging materials company to a large company producing primary aluminum—yet it was virtually unknown to the rest of U.S. industry. It also faced the challenge of making its optimistic belief in aluminum's growth come true. To solve both problems it conceived the sales strategy—unique for a basic materials producer—of putting aluminum into the hands of the public and letting it sell itself. Reynolds accomplished this by introducing household aluminum foil—Reynolds Wrap —in 1947, and making it the keystone for advertising and promoting the entire line of Reynolds aluminum products. This thin sheet of metal (only 0.0007-inch thick) went into America's homes and demonstrated many of the remarkable properties of aluminum—it was lightweight, non-rusting, non-toxic, a rapid heat conductor to aid cooking and refrigeration, excellent for storing and refrigerating foods because it sealed moisture in or out, was odor-proof and light-proof.

Reynolds Wrap taught Americans the versatility of aluminum—and made Reynolds Aluminum a household word. The company was the first aluminum producer to advertise on network radio and the first basic materials producer to advertise on network television. It not only advertised Reynolds Wrap but other new aluminum products being developed in the company's laboratories—aluminum siding and windows, aluminum boats, etc.

In the twenty-five years R. S. Reynolds, Jr., has been at the company's helm sales have grown nearly tenfold—from $149 million to $1.2 billion. Reynolds has expanded worldwide with subsidiaries and associated or related companies in twenty-three countries abroad. Its largest overseas step took place in 1959, when Reynolds and Tube Investments Ltd. of Great Britain purchased The British Aluminum Company, Ltd.

Today Reynolds supplies molten aluminum to the automotive industry for the all-aluminum engine block, forms sheet into beverage cans, manufactures aluminum building products, machines wingskins for superjets, forms and prints an array of aluminum packaging materials and supplies aluminum for thousands of applications as diverse as the economy itself.

Reynolds is today the world's largest producer of the aluminum beverage can, which it developed and pioneered in 1963. Concurrent with its efforts to market the new can, the company developed a unique recycling system, under the leadership of David P. Reynolds, executive vice president and general manager of the corporation. The system harnesses aluminum's high salvage value to help solve the nation's litter and solid waste problems—first through an incentive system for consumer collection and return of aluminum cans and, ultimately, through municipal recycling systems which aluminum could help mightily to make economic.

The system includes strategically located major Reynolds centers equipped with separation and shredding equipment, roving mobile recycling units and facilities for remelting the cans and processing them into new cans in classic, closed-loop recycling. The public brings its aluminum cans and other household aluminum scrap not only to the Reynolds centers but to satellite collection stations operated in every state by beer and soft drink distributors. Reynolds has carried on public education programs designed to generate return of the cans in the volumes necessary for an economical operation of the system. The cans are worth ten cents a pound at collection centers, and consumers are paid this amount.

The company is actively working on development of advanced technology for separating aluminum from mixed waste at the municipal level, and Reynolds is participating with government and other institutions and industries in total recycling projects.

Reynolds' innovative leadership in recycling has stimulated similar efforts by other companies and industries. It also has another interesting facet: Since an aluminum can is recycled in a process that consumes virtually no electricity and requires only a small fraction of the energy required to produce the original aluminum, the can in effect becomes an energy bank —on which the system draws over and over again as the metal is repeatedly recycled.

The aluminum can and the innovative recycling system are typical of the many uses and applications of aluminum pioneered by Reynolds. Not only because R. S. Reynolds, Sr., saw the potential of aluminum, but because he and his sons had the foresight to hire people who had the same kind of enthusiasm for aluminum.

A lot of critical decisions figured in the company's growth, but the steps taken in the 1940s were perhaps the most important. They were based on the courage and faith of a man who believed in an idea and in the future of a metal—aluminum.

SANTA FE

□ □ □

The Man Who Met the Longhorns
with a Railroad

Maybe it is just a coincidence that the year Cyrus K. Holliday was born the first railroad was built in this country. Yet as the man matured and the rail industry grew, each seemed to have a profound influence on the other. Jointly their accomplishments helped shape the development of the West.

The year was 1826. The nation's size had more than doubled with the Louisiana Purchase twenty-three years earlier. Rivers, canals, lakes and roadways, such as they were, carried commerce. In the West there were the paths of Indians and fur traders, and the Santa Fe Trail.

In Massachusetts a railroad was being built. It was only a three-mile line to haul stones for construction of a monument at Bunker Hill, but it represented the birth of an industry.

And at Carlisle, Pennsylvania, on April 3, Cyrus Holliday was born. Eventually he would be known as Colonel Holliday, founder of the city of Topeka, Kansas, and the driving force behind the building of The Atchison, Topeka and Santa Fe Railway Company.

It is hard to say just when these particular ambitions first planted themselves within the young Pennsylvanian, but they seemed to be triggered soon after he was graduated as a lawyer from Allegheny College at Meadville, in his home state. Local promoters, planning a railroad through Meadville, needed a charter. Young Holliday, recently married, needed

The "Cyrus K. Holliday," a replica of a Santa Fe train of the old days. Arrival of a train such as this one was a big event at the depot (shown below is the station at Topeka, Kansas, in 1880).

a client. Both were short of funds. As his fee for the drafting Holliday accepted stock in the company rather than cash. He had explored the new venture thoroughly and was excited by its prospects.

His decision was a wise one. Two years later he sold the stock—for $20,000. This "fortune" provided the spark. He headed west to Kansas—determined to found a town and to build a railroad. He was twenty-eight years old.

In the East the rail industry continued to grow by building short lines connecting established communities. Between Kansas and the Pacific Ocean, however, except perhaps in New Mexico and the Mormon settlement in Utah, there were no established towns of any real importance.

Holliday's dreams were of a railroad to Santa Fe—and maybe even beyond.

After arriving in Kansas in 1854, he soon set out up the Kaw River (Kansas River) with a small group of men to find a place on the Western emigrant trail. They selected a place called Papan's Ferry, and with a watch-charm compass and some twine laid out a town. Holliday, with customary optimism, set aside 20 acres for a state capital. The name Topeka was chosen and Holliday was elected "president" of the place. Within six years Topeka was the capital of the state, largely through his efforts. By then he was a member of the legislature.

These were uncertain times. Slavery was a burning issue. Already pitched battles were being fought—particularly in eastern Kansas between men of proslavery Missouri and those of free-soil Kansas. Holliday, strongly antislavery, was made colonel of the Second Kansas Regiment. The fighting ebbed and flowed and eventually erupted in all-out war.

But through it all pioneers continued their relentless movement westward and Colonel Holliday dreamed of a railroad. By 1859 he had drafted a charter for his new line, projecting it "to such a point on the southern or western boundary of Kansas Territory in the direction of Santa Fe as may be convenient and suitable." Almost as an afterthought, he included a branch "to any points on the southern boundary of Kansas Territory in the direction of the Gulf of Mexico."

A railroad to the west and south, he figured, would intercept thousands of beef cattle and provide revenue for the young line as it moved westward. It was shrewd and correct reasoning. For many years the herds would pound up the storied trails from Texas to be loaded on cars at Newton, Wichita, Dodge City and a dozen other railroad towns across Kansas. Colonel Holliday's railroad moved westward.

Other men would follow the colonel in a leadership role as the railroad continued to progress. They would demonstrate his qualities of leadership and vision, and these very qualities would become the hallmark of Santa Fe's philosophy of doing business.

Perhaps symbolic of the spirit that has epitomized Santa Fe's leadership are the circumstances surrounding the explosion at Ardmore, Oklahoma, on September 27, 1915.

A tank car of highly volatile casing-head gasoline was on a spur at Ardmore, when employes noticed a whistling sound of vapors escaping through safety valves. A refinery representative was called, and he removed the dome cap. A stream of gases and vapor shot upward, and without warning a terrific explosion rent the air. The blast was heard for twenty miles, and when the final tally was completed, forty-eight citizens of Ardmore were dead and ten times that many had been injured. Property damage was immense.

Government investigators rushed to the scene, and there was much debate over responsibility. Representatives of the railroad believed that the company would probably be exonerated in any litigation, but the whole thing became academic on October 4, when President E. P. Ripley sent the following wire to the mayor of Ardmore:

> During its entire life the Santa Fe has never declined to pay any just claim, and in the face of the terrible calamity which has overtaken the people of Ardmore, I am not disposed to await the judgment of the court upon the liability of the railroad company.
> I therefore propose that a careful investigation of claims for death, personal injury and property be entered upon by the committee of your citizens which you have appointed

and that a statement be prepared and submitted to us with a view to prompt adjustment of such claims in cash upon a reasonable basis.

No action could have been more warmly received. Ardmore citizens promptly erected a large billboard on which appeared a Santa Fe emblem with the words: "Great is the Santa Fe—One Corporation with a Soul."

A committee of six leading Ardmore residents received the claims and negotiated with representatives of Santa Fe. Most of the settlements were made within a month, and by May, 1916, a total of 1,967 cases had been settled involving 48 fatalities, 504 personal injuries and 1,415 property claims. Only one lawsuit was tried, the plaintiff receiving $1,000 less than the committee had recommended.

There have been many other examples of Santa Fe's philosophy. It isn't unusual for some of the arid communities Santa Fe serves to run short of water during periods of drought, and it has been standard practice to haul in free tank cars of water to tide them over the emergency. When steam locomotives were displaced by diesel locomotives, many of the lakes the railroad had used for water supplies were given to local communities to form the nucleus for a new recreational facility. Some forty-six of the locomotives themselves, each worth many thousands of dollars in scrap value alone, were donated to parks and museums along the way to serve as a reminder of the days of steam.

In the early days the company sent agricultural agents into areas under development to aid immigrants in planting and harvesting their crops. Later, if a community seriously wanted industry, Santa Fe sent people to advise and help them in locating it. The whole business philosophy recognized that the success of the company was dependent on the success and good will of the communities it served. It further recognized that success could be achieved only by keeping up to date, perhaps even one step ahead of the times. Eventually this philosophy would be summed up in the phrase. "Always on the move toward a better way."

Out of the lawyers and merchants and farmers who dreamed
of it, built it and operated it, the Santa Fe made not a single
millionaire. But it created enough wealth out of almost nothing to make thousands of people wealthy and millions prosperous. For years it was the greatest corporation of the plains
with which settlers, traders or workers came in contact.

The Santa Fe Railway recently celebrated an anniversary
along its 13,000-mile-long system. It had been one hundred
years since the colonel had turned a symbolic shovel of
dirt in Topeka to start his railroad. Before his death in
1900 he had seen the product of his dreams reach westward
to the Pacific Ocean, eastward to Chicago and southward to
the Gulf of Mexico—opening new lands and new opportunities to the thousands upon thousands of persons who followed.
He had witnessed commerce and industry develop and towns
grow where none had existed before.

As the railroad prospered, so did the West. Perhaps it is
just a coincidence. Or is it?

SCHLITZ

□ □ □

That Milwaukee Slogan
Stems from Chicago's Fire

Milwaukee is one of the world's few cities whose name is part of an advertising slogan for something other than itself. The advertised product is billed as spreading the fame of Wisconsin's largest city, and there appears to be more than a little justification for this rather bold claim.

The slogan is, of course: "The beer that made Milwaukee famous." It accomplishes what Madison Avenue practitioners of the advertising art earnestly hope for when they crank out their catchy phrases and jaunty jingles—product identification is immediate. It seems safe to surmise that upon hearing these six words, most people know the product referred to is Schlitz beer.

The durability of this world-famous slogan is indeed remarkable. It first appeared in an ad for Schlitz beer on May 15, 1894. It was subsequently trademarked and has been used continuously since that time. As a result, this unusually successful phrase, coined in an era when advertising was not the sophisticated phenomenon it is today, has had considerable time to work its magic.

There have been other advertising slogans over the years for Schlitz beer, and some of them have achieved a degree of recognition. Among these was one describing the taste of the brew—"Just the kiss of the hops." Another called attention to the height of despair—"When you're out of Schlitz, you're

The Jos. Schlitz Brewing Company cooperage shop in 1878.

out of beer." However, only one advertising slogan is promi-
nently displayed on every bottle and can of Schlitz, and that's
the one first used eighty years ago. It is as much a fixture as
the familiar Schlitz rhomboid.

The emergence of the slogan can be traced back, strangely
enough, to the great Chicago fire of 1871. After that fire
Chicago was desperately short of water (not to mention beer
—Chicago breweries were virtually destroyed and those still
operating, of course, lacked water). A small brewery to the
north, then known as the August Krug Brewing Company
and in its twenty-second year of operation, sent a ship loaded
with beer down Lake Michigan to its parched southern
neighbors.

Chicago's thirsty citizens welcomed the Milwaukee beer,
and long after the fire cooled and the water supply was re-
stored, they remembered that wonderful brew from Wisconsin. They wondered how they could go about getting more.
And Joseph Schlitz, who was head of the Krug brewery and
gave it his name in 1874, saw to it that Chicago was kept well
supplied.

In 1870, the year before the fire, Krug sales had risen to
8,700 barrels. After the Chicago conflagration the Milwaukee
firm became a "shipping brewer." By 1880 annual sales had
jumped to nearly 200,000 barrels.

Schlitz had literally made Milwaukee beer famous outside
the city limits. The beer's fame grew, and with it the fame of
Milwaukee, which was eventually to be known as the "beer
capital of the world."

About twenty years after the fire Baron Alfred von Kotzhau-
sen, president of the Milwaukee Fine Arts Company, a litho-
graph firm which made Schlitz labels, and Ernest Bielefeld, a
Schlitz employee, approached August Uihlein, head of the
brewing firm (Schlitz had died in a maritime accident in
1875), about capitalizing on the firm's Chicago gesture and
resulting success. The slogan was suggested, approved and
used. And it's been used and used ever since then. So one of
the most recognized and successful slogans ever devised would
probably never have come into being had it not been for the
tragic Chicago fire more than a century ago.

The tiny brewery that August Krug, a German immigrant, founded in Milwaukee in 1849 is venerable in age but remains a vigorous and progressive company. It is the world's second-largest brewer today and has achieved a new annual sales record in each of the past eleven years, nearly tripling in size during that short span. The company is still operated by direct descendants of the founder.

A year after he opened his brewery in Milwaukee Krug hired Joseph Schlitz, a young man of twenty, to be his bookkeeper. The same year Krug also brought his eight-year-old nephew, August Uihlein, from Germany to live with him. Krug passed away in 1856 and Schlitz assumed management of the brewery. Sometime later he married Krug's widow, and subsequently gave the brewery his name. After Schlitz perished in 1875 when the steamer *Schiller* went down in the Irish Sea, management of the brewery passed to August Uihlein and his three brothers, Henry, Alfred and Edward. Robert A. Uihlein, Jr., president and chairman of the company today, is a grandson of August. Stock in the company is traded on the New York Stock Exchange but a majority of the shares are held by the Uihlein family and Schlitz remains one of the few major American firms owned and operated by direct descendants of the founder.

The growth of Schlitz from a local brewery to a national shipper began with the Chicago fire more than a century ago but the company's greatest expansion has come since World War II. Spurred by increased consumer demand following the war, Schlitz undertook major expansion of its Milwaukee brewery—at that time its sole plant. In 1949 the company felt the need for additional production facilities and purchased a brewery in Brooklyn, New York (since closed). The multiplant concept was further advanced five years later when Schlitz built a new brewery at Van Nuys, California, and in 1956 when it acquired a Kansas City brewery, which it remodeled and enlarged. In 1959 the company built a plant at Tampa, Florida, and five years later acquired the Hawaii Brewing Company of Honolulu. In 1966 Schlitz built a brewery at Longview, Texas, to serve the Southwest. Another new brewery was opened in 1969 at Winston-Salem, North Carolina, and an eighth began operations in 1971 at Memphis, Tennessee.

In addition to these operations Schlitz has minority interest in three Spanish brewing firms—La Cruz del Campo, S.A., of Seville; Henninger Espanola, S.A., of Madrid, and Cerveceras Asociadas, S.A., of Barcelona. The company also operates a can manufacturing division with plants at Milwaukee and Tampa and has two subsidiaries: Geyser Peak Winery at Geyserville, California, and Murphy Products Company, Inc., of Burlington, producer of animal feeds and feed concentrates.

Schlitz markets four brands of beer—Schlitz, Old Milwaukee, Primo (a Hawaiian brand), and Encore—and Schlitz Malt Liquor.

In perfecting precise quality control in brewing the Jos. Schlitz Brewing Company has chalked up many "firsts" in the industry during its long history. It was the first company to brew beer from a pure yeast culture and the first to give beer complete protection from air at all critical stages in the brewing and packaging processes. The company also has been responsible for many packaging innovations.

August Krug would scarcely recognize the vast brewing operation which has grown from the tiny brewery he started so long ago. But he certainly would recognize the constant preoccupation with quality through better ingredients and processes, for he began that tradition the same day he began his brewery in 1849.

SCM

□ □ □

A Takeover Attempt Was
the Turning Point

If American businessmen learned anything from the rash of mergers and acquisitions in the 1960s, they learned that once a company is involved in a serious takeover attempt, win, lose or draw, that company is never the same again.

In the late 1950s what is now SCM Corporation was a small company ($35 million sales) with a narrowly channeled product line (typewriters), headquartered in Syracuse, New York. Today it is a diversified manufacturing company with five operating divisions and annual sales of more than $900 million. Obviously something happened.

What happened was that SCM was involved in two take-over attempts. The first attempt was in 1956 and involved Smith-Corona, the predecessor company to what is now known as SCM. The second was in 1967 and involved the Glidden Company, which now is a part of SCM and accounts for more than half of the company's sales and profits.

The first attempt featured a clash of wills between two forceful and dynamic men: the late Edward H. Litchfield, former chairman of SCM's board of directors, and Meshulem Riklis, now chairman of Glen Alden Corporation.

The story of the first attempt begins right after World War II. The postwar typewriter industry was described in a 1961 Harvard Business School study as "staid, content and optimis-

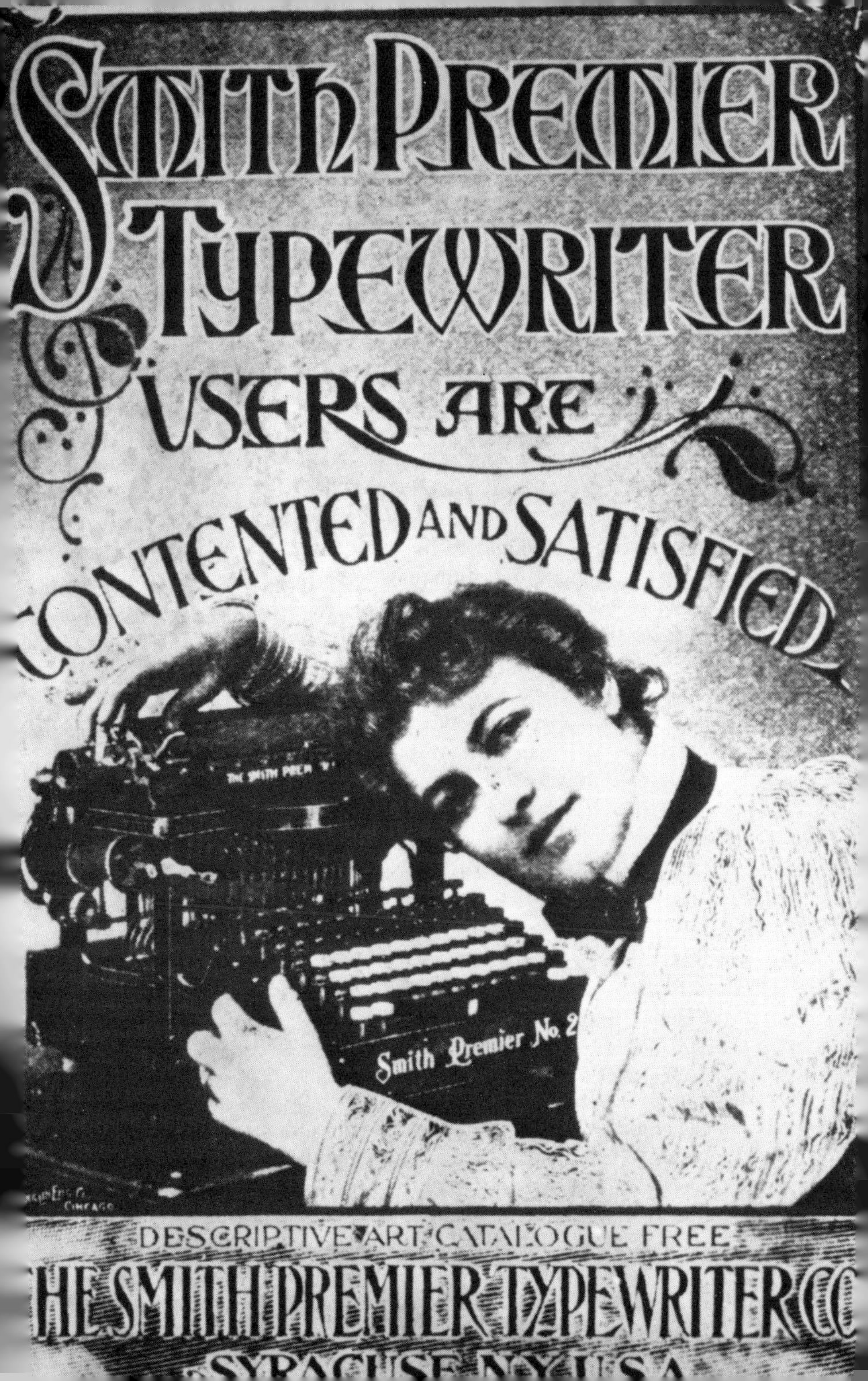
Smith Premier
Typewriter
Users are
Contented and Satisfied
The Smith Prem
Smith Premier No. 2
Descriptive Art Catalogue Free
The Smith Premier Typewriter Co.
Syracuse N.Y. U.S.A.

tic, seeing no threat to its ever-increasing sales." But the old-line companies—Smith-Corona, Remington, Underwood and Royal—were not to enjoy that euphoria for very long.

Up to that point there had been a tacit assumption that only the U.S. economy was sophisticated enough to provide the world with precision-manufactured items like typewriters. But industrial societies in Europe and Japan had favorable wage differentials and were aided by an almost impregnable tariff wall as war-torn economies were nursed back to health. Within a short time not only were American typewriters less able to penetrate foreign markets, but foreign machines were making vigorous inroads here.

At the same time, partly in response to these pressures, and partly, too, in response to the growing impact of technology, American typewriter companies were turning to other facets of what soon became known as the office equipment industry. Most of them turned too late. None of the old-line companies now resembles what it was twenty years ago. Most, in fact, have become parts of much larger organizations. Remington is a part of Sperry-Rand, Underwood has joined the vast Olivetti organization, Royal is a part of Litton Industries, and so on. Only Smith-Corona represents an independent company that can trace its history back to its founding in the latter part of the nineteenth century, a matter of considerable pride to people at SCM. Moreover, Smith-Corona is the only typewriter manufacturer to still make portable machines in the United States. In fact, it is the largest maker of portable typewriters in the world.

In 1953 the board of directors commissioned a study that strongly recommended that Smith-Corona consider diversifying, making it clear that the typewriter business alone was no longer going to be sufficient to support a major American company. One of the study group's first recommendations was that Smith-Corona attempt to acquire Kleinschmidt Laboratories, a small but growing telecommunications company in Deerfield, Illinois.

Shortly thereafter Meshulem Riklis began taking an active interest in Smith-Corona's affairs. He was astute enough to recognize that the company's real future was in diversification into a number of fields only tangentially related to its original business of manufacturing and selling typewriters and related office supplies. Riklis obtained a 20 percent interest in Smith-Corona in 1955. With it came two seats on the board, which he and his counsel occupied.

Smith-Corona and Kleinschmidt had been talking on and off about a merger before Riklis arrived on the scene. In fact, he made no bones about the fact that the proposed association with Kleinschmidt was one of the things that made Smith-Corona a prime takeover candidate. It was a company about to be heard from, he felt. In retrospect Riklis can take part of the credit for stirring the Smith-Corona board into moving more promptly than it otherwise might have.

The influence of the Smith family was still dominant in Smith-Corona affairs. Hurlburt W. Smith, youngest of the four Smith brothers, had died in office at eighty-six years of age and Elwyn Smith had taken over as president in 1951. Practically the entire board was more or less close to the Smith family. The major thrust of the company had been in typewriters and the board was not inclined to embark on a course as radical as one involving merger with anything other than another typewriter company. But that course of action had been rather effectively foreclosed by the 1950 Amendment to Section 7 of the Clayton Act.

The predisposition of the Smith-Corona board members became academic, however, when it became apparent that Meshulem Riklis had quietly increased his ownership control to fully 40 percent of the outstanding common stock. The board quickly concluded that none of its members had sufficient mastery of the legal and technical aspects of takeover attempts and the necessary leadership qualities needed at this time in the company's history. These qualities were all possessed, however, by the dean of the Graduate School of Business and Public Administration at nearby Cornell University, Edward H. Litchfield. Dr. Litchfield, just forty, was vigorously proposed for election to the board.

Litchfield proceeded to lead the fight to repel what the

board unanimously concluded to be a raid. The battle turned on the proposed acquisition of Kleinschmidt.

Litchfield was quick to understand the potential benefits of Smith-Corona joining forces with Kleinschmidt. Manufacturing methods for teleprinters were similar to those for typewriters, but Kleinschmidt had made considerably more progress in automating production techniques. And, of course, the tie-in of Kleinschmidt's data handling ability with Smith-Corona's strong position in the office equipment market made the acquisition a natural. The question was: Should the acquisition be made for cash or stock? It was clear that Smith-Corona's capital structure would most benefit from a stock transaction. But from the standpoint of the Riklis group, issuing a large block of stock to a new group friendly to management would have the effect of diluting their interest in Smith-Corona by 10 percent.

Riklis sued for an injunction against the acquisition of Kleinschmidt by Smith-Corona's management for stock without first calling a special shareholder meeting to consider the method of acquisition. He lost—in part because everyone agreed the merger was desirable from the standpoint of the shareholders—and by August, 1956, the merger was completed. At this point Riklis sold his shares (at what people like to call a tidy profit) and has taken no further interest in the company.

That should have been the end of the story. But when the dust had settled, Smith-Corona was a different company. It had begun to make basic changes in management philosophy.

The board installed Litchfield as chairman in 1956, partly in recognition of his leading role in the takeover battle. Within a comparatively short time, partly because of the advanced age of the board members, and partly because of Litchfield's objectives for SCM, practically the entire board had been reconstituted. He was instrumental in setting what was a relatively small and vulnerable company on the course that eventually brought it to the forefront of American industry. His career in education and foreign affairs, as well as in the business world, was cut cruelly short when he died,

with almost his entire family, in a private airplane crash in
March, 1968.

The second takeover attempt was somewhat less dramatic,
but equally important to SCM. The Glidden Company, with
headquarters in Cleveland, was for years well known for its
Glidden Spred Satin paints and Durkee foods. It was a solid,
well-managed but rather conservative company whose stock
was well thought of by institutions and income-minded shareholders alike. It was also well thought of by a group of Texas
financiers, especially Troy V. Post, chairman of a company
called Greatamerica Corporation. Greatamerica was originally an insurance holding company but had expanded to
include Braniff Airways and Wilson meat packing and sport-
ing goods in its corporate stable. One Friday in early May
of 1967 E. Grant Fitts, president of Greatamerica, presented
himself in the executive office of Glidden and announced that
his company was going to offer a cash tender to Glidden
shareholders and suggested that Glidden management en-
dorse the move. He received a cordial reception, an office
was provided and coffee was ordered. After meetings with
Glidden management he and his aides left with the impres-
sion that the tender would receive no important opposition
from Glidden.

He was wrong. Glidden resisted the takeover with everything it had, which was not too much. But one way to beat
a tender is to merge with a friendly company. Glidden was
determined not to be taken over by some strangers from
Texas who might sell off one or more of the several profitable Glidden businesses. These businesses had been valuable
members of Glidden for a long time and selling them seemed
like auctioning off part of a closely knit family.

Sometime before the tender offer Glidden had been talking
to a few large companies about the possibility of a merger,
but nothing had gotten much past the talking stage. One
was SCM, but contacts had not been active for some time.
The best choice for Glidden of several possible alternatives
was SCM. Contacts were renewed. There were no impedi-
ments to a lawful marriage and each was eager to join in

the merger. Agreement was reached in late May and the merger became official in September, 1967.

What has happened to each party since the merger? Glidden itself, which became Glidden-Durkee Division of SCM, remains relatively unchanged and prosperous. Management and employment has remained stable, though some movement was experienced, most of it upward—Glidden-Durkee people have moved to SCM corporate headquarters in fairly large numbers. Former Glidden people now have SCM titles of division president, vice president–employee relations (second of two Glidden people to hold that position), vice president–purchasing and transportation, vice president–treasurer, assistant treasurer, and managers of insurance, public relations, cash control and personnel development. Glidden-Durkee remains intact and has grown considerably larger. Several new plants have been built and a large research center completed.

The merger with Glidden had a profound impact on SCM. The company, which was generally known as a producer of office equipment—typewriters, copiers, and calculators, plus a line of kitchen appliances—found itself a major producer of paint and industrial coatings, a variety of food products and several specialty chemicals. In 1966 sales were a little more than $240 million and the next annual report showed sales of $640 million. The merger gave SCM several strong consumer trade names and a good grounding in the industrial market, which it lacked before. Glidden management was strong and deep, which aided the corporation and other divisions as well, and Glidden brought a capability in advance research.

Thus two takeover attempts, while certainly unwelcome at the time, exerted what turned out to be positive and lasting effects on the company. A smallish typewriter company became a power in the office equipment industry. Glidden found itself virtually unchanged but larger in operation with its management playing on a much bigger stage. And both medium-sized companies together became a giant.

SINGER

The Suit That Led to Triumphs in Sewing

The early success and worldwide reputation of The Singer Company can be traced to an improbable allliance, formed late in 1851, between Isaac Merritt Singer and Edward Clark. Singer is generally credited with the invention of the sewing machine; Clarks contribution to history is not as well known.

Singer had built a sewing machine a year earlier. As a relic in the Smithsonian Institution shows, his version was the first practical sewing machine and the first to resemble present models. It was not, however, the first sewing machine. Elias Howe, Jr., is historically credited with a patent on a machine employing an eye-pointed needle with a shuttle. When Singer and two other sewing machine makers appeared with improved machines in 1850, Howe sued them.

Singer turned for help to the New York law firm of Jordan and Clark. For an interest in the company Edward Clark agreed to fight the legal battles, and he and Singer became equal partners in I. M. Singer and Company in 1851. The Singer organization dates from that year.

Clark and Singer were very different men.

Born of poor German immigrant parents, Singer had little education and left his Oswego, New York, home when he was only twelve. He was a farmer, a machinist, an actor and an inventor of machines for excavating rock and carving wood—all without success. He was a truculent man of lusty appetites.

A Singer sewing machine in use in the 1860s; below, Singer's original workshop.

Clark, who also was from upstate New York, was a successful lawyer. He was a graduate of Williams College and had a remarkable aptitude for business.

His presence and legal advice paid several dividends in the company's crucial early years. He ended the "sewing machine war" by organizing the Sewing Machine Combination, America's first patent pool. Howe, Singer and two other companies were in it, and other manufacturers were also licensed to use the pool patents. Each paid a $15 royalty for every machine it made, and this was divided among the four companies that organized the pool.

Another contribution of Clark was the introduction of installment selling in 1856. The earliest Singer sewing machines were heavy and designed for manufacturing. But in 1856 the lighter Turtle-Back machine was added for the home. It enabled housewives to sew in one hour what took ten to fourteen hours by hand. But since the average family income at that time was only $500 a year, the $125 purchase price was a serious obstacle. Clark's "hire-purchase" plan put Turtle-Backs in homes at $5 down and $3 a month. This was the prototype for all installment selling. He increased volume with trade-in allowances and lower prices, additional "firsts" in American industry.

By 1863 sales of Singer sewing machines had climbed to about 20,000 machines a year, most of them outside the United States. That year Isaac Singer retired and moved to Europe, where he died in 1875.

With establishment of its own cabinet factory at South Bend, Indiana, in 1867, Singer became virtually a maker-to-user manufacturer and has remained so ever since.

The company makes its own sewing machines in some sixty models. It makes its own needles in more than 8,000 types and sizes, and its own electric motors. Most important, it sells nearly all its machines directly to the user through a worldwide network of 4,000 retail outlets.

Singers are found in all sorts of places. Nearly every ship carries at least one. They are used in prisons, leper colonies and mental institutions, where the satisfaction of creating something is an important factor in rehabilitation.

The Wright brothers stitched the wings of the first airplane on a Singer. Admiral Richard Byrd took six Singers with him to the Antarctic. Both the gowns and the shoes of Queen Elizabeth of England are made on Singers and Westminster Abbey has a Singer for repair of the ceremonial robes of the British royal family.

Singer was one of the first truly international companies. From its earliest days it regarded the world as its area of operations. Within ten years after it was founded, the company was selling more sewing machines overseas than in the United States. It began manufacturing abroad in 1867 at Glasgow, Scotland.

The company's worldwide expansion was interrupted by World War I. In Russia its extensive properties, valued at more than $100 million, were confiscated. Other serious losses were suffered in World War II, but the company's mettle was proved as its factories throughout the United States converted to production of intricate fire control devices, airplane parts and other military items.

For a number of years after the war Singer remained essentially a one-product enterprise, with nearly 95 percent of its business concentrated in the production and sale of sewing machines. Then, in the late 1950s, the company undertook a diversification program. It adopted a plan for future growth that was systematic, deliberate and bold. Its goal was to put Singer into the mainstream of modern business and industry by acquiring expertise in major new fields, where the company would be in a position to serve significant and broad needs of the future.

The company began by entering the textile machinery field, which was closely allied to its traditional business. To expand its technological base, Singer acquired a highly technically oriented company engaged in defense work and several small electronic instrument companies. Numerous other acquisitions followed. The most important were Friden, Inc., a manufacturer of calculating machines, and General Precision Equipment Corporation, an electronics company.

Once known solely as a manufacturer and marketer of sewing machines, Singer today is a high-technology company that produces an almost endless variety of products.

It manufactures a broad range of advanced electronic calculators, small-scale data processing systems, adding machines, automatic writing machines and other office products. It is a leading producer of electronic cash registers, sophisticated machines that record information at the point of sale and transmit it to a central computer for detailed and instantaneous sales reports.

The company is a major supplier of textile machinery, metering and regulating equipment, controls products and water resources equipment. It is the world's foremost manufacturer of aircraft and spacecraft simulators. Its aerospace and marine products range from microwave instrument landing systems for commercial airliners to underwater acoustics systems.

Singer builds homes and apartment complexes, manufactures a complete line of home furniture, constructs heating and air-conditioning systems and offers a variety of educational products and services.

The diversification program has dwarfed Singer's previous success, tripling its business volume. Annual sales now exceed $2 billion. Consumer products account for half of this business, and sewing machines still set the pattern. The company remains preeminent in the field of household sewing products, but these products now account for less than a third of Singer's total business.

With nearly 40 percent of its sales outside the United States, Singer is a leader in global marketing. It has many more retail outlets overseas than in this country, and still sells more sewing machines abroad than in the United States. More than half of its nearly 120,000 employees live and work in other countries.

Today Singer helps man control his environment, improve his tools, move his mountains of paper. A vast array of Singer machines and appliances helps him to house and clothe himself, furnish and clean his home, cook and preserve his food.

With Singer equipment he can solve complex problems in

seconds and write at unprecedented speed. Singer instruments probe the invisible world around him.

The improbable alliance of Isaac Merritt Singer and Edward Clark in 1851 has grown into a large, diversified, multinational corporation with new ideas, broad resources and growing technological capabilities to meet the needs of people around the world.

SOUTHERN RAILWAY

□ □ □

Highballing Along with Innovations

When forty-seven-year-old Samuel Spencer journeyed to Richmond, Virginia, on June 18, 1894, to accept election as the first president of Southern Railway Company, he was under no illusions about the magnitude or complexity of the task facing him. To it he would devote the remaining twelve years of a brilliant career that was to end in tragedy.

It wasn't only that more than thirty formerly separate corporations had to be brought together and made to work as one under the Southern Railway banner. The affairs and securities of these corporations had been interlocked in every conceivable way, and the situation was one of hopeless confusion. Worse, all were in receivership, victims of a prolonged nationwide business depression.

Efforts to reorganize the thirty-odd properties had been tried before and failed—not once, but twice. The third try, directed by John Pierpont Morgan, had produced the miracle: a plan acceptable to all interested parties. As president of the new company, Spencer's assignment was to transform the plan into a viable operating railroad.

He came to the job with impeccable credentials. As the top authority for Drexel, Morgan & Company of New York, the nation's leading bank, Spencer had been midwife at the new corporation's birth. Before that he had made his mark in railroading itself, rising from a clerical job to the presidency of the Baltimore & Ohio Railroad.

A replica of the wood-burning "Best Friend of Charleston," the first locomotive for regular railroad service built in the United States.

Samuel Spencer, the first president of Southern Railway (1894–1906).

Spencer wasted no time in demonstrating that he was the right man for the job at Southern. By the end of the first year, he was able to report net income of $896,000 on a gross of $17.1 million. By the turn of the century Southern's mileage had more than tripled to 7,200 and the company was solidly in the black. Three years later traffic volume on the Washington-Atlanta main line had so increased that the line had to be double-tracked to handle the load.

But three years later, in November, 1906, tragedy struck. In one of the bitter ironies of history the railroad to which Samuel Spencer had contributed so much was to become the instrument of his death. While he was asleep in his office car at Lawyer's Station, Virginia, on the night of November 29, a mixup in signals sent a fast train from Atlanta crashing full speed into the car, killing Spencer and three guests.

Of this formative period in the history of Southern Railway, Spencer's lifelong friend and associate, Judge Alexander P. Humphrey, of Louisville, Kentucky, was to say: "The twelve years that elapsed from 1894 to 1906 were strenuous years, no one without its peculiar difficulty to be encountered or obstacle to be overcome. In the accomplishment of this great work his fame is secure. For it is a work that takes hold not alone upon the present day but upon a future of broad expanse. It belongs to few men to have such an opportunity, and to only a handful to meet and fulfill its every demand."

The news of Spencer's death brought forth expressions of sadness and a sense of deep loss in the nation. In quoting at length from his last public address, delivered a month before he died, the New York *Sun* editorialized on November 30:

> We make no excuse for the extent of these quotations, for they will afford to the discerning a picture of the mind of the remarkable man whose life of public usefulness ended yesterday in tragedy. Those who can read character aright when it is written in autograph will need no further assurance of the uniform sincerity of Mr. Spencer's mental attitude, the honesty and great energy of his intellectual processes, the sturdiness of his thought and morals. These

characteristics that are so apparent in his literary style and philosophic methods of statement and reasoning distinguished likewise the individual in all his relations to others, and won for him not only his just due of admiration and esteem, but also a wealth of personal affection.

An account of his funeral headed "Spencer at Rest" was the lead article in the Washington *Post* of December 2, 1906, occupying the entire righthand column on page 1. The article said in part:

> For five minutes yesterday every wheel along the steel railed miles of the Southern Railway was stilled, every voice was hushed and every head bowed as the wires flashed along the lines that the funeral rites had begun over the body of Samuel Spencer, president of the Southern, whose tragic death on his own railroad on the morning of Thanksgiving Day shocked the peoples of two hemispheres.

Immediately following the funeral the voting trustees and members of the Southern Railway board of directors held a joint meeting in Washington, D.C., and upon the motion of J. Pierpont Morgan adopted a resolution that read in part:

> The mighty fabric which for twelve years he has been moulding must continue under others to develop, and to improve in the service that it shall render to the public, but never can it cease to bear the impress, or to reveal the continuing impulse of the master mind of its first President. In the height of his usefulness and his powers he has been called away, but the inspiration of his shining example and his lofty standards must ever animate his successors.

Although Spencer's untimely passing deprived Southern prematurely of the first of its many great leaders, he had launched the company on a sound path that others would be able to follow. The corporate policies he established, continued by his successors, have served both the company and the people of the South well.

One of Spencer's first official acts in 1894 was to appoint an agent to help encourage the growth of the territory served by Southern. This function has been continued and expanded by succeeding administrations. Assisted by a continuing advertising and promotion program, it is carried on today by Southern's Industrial Development Department. It was during Spencer's administration that Southern Railway inaugurated the first of many improvements in technology which were to earn for it in later years a reputation as the railroad that gives "a green light to innovations." A large-scale installation of the block signal system, which continues today to be the heart of railroad traffic control, was first made on Southern's main line to Atlanta in 1905 and attracted nationwide attention.

A list of some Southern Railway "firsts" reads almost like a chronology of landmarks in railway technology:

Southern was the first railroad to use diesel-electric power in main line freight operations and to become 100 percent dieselized.

It was the first to develop the machinery that mechanized track work, eliminating manual labor by huge section gangs.

It was also the first to install a wireless centralized traffic control system and to build a modern electronic classification yard in the South.

More recently Southern has pioneered with such significant developments as unit trains for the low-cost movement of coal and the use of microwave communications. Southern was also among the earliest pioneers in the use of computers and is today one of a handful of railroads equipped with third-generation computer capability.

Unlike many other U.S. railroads, which in recent years have followed a policy of diversifying into various manufacturing and other nontransportation-related enterprises, Southern's declared policy is to remain transportation-oriented by limiting diversification to other transportation modes or transportation-related businesses. In keeping with this policy Southern offers its customers a rapidly growing intermodal service of rail, highway and water transportation. In the early 1970s it sought and won Interstate Commerce Commission approval to establish and operate a barge line on the Ohio River for the movement of coal.

Also, Southern's Central of Georgia Railroad subsidiary owns and operates the Central of Georgia Motor Transport

Company, and a newly established subsidiary, Southern Region Distribution Services, Inc., has been formed to build and operate several public warehouses along Southern's lines. Early in 1973 a new service for hauling shredded, compacted and baled municipal waste to abandoned strip mines or other areas to be reclaimed as land-fill was initiated with the signing of a contract to provide such a service for the city of Atlanta.

Although the long-term trend of Southern's growth has been upward, the climb has not been without its hesitations and pitfalls.

William W. Finley, who succeeded Spencer as president, was only months in office when the nation was plunged into a deep recession that lasted for years. Bankruptcy was avoided only by the narrowest of margins, when Fairfax Harrison, who assumed the presidency in 1913, succeeded in a desperate effort to arrange an emergency loan.

Nor was Harrison's administration, which lasted twenty-four years, to fare better. Although the nation was enjoying unprecedented prosperity when he took over, he had the task of seeing Southern through the agonizing period of federal control of railroads in World War I, and then the great Depression of the 1930s.

When Ernest Norris succeeded Harrison in 1937 a loan which he arranged personally from the Reconstruction Finance Corporation was necessary to save Southern from receivership. However, before his administration was four years old, Norris had the immense personal satisfaction of seeing the loan repaid in full with interest. More important, it was under Norris that Southern was launched on a period of unprecedented prosperity, which expanded during the succeeding administrations of Harry A. DeButts (1952–1962) and D. W. Brosnan (1962–1967), and continues to expand today under W. Graham Claytor, Jr.

The relatively fortunate financial position which Southern now enjoys can be credited in no small part to two basic company policies: continuing emphasis on improvement, and on assisting the growth of the territory it serves.

SWIFT

□ □ □

Try an Icebox on Wheels—
and Change an Industry

Swift & Company has for more than a century been part of
the dynamic growth of our nation, developing in an era of
dramatic business and sociological change. Historically a
meat and food processor, the company became part of the
American scene during a time of constant and drastic innovations in selling and servicing. Those were years of vital decisions and driving determination on the part of business
leaders—men who had the ability and imagination the times
required. It was this pattern of determination and decision
that formed the foundation of Swift as a major factor in
worldwide industry.

The time was the 1870s. Gustavus F. Swift, who started in
the livestock-meat business in Massachusetts, watched as
cattle markets moved westward. To him the course was clear.
He also moved westward, basing his headquarters in Chicago.
The year 1875 found him among the cattle buyers in that city.

Events moved rapidly toward decisions that were to be the
basis for vast changes in business procedures and practices of
the nation. The demand for meat in populous areas in the
Eastern United States had grown far beyond the regional
supply. This was one of the prime circumstances that led
G. F. Swift from cattle buying into the meat business.

A conviction grew that the meat industry would be trans-

Gustavus F. Swift about 1885, ten years after he followed the cattle markets westward.

Swift was quick to see the possibilities in refrigerator cars such as the "Tiffany" (named for its inventor). By 1877 Swift had ten refrigerator cars shipping beef to the East Coast.

formed from traditional curing and packing functions to supplying fresh meat over a wide geographical area. In the background was an invention that was the key to the far-reaching program—the refrigerator car. This was the development of more than one of the men of vision of the era, and several patents existed, but the concept had not been successfully tried and proven. There were serious questions about whether the refrigerator cars could be utilized successfully.

The vast potential began to be realized when Swift decided on independent action. He arranged for a few refrigerator cars to be built—incorporating the best available features—and started shipping dressed meats, with one railroad cooperating.

An economic, industrial and social battle was on, and the opposition was formidable. Eastern stockyards and local butchers saw a threat to their business. Railroads feared a loss of revenue in handling fresh meat, as it offered only about half the tonnage of live cattle. Swift tried to convince them that his plan was economically sound and would be quite profitable for the carriers in the long run. His belief was that production costs could be lowered by shipping dressed meat as opposed to live cattle because it would eliminate shipping inedible portions of the cattle as well as cut down on cattle weight loss during shipping.

The Trunk Line Association, the direct-line railroads to the Eastern United States, displayed their opposition by refusing to bargain on shipping rates. They simply demanded an exorbitant rate and Swift was forced to comply or suffer product deterioration due to prolonged shipping time.

Over a period of ten years Swift and the chairman of the Trunk Line Association argued over the shipping rate of dressed beef, but it was not until the Interstate Commerce Act was passed in 1887 that the Trunk Line was forced to lower their rates to a more reasonable level and discontinue discriminatory practices against the meat-packing industry.

Technologically overcoming the hazards of the shipping process itself was a giant undertaking around 1875. Winter shipping was particularly problematic because the beef would often freeze before leaving the Midwest, only to thaw out once the freight cars passed through warmer climes on its eastward journey. The meat might freeze and thaw again before reaching its final destination. These drastic temperature changes naturally took their toll on product quality.

Another segment of the food industry that also had an inherent interest in the development of an efficient refrigerator car was the fresh fruit and vegetable industry. Farmers along the Pacific Coast desperately needed a means to transport their abundance of fruit to Eastern markets. In fact, Swift utilized some of these fruit refrigerator cars for his own meat shipping purposes.

Eventually Swift had a refrigerator car designed which incorporated all of the best features of the existing cars. He was financially aided by the Michigan Car Company of Detroit. By 1880 the refrigerator car was an indisputable success.

However, the built-in prejudice against anything new or different had to be combatted. Here, the tempo of the times and the growing need for sweeping changes in food distribution supplemented the determination of the industrial pioneers. The decision to ship chilled beef to Eastern markets from Chicago, the conviction that the refrigerator car would work and the persistence in opening doors to new markets were the factors that led to new concepts in marketing and distribution. The business grew and spread. Branch houses were established in all major cities.

By 1880 a successful enterprise existed, built by Swift and other men of business stature and know-how. Against tremendous odds, prejudices and objections, a far-reaching system had been established, while solid business facts were hammered home: the savings in distribution costs, the availability of improved products and dollars-and-cents benefits to consumers and livestock producers.

From the basic meat business Swift & Company progressed and expanded into many fields, moving ahead in new directions, adding, changing, realigning and restructuring. It has evolved into a diverse international corporation with major interests in food, but also chemicals, insurance and business services and petroleum.

Most recently Swift has reorganized into a new holding company complex—Esmark, Inc.—of which Swift & Company is one of four subholding companies. In the new Esmark complex Swift owns the food businesses; Estech, Inc., the chemical and industrial products companies; GSI, Inc., the insurance and business services firms; and Vickers Energy Corporation, the petroleum activities. The company has annual sales of over $3 billion, making it one of the largest industrial corporations in the United States.

Swift has moved with the nation and with the times. Determination and daring decisions in an earlier era still provide a traditional backdrop and inspiration for its continued business enterprises and operations.

WELLS FARGO

□ □ □

They Struck It Rich by Not Rushing to the Gold Rush

It was an awesome, unbelievable spectacle. Supposedly sane men left crops unattended, abandoned their herds, kissed wives and families a hasty goodbye and set out for the wild, uncivilized "wastelands" of California. Ships arriving at a village called San Francisco were abandoned by their crews and left to rot in the harbor. All humanity, it seemed, using any conveyance, any means, was bent on a wild, reckless flight westward.

The reason rested in the river beds and rocky crags of the Sierra Nevada Mountains, where a few shiny yellow flakes of gold discovered at Sutter's Mill in Coloma in 1848 touched off one of the wildest rushes for wealth in history.

All of this was observed with interest by two men 3,000 miles away in New York. Vermont-born Henry Wells and New Yorker William G. Fargo were established, experienced expressmen. Wells had demonstrated his imagination and gumption by engineering the delivery of fresh oysters from Albany to Buffalo. Fargo had already overseen a thirty-mile mail route at the age of thirteen.

Putting their bearded heads together, Wells and Fargo saw a need for a dependable banking and express operation to serve Gold Rush California. As hordes of people swept across the country to seek their fortunes in the gold fields, other banks and express companies raced to San Francisco to set

Wells Fargo and Company opened for business on San Francisco's Montgomery Street in July, 1852.

up shop. But not these two gentlemen. With characteristic prudence and careful planning, they waited and watched. Was the rush to California a passing fad, or would it bring stability and lasting prosperity to the area?

By 1852 Wells and Fargo knew that the migration westward was irreversible. The time had come to act. They met on March 18, 1852, at New York's plush Astor House and formally launched a banking and express company to serve Gold Rush California. The new venture, Wells Fargo & Company, may have been born amid the staid comforts of the East, but it would become synonymous with the wild and daring days of the Old West. It was a name that would forever conjure up images of stagecoaches plying rugged Western trails, of treasure boxes laden with gold, of gallantry, gumption and derringdo.

Shortly after the historic meeting banker R. W. Washburn and expressman Samuel Carter were dispatched to San Francisco to open an office on Montgomery Street, then as now the center of the city's financial life. The "wait and see" policy of Wells and Fargo before venturing westward paid off. Although when Wells Fargo & Company opened its doors in July, 1852, there was already considerable competition, their sound business practices, based on a lifetime of experience, soon made a difference. The company grew and expanded rapidly, and early in its corporate existence established a reputation for honesty and dependability. In 1855 failure of an Eastern bank caused panic in San Francisco. Every bank in town—with the exception of Wells Fargo— closed. Two or three later attempted to reopen, but have since disappeared into history.

From the start Wells Fargo & Company offered a broad range of banking and express services: protecting gold and other monies, exchanging gold and greenbacks, making purchases, selling merchandise, collecting on notes and waybills, paying taxes. No task was too large, no assignment too small. One of its most important services in those fledging days was the delivery of the United States mail. Wipe the dust from the side of a stagecoach and you'd be likely to see the emblem miners in distant gold camps found most heartening—*Wells Fargo, U.S.M.*

How did Wells Fargo agents in distant mining camps run their offices and what did their work consist of? A pretty good idea can be gleaned from a series of letters written in the 1850s by John Q. Jackson, Wells Fargo's agent in Auburn in the heart of California's mother lode country:

> All my letters are to be written—always five or six each night and the same number during the day. The gold dust bought during the last two days is to be cleaned, weighed, sealed and packed ready to forward in the morning. My books must be balanced and letters sorted for the different offices to which they are to be forwarded, and a list made of those received from Sacramento today and bundled for the river messenger who leaves at daylight. This must be done with half a dozen other things before I go to sleep— I have no trouble except simply owing to the care of the treasure which is placed on this office. Were it not for this feeling of responsibility and trust I would be lighthearted and happy as a bird.

Wells Fargo established a reputation among Westerners that commanded absolute faith, so much so that even wives and children were shipped as "express." Wrote one 1866 journalist:

> A billiard saloon, a restaurant and a Wells Fargo office are the first three elements of Pacific or Coast mining towns. It is the omnipresent, universal business agent of all the region from the Rocky Mountains to the Pacific Ocean. Its offices are in every town, far and near. Its messengers are on every steamboat and railcar and stage in these states. It is the ready companion of civilization, the universal friend and agent of the miner, his errand man, his banker, his post office.

A milestone was reached in 1866 when Wells Fargo & Company's staging empire hit its peak with the consolidation under its own name, ownership and operation of the entire Great Overland mail route from the Missouri to the Pacific, as well as thousands of additional miles of stagecoach lines in California, Nevada, Utah, Idaho, Montana, Wyoming, Colorado, Kansas, Oregon and Washington.

The stagecoach, of course, was the fastest way for a traveler to reach California overland in 1866—about twenty-one days from St. Joseph, Missouri, to Sacramento, California, at a cost of around $300. The famous Concord stagecoaches with their six-horse teams averaged around twelve miles an hour. Station stops were located about every twenty or twenty-five miles.

What was it like to travel across country on a stagecoach? One nineteenth-century passenger described his trip as "a through ticket with 15 inches of seat space, a fat man on one side, a poor widow on the other, a baby in your lap and a hatbox hanging over your head."

Though it was an adaptation of the English mail coach, the Concord coach used by Wells Fargo was strictly American, designed to meet the needs of the rugged American West. Built for trouble and rough conditions, it was slung close to the ground, permitting it to take sharp curves at speeds that probably made passengers hold their breath.

To one driver the coach was "as tidy and graceful as a lady, as inspiring to a stagefaring man as a ship to a sailor and has, like the lady and the ship, scarcely a straight line in its body."

The Concord coaches took their name from the capital of New Hampshire, where they were built by Abbot, Downing & Company. The precision and care in their construction was matched by the careful selection of materials. Spokes were made from the finest ash and were hand-picked and hand-fitted to rim and hub. Wood was seasoned to withstand any climate.

As an example of how rugged and durable these vehicles were, consider the story of one coach that had the misfortune to be on a ship that sank just before it reached its destination. The coach was fished out of the water several weeks later and put into service, where it reportedly remained for fifty years.

While these were active, exciting years of expansion for the express portion of the business, they were times of quiet, steady development for the banking end, which continued to be centered in San Francisco. The banking and express arms went their separate ways in 1905, and in 1918, under wartime restrictions, the express portion was merged with other express firms into the American Railway Express.

The bank grew and expanded. In 1969 when it decided to form a one-bank holding company—at the time it had well over 250 branches in California—it seemed only appropriate that it take as its name the same legendary, pioneering one of a century earlier. Wells Fargo & Company had come full circle.

Today Wells Fargo is something more than a large financial institution. It is a treasure house of the past. Much of the history and hardware of the Old West is preserved in the museum in its San Francisco head office. There, among gold pieces, six-shooters, treasure boxes—and large portraits of Wells and Fargo—you can see the only stagecoach on Montgomery Street.

WESTERN UNION

□ □ □

Tying a Nation Together — by Wire

The year was 1861. The nation was poised for two great events that would forever change its history: the Civil War and the opening of its Western lands.

In the North a few men were beginning to realize how important the West—particularly California and its gold—was going to be in the outcome of the Civil War.

Close ties were essential, but California lay 2,000 miles and many days away (by stage or rider) from the government in Washington. The westernmost telegraph terminal at the time was at St. Joseph, Missouri. The Pony Express was, at best, a fragile link to connect a nation. There was real danger that the wealth and support of the Western lands would be lost to the Union cause—cut off by time, distance and the dangers of passage.

Among the men who shared the government's concern was Hiram Sibley, president of the Western Union Telegraph Company. This was the company that, by acquiring eleven small competing telegraph companies operating north of the Ohio River, had by 1856 created a unified communications system—the only consolidated system running east and west.

On July 4, 1861, less than three months after the firing on Fort Sumter, the first pole was set for Western Union's 2000-mile line between Omaha and Sacramento. On October 24, the first transcontinental telegraph line stretched unbroken from ocean to ocean. Here is an early view of the line near Carson City, Nevada, as it crosses the Sierra Nevada Mountains.

For Sibley patriotism and business sense went hand in hand. He knew the Union side needed a telegraph line to the Pacific. And he knew his company was the one that could build it.

Not many men shared his optimism. Engineering experts predicted the project would take ten years to complete, if, in fact, it could be done at all. The obstacles seemed almost insurmountable: between the St. Joseph telegraph terminal and the Pacific lay the treeless miles of the Great Plains, the unmapped Rockies and hostile Indians.

Abraham Lincoln warned Sibley: "I think it is a wild scheme. It will be next to impossible to get your poles and materials distributed on the plains, and as fast as you complete the line the Indians will cut it down."

But Sibley persisted. He knew it could be done. In fact, two years previously he had commissioned a remarkable young man named Edward Creighton to show how the project could be carried out.

For two years Creighton surveyed a route. Traveling alone, he set out from Omaha and almost immediately suffered a setback that would have stopped a less determined man—the loss of his horse and all his equipment while crossing the icy Platte River. Barely escaping with his life, Creighton nevertheless pushed on. In Salt Lake City he was befriended by Brigham Young, the Mormon leader, and received promises of help from him.

In midwinter, despite warnings, he left Salt Lake City to attempt the 500-mile journey to Carson City, Nevada. Pushing on alone, often on foot, through country inhabited only by trappers and Indians, he headed through the Humboldt Valley toward the icy Sierra Nevadas.

Creighton nearly didn't make it. When he stumbled into Carson City, more dead than alive, he was snow-blind and exhausted. But after a few days' rest he moved on and finally reached Sacramento.

His heroic feat was proof enough for Sibley. Planning for a telegraph line began immediately. Creighton was to command a work party heading West to Salt Lake City. From Sacramento a second force was to head East. As if the undertaking itself were not enough of a gamble, the two teams bet on who would reach Salt Lake City first. The losers would have to pay the winners $50 a day for every day they were late.

Symbolically, the first pole was set on July 4, 1861. Expeditions of hundreds of men driving oxen, mules and herds of cattle for beef to feed the workers moved slowly over mountain trails and the Great Plains. The route was marked by names echoing the wilderness: Mud Springs, Sweetwater, Three Crossings, Rocky Ridge, Fish Springs and Deep Creek.

Tough and determined crews advanced ten to twelve miles a day, setting up as many as twenty-five poles every mile. Behind them stretched a telegraph line.

One day it brought news of the Union defeat at the first Battle of Bull Run. Their mission now seemed doubly urgent. Overcoming weather and terrain, winning over the Indians, and helped by Mormon contractors who hauled poles across the endless plains, Creighton's group reached Salt Lake City on October 16, 1861. They were first—but only by a week. On October 24, just three months and twenty days after this supposedly impossible enterprise had begun, two strands of wire were joined at Salt Lake City. A telegraph line now stretched unbroken from the Pacific to the Atlantic.

The building of the first transcontinental telegraph line was one of the earliest and most successful examples of project management in American history. Here was a logistical nightmare turned into a triumph of planning and coordination.

The achievement set a standard of performance for Western Union ever since. Today the company is once again responding to the public's need for new types of communications by putting into place a vast new nationwide communications system. For this system the planning and coordination deals with satellites, microwave radio beams and electronic switches rather than poles and cattle. Just as revolutionary as the first cross-country telegraph, the new network will join into one complex facility the most advanced communications system anywhere.

Only the best will do because the public's need for communications has changed dramatically over the years. The telephone system has had to be supplemented by a network that allows record communications like teletype messages and data to be sent everywhere. Businesses, institutions, government agencies and nearly every organization now needs to move information faster than the mails and with more convenience. At the same time, computers are generating ever greater quantities of information and making it possible for organizations to set up private information systems to improve efficiency.

The new Western Union network—completely modernized, greatly expanded and offering completely new capabilities— is a direct response to the need for information, especially in data form.

Data transmission is an infant industry now, but is expected to become a giant. In large part its growth will depend on how carriers like Western Union meet users' requirements for lower charges, greater flexibility and more capacity. Fortunately technology in the form of satellites and computers is available to meet this challenge. The new Western Union is well along in integrating this technology into its new multi-element network.

One element will be the country's first satellite network for domestic communications. Entirely owned by Western Union, this system, consisting of Westar satellites in orbit and ground stations near population centers, is opening new possibilities for communications users. The same basic system can handle broadcast television, cable television, data, telegrams, Mailgrams or other types of communication for which there may be public demand.

As complex as the Westar system is, it is only part of a larger network including a coast-to-coast microwave radio relay system for moving communications economically during the ground portion of their journey. The network is being upgraded and extended to permit the transmission of computer data at lower cost and with high accuracy. This expanded terrestrial facility and the satellite system greatly increase the capacity of the nation's principal means of handling record communications.

To use this capacity efficiently other massive systems are being installed. These are the computerized switching systems that route and switch messages over the transmission network from destination to destination. Some of the switches complete circuits that allow dial-up connections like telephone service but which provide written, rather than voice, communication. Other Western Union switches being installed store and process incoming messages before routing them to destinations. Public, business and government users of communications require both types of switching. As the use of computers grows, so will the need for switching.

Great demand for data communications is the mark of a great and growing nation. By forging and operating a flexible high-capacity network to make modern data and traditional communications possible, Western Union plans to keep aiding this growth as the leading supplier of record communications facilities.

WEYERHAEUSER

□ □ □

The Tree Farm and How It Grew

As the nineteenth century drew to a close, the farsighted had already realized that the time had come for America to change its resource policies.

Resources no longer seemed infinite, but one of them, timber, had the recognized potential for infinite renewal. Thus there was great optimism and an era of private-governmental cooperation to find forestry solutions seemed about to begin. In 1902 and 1903 Weyerhaeuser Company began forest management studies of its newly acquired timberlands, and in 1904 it began fire prevention and control programs.

In 1905 F. E. Weyerhaeuser, a son of the company's founder, told a national forestry conference that forestry on private lands was practical but that "only by tremendous effort can the lumberman himself, the legislator and the voter be made to realize its importance and its possibilities." He had reason to believe that that effort was about to get under way. Gifford Pinchot had shown him an advance copy of a speech prepared for Theodore Roosevelt, twenty-sixth President of the United States, for delivery at the same conference. It was a strong bid for government-industry co-operation, which could mean "the difference between mere agitation and actual execution."

Roosevelt didn't read the Pinchot-prepared remarks. For

CLEMONS TREE FARM

Growing trees for you — your children — and your grandchildren Weyerhaeuser

reasons still unexplained, he opted instead for agitation, for a "confrontation" staged before the nation's press. He launched a slashing attack upon his audience, calling its members (who had, after all, gathered to discuss forest conservation), "skinners of the land," "despoilers of the national heritage." The media took up the cry. The animosities created at the conference set back the practice of private forestry for a generation; the mythology perpetrated still clouds the nation's consciousness.

The charges went mostly unanswered. The timbermen had been attacked for past practices. The practices of the future were in the theoretical state and their worth could not be demonstrated for several decades.

Frederick Weyerhaeuser, the founder of the company, with his associates made the basic decision in 1900 to hold onto Weyerhaeuser Company's lands. The company would not "cut and run," and it would limit the amount of its cutting.

Eight years later, at the age of seventy-three, he delivered a mild rebuttal to the Roosevelt charges before a Congressional committee. He discounted reports of impending "timber famine," urged federal action on fire control laws and recommended laws regulating the practices of loggers in order to preserve seed sources and safeguard against soil erosion. He pointed out that property tax systems designed in pioneer days to speed the conversion of forested lands to row crop agriculture, rather than owner reluctance, were the chief deterrents to forest reproduction.

The company continued to experiment with forest regeneration and to urge a rethinking of state tax philosophies. A body of knowledge was accumulated about forestry, and in 1929 Oregon became the first state to make reforestation, rather than deforestation, a declared objective of its public and tax policy. A trend seemed established. Weyerhaeuser committed itself to the sustained growing of trees.

J. P. (Phil) Weyerhaeuser, Jr., then thirty-five, executive vice president of Weyerhaeuser Company, directed the first full-scale implementation of this policy in 1934. In 1936 the shareholders were told what was going on, and the company began to promote the slogan "Timber Is a Crop" within the industry and within its plant communities. The response, in many cases, was either a chuckle or a show of resistance. After all, some 300 years of industry tradition were being challenged, and with techniques that most operators felt were still unproven.

Thus by the late 1930s Phil Weyerhaeuser had become convinced that two things were necessary—a large demonstration tract to offer physical proof, and a campaign to publicize it within the forest industries. He picked what was known as the Clemons tract in southwestern Washington, where the company owned 130,000 acres of mostly fire-devastated land. Here foresters could conduct a comprehensive demonstration program without interfering with the activities of logging bosses.

The Clemons became the site of "Operation Rehab." By 1941 the progress of "Operation Rehab" made it apparent that the skeptics could be convinced. Roderick Olrendam, a company public relations executive, had come up with a suggestion that would make the sales job easier. He recommended that the "Operation Rehab" tract be called a "Tree Farm."

The Clemons was dedicated as the nation's first Tree Farm, with accompanying regional and trade press publicity, in public ceremonies at Montesano, Washington, in June, 1941.

It led to a movement which has brought the application of scientific forestry to more than 70 million acres of privately owned lands in the forty-eight contiguous states, and which, as much as any other factor, reversed the long-term destruction of America's forest resource. It probably accomplished more in a shorter time than any single conservation program in world history. Tree farming became an accepted fact of rural American life by the start of the 1950s.

The United States, however, had become an urban nation, and urban voters, when they thought of the forest at all, continued to think of it in the terms popularized in the Teddy Roosevelt era—terms such as "Timber Barons" and "Timber Famine." Four out of five, according to 1952 polls, felt that the federal government should confiscate or control privately owned forest lands.

The industry, which by now had a solid story of accomplishment to tell, was unable to tell it. It was fragmented among tens of thousands of timber owners and forest product manufacturers divided by product competition and regional concerns. The industry lacked a voice.

Weyerhaeuser Company in 1952 was a relatively small factor within the industry. It was basically a Pacific Northwest lumber and pulp producer, little known nationally, with its stock traded over the counter. Nevertheless, Phil Weyerhaeuser decided that if the industry wasn't in position to tell its own story, Weyerhaeuser Company was.

"Unless an institution merits good will and understanding, it cannot maintain its position as part of our American industrial structure," he said. "We have an honest story to tell. Through public opinion polls we learned that . . . our enemies by and large were the uninformed. Today, the world is groping its way toward new concepts, new objectives, and new social standards. New emotions, new pressures, new influences are at work. But sound principles will remain if we have the courage to fight for them."

So, forty-seven years after the 1905 conference, Weyehaeuser began to respond for the industry to Teddy Roosevelt's charges. Eleven years after dedicating the first tree farm, the company launched a classic "corporate" communication effort—with advertising designed not to sell products but to sell the concept of timber as a perpetual resource. The "Weyerhaeuser Wildlife" series in magazines was the longest continual print-media ad campaign built around a single theme ever to be carried out in the United States. In its original series format it ran for fifteen years.

The educational effort via advertising was transferred to national television in the 1960s. This has turned out to be an excellent medium for the purpose, because, as one Weyerhaeuser executive puts it: "Through TV, we can actually take millions of viewers out into the forest to see what's being done in advanced management of the forest resource."

Typical TV commercials on this theme show various steps in Weyerhaeuser's forest management, starting with the careful planting of selected tree seed in the company's six big nurseries located around the United States. Seedlings grown in these nurseries are lifted and moved to field locations where they are planted by skilled planting crews or, where the terrain permits, imbedded by the thousands behind specially designed mechanical tree-planting machines.

Weyerhaeuser's system of forest management took a quantum jump in computer-based scientific complexity during the 1960s, based on years of patient and painstaking research in the combined art and science of growing new forests. The objective of this new "high-yield forest" program is to grow one-third more wood per acre. This is made possible by genetically superior seed sources and planting stock, scientifically managed thinning of the young forest to speed growth and aerial fertilization. In terms of North American forestry, these have been pioneering moves on a fully operational scale.

High-yield forestry is a far cry from the earlier mode of forest management, which consisted largely of such necessary but passive measures as protection against fire and forest pest outbreaks. The new concept has been incorporated into Weyerhaeuser's total communications program.

Advertising remains a key of this educational effort directed at the American people. Television continues to be used, augmented by print media directed to selected audiences, such as opinion leaders and the recreationist audience, including the populace of communities across the nation where Weyerhaeuser has significant timber holdings and manufacturing operations. One challenge of this effort has been to reach new regional audiences. The company expanded in the 1960s into geographical areas such as Arkansas and Oklahoma where it had not previously owned forest lands or manufacturing plants.

Advertising is only part of the expanded program of "telling it like it is" in high-yield forestry today. A company film on forestry, *To Touch the Sky*, is distributed through a national booking agency and to date has been seen by 22 million viewers. Tours for political and media leaders are hold by Weyerhaeuser to give these key figures a firsthand look at what the company is doing in its intensive forest management program. In Weyerhaeuser operating regions civic leaders and students are taken on such forest tours. Self-guided tours in forest demonstration areas have been used by the company, along with roadside mini-tour setups using full-time guides.

A main feature of Weyerhaeuser's high-yield forestry is a drastic step-up in reforestation. While the company once relied on reforestation via natural seeding from blocks of standing timber left for that purpose, today's operations call for immediate replanting or serial reseeding of harvested areas. Backed by a massive nursery program of its own, Weyerhaeuser is planting 102 million seedlings in 1973 and aerial seeding 35,000 acres in addition.

Information on this reforestation effort, the biggest in American history within the private enterprise sector, was disseminated early in 1973 in an educational campaign estimated to reach over 100 million Americans. Television, radio, magazine and newspaper media were used, along with a series of commemorative tree planting ceremonies at each of the company's nursery facilities, attended by local governors, senators and congressmen.

Weyerhaeuser Company is keenly aware that doing an outstanding job of forest management by itself is not enough. In today's environmentally concerned world the story of that forest stewardship must be told on the widest possible scale and with maximum credibility backed up by solid facts and tangible achievements.